E D E N
B U I L T   B Y
E V E S

EDEN BUILT BY EVES

THE CULTURE OF WOMEN'S MUSIC FESTIVALS

BY BONNIE J. MORRIS, PH.D.

PHOTOGRAPHS FROM THE COLLECTION OF TONI ARMSTRONG JR.
AND OTHER WOMEN ARTISTS

alyson books
los angeles | new york

MANUFACTURED IN THE UNITED STATES OF AMERICA.
PRINTED ON ACID-FREE PAPER.

THIS TRADE PAPERBACK ORIGINAL IS PUBLISHED BY ALYSON PUBLICATIONS INC.,
P.O. BOX 4371, LOS ANGELES, CALIFORNIA 90078-4371.
DISTRIBUTION IN THE UNITED KINGDOM BY TURNAROUND PUBLISHER SERVICES LTD.,
UNIT 3 OLYMPIA TRADING ESTATE, COBURG ROAD, WOOD GREEN, LONDON N22 6TZ ENGLAND.

FIRST EDITION: APRIL 1999

99 00 01 02 03 a 10 9 8 7 6 5 4 3 2 1

ISBN 1-55583-477-9

LIBRARY OF CONGRESS CATALOGING-IN-PUBLICATION DATA
  MORRIS, BONNIE J., 1961–
    EDEN BUILT BY EVES : THE CULTURE OF WOMEN'S MUSIC FESTIVALS /
  BONNIE J. MORRIS.—1ST ED.
    INCLUDES BIBLIOGRAPHICAL REFERENCES AND INDEX.
    1. MUSIC FESTIVALS. 2. LESBIAN MUSIC. 3. FEMINIST MUSIC. I. TITLE.
  ML35.M67 1999
  780'.79—DC21   98-54780 CIP   R98

CREDITS
• COVER PHOTOGRAPHS BY TONI ARMSTRONG JR.
• MATERIAL FROM *ORIGINAL SINS* © 1981 BY LISA ALTER INC. REPRINTED BY PERMISSION OF
  ALFRED A. KNOPF INC.

For Alix Dobkin and Toni Armstrong Jr.,
my beloved role models in lesbian culture.
"When the pupil is ready, the teacher appears."

For Jeanette Buck, Sherry Hicks, and Karen Kane,
just three of the hundreds of festival workers
who gave their best energies to the stage.

CONTENTS

CHAPTER TEN – 291

How I Spent My Summer Vacation—hostile cynics declare that women's music is dead. Certainly the lack of mainstream press coverage would suggest so. Then why do festivals continue to attract thousands of women annually? Why do so many women volunteer unpaid skilled labor and demanding work hours to perpetuate this lesbian subculture? Will festivals continue in the next century?

APPENDIX A – 313

Voices of Festiegoers—selected first-person responses from a ten-year survey of over 800 festiegoers; written testimony to the durable appeal and importance of festivalgoing.

APPENDIX B – 359

A Lexicon of Festivalese—festival slang and terminology.

BIBLIOGRAPHY – 369

Festival, Cultural, and Women's Music Sources

FESTIVAL HERSTORIAN'S PREFACE

Filling Up the Jam Jars With Festival Preserves

*I create myself as a mythical hero, and I don't think this is any less
accurate than any other projection of reality.*
—Alix Dobkin

Women's voices are a moral template, the narrative of survival. And all who listen are changed forever.

I grew up in the 1960s, listening to women's folk music recordings by Judy Collins and Joan Baez. My mother played these albums over and over in our California living room when she did her modern dance exercises. I became convinced that both Judy and Joan were simply artistic extensions of my own mother. As a result of my early exposure to women artists of the 1960s folk and antiwar movements, I saw women as the moral and musical authorities of what was then a male-dominated and commercial "protest" genre.

By the time I reached puberty, I also knew I loved women; I wrote love letters and sent poems to girls I had crushes on. When my family moved to the East Coast, I began attending an alternative school where women's studies courses were a regular part of the curriculum, and thus I found academic feminism at age 12. As a bookworm, I learned about lesbian culture through *Ms.* magazine and novels, but like most baby dykes of the mid 1970s, I found few popular songs expressing my feelings for other girls. When at 14 I formed an intense relationship with my best friend, we had no music for our special connection other than the mainstream pop songs on the radio. I stood in the light spill of women's music just once, not realizing my anointment: There was an arts festival called Womansphere held near my home in October of 1974, and there, as a lonely 13-year-old prowling Glen Echo Park, I walked right past Meg Christian, Margie Adam, and Cris Williamson's performances in my haste to purchase a woman's symbol necklace.

Then one day in 1975, home from school with the flu, I heard a radio advertisement for the new Deadly Nightshade album. These three women sang unabashedly feminist music and had just released a song called "High Flying Woman." Their voices filled my yearning bones. Within three years I discovered Cris Williamson's album *The Changer and the Changed*, and when I finally came out at age 18, I plunged into the burgeoning culture of lesbian music albums, concerts, and festivals.

In August of 1981, I attended my first women's music festival. I had just received a beautiful Minolta camera for my 20th birthday, a gesture of love from my parents, but I decided not to bring the camera with me to Michigan that first time. I was concerned about carrying such a valuable item into a crowded festival where I knew no one. And so I have no pictures of myself as a "festie virgin," of my first immersion in the culture that has been my home ever since.

When I arrived in Hesperia, Mich., that summer, I found myself joining a festival culture so responsible and caring that I mentally kicked myself for thinking I or my camera might not be safe. Lacking the means to make a photographic record of my first impressions, I wrote frenzied journal entries describing everything I saw and heard: the land, the music, the women dancing sensuously beneath green summer trees. On the last night, I slept in a group tent and joined an all-night singalong with women from all over the world. As dawn broke, I pulled out my journal and passed it around, asking any woman who might be interested to write *her* festival impressions in my notebook. Then on the long bus trip home, I read with increasing delight the sisterly words others had entrusted to me. It was my first clumsy attempt at starting a festival yearbook.

Now, 17-plus years later, I have collected a full archive of festival herstory through my working tools: journal, camera, tape recorder, eye, ear, and other senses.

These personal archives of recordings, photographs, and documents capture the images and voices of women from all corners of the globe—women who, like me, return over and over to the various festivals where an authentic lesbian culture is created and sustained by our own efforts. In the long winter season between festivals, I rest beneath my quilt and look at my scrapbooks or listen to these tape recordings of crackling campfires, rain on a dome-tent roof, stage announcements, the shrieks of raffle winners, and the sounds of 9,000 women laughing together in a field.

More significant than my own personal rejuvenation, however, is this maintenance of a true record of festival energy. Conflicts, scandals, new music, weather, work, and stage personalities determine the character of each separate festival, but these instant villages of women, chronologically added together, build a lesbian nation well worth remembering as we tumble toward a new century. Women's music festivals are a culture as tribal and ritualized and sustaining to the participants as any spiritual movement, and this is because the diverse contributions of the women involved have forged a sum of art and politics that is richly nourishing.

From spring to fall, women fill up their jam jars of inspiration and memory with enough festival preserves to last all winter long. Perhaps no sentiment is more commonly heard than "I live off this week all the rest of the year" or "I'm here again to have my batteries recharged" or "Only in festival time do I get to experience total personhood." Festival season means regeneration as well as recreation. We go because festivals offer the possibility of what our lives *could* be like year-round if we lived each day in a matriarchy actively striving to eliminate racism and homophobia. Living tribally one season per year, all of us share a life together in that concentrated bank statement of time, a wealth of women's culture(s) as the bottom line of accumulated principal. Like the period of weeks between Thanksgiving and New Year, festival time is a packed *family* celebration on which the emotional year turns in heart and memory. And for the most part, we "festiegoers," producers, performers, and technicians must serve as our own biographers, declaring our festival stories and memories to be important and revolutionary—because mainstream society refuses to acknowledge our gatherings, our contributions, our music, our ideas.

It is high time we had a book of our own. In my heart this book was envisioned as a vibrant and soaring tribute to all our work, not as a dry scholarship of festival culture. I write frankly from my biased perspective as a festival veteran and insider—"Dr. Bon" to my friends and festival audiences. At different festivals I have been a stage performer, a backup singer, an emcee, a workshop presenter, a coordinator, or an anonymous paying festiegoer; these contrasting roles have enabled me to study festival work and politics from nearly every angle. My perspectives here are those of a woman immersed in festival culture from age 20 to age 36, the time turf of energy and commitment.

But I also earn my living as a women's history professor and since earning my Ph.D. in 1989 have learned to define my festival research as serious work. To this end I owe tremendous debts of gratitude to those festival producers in the United States—Deedy Breed, Mary Byrne, Michelle Crone, Lin Daniels, Lee Glanton, Janet Grubbs, Wanda and Brenda Henson, Kim Kimber, Maile Klein and Marina Hodgini, Tam Martin, Boo Price, Robin Tyler, and Lisa Vogel—who have granted me trust and affection in creating the means for my involvement as a festival herstorian.

Few universities regard festival culture as a legitimate subject for study and preservation, and carving out the academic writing time for this project has been an exercise in being out and proud as a lesbian scholar. Despite the explosion in women's studies and lesbian publishing, academia retains a homophobic and misogynistic climate. A handful of institutions offer graduate programs in women's history—but just try to find a lesbian voice in the curriculum. Regrettably, to find employment as a professor of women's history, one must write about topics that will not alarm the men (and straight women) who hire historians and fund or publish our research.

I spent six years in graduate school working toward my doctorate in women's history. During those years, which roughly corresponded to the blossoming of festival culture all over the country, I lived two lives. I sat in university classes where a lesbian perspective never appeared in our assigned readings; I learned through my training as a future history professor that the development of my own women's community did not count as "real" history and was unthinkable as a serious research project. Nevertheless, when I was not on campus I was at festivals, at women-identified concerts and performances, at lesbian conferences and camp outs and celebrations—my journal and camera and tape recorder purring back to me, *Yes, this is real.* This is herstory in the making. And I realized that I, as participant, could both create and record the phenomena of this movement, even if the history texts of higher education forever deny our events, growth, and change.

I might have remained a split personality—my festival work and published lesbian writing kept on a wholly different resume from my *scholarly* work—had I not forged an alliance with Toni Armstrong Jr., editor of *HOT WIRE: The Journal of Women's Music and Culture.* Writing for *HOT WIRE,* the one publication dedicated to exploring highlights of festival culture, I found my name on a masthead with other writers who were all laboring—unpaid—to give back to the women's community the best writing and research we could offer. Toni, our editorial dominatrix, expected no less than perfect journalism, confronting me at a critical moment in life (I had just spent a year teaching at Harvard) with this question: "Why *don't* you consider writing for the women's community your primary work? The community needs writers. If you value festival culture, why aren't you publishing your perspectives in your own community?"

I was flabbergasted to be taken seriously as a festival writer, and my alliance with Toni soon became a pretty terrific spiritual partnership. This is an acknowledgement I must make, as it is Toni who asked festival artists and producers the hardest questions, assigned writers the most difficult *HOT WIRE* articles, and called for the highest standards in festival journalism. Since the final issue of *HOT WIRE* in fall 1994, we as a festival community have been without a primary published medium for celebrating artists and workers alike. Some of *HOT WIRE*'s legacy is recapped in the chapters to follow, and throughout this festival herstory I quote heavily from Toni's experienced wisdom. In utilizing Toni's excellent festival photographs to enhance this book, I have also learned anew the difficult price of homophobia: We selected no "crowd" shots of happy women at festivals, lest we unwittingly print the face of a woman who, so revealed, might lose her job or her kids. The photos herein are primarily of artists we know, who could clearly give consent.

There is sufficient material in my own festival archive—and in the knowledge of the savviest producers and the veteran performers and workers—for several books; this is just the first, and I have all my life to write more, I hope. Writing this first volume has been an act of homage to the artists, techies, and festival friends I deeply love. I should be on my knees for every line I write, as though in reverent prayer; in such posture my chin would just barely rest atop the writing table, as it did when I was a toddler pulled hypnotically toward large school desks. Perhaps we are all striving for that mingled feeling of awe and belonging in our work, that sense of being a cog in something larger than ourselves. I do indeed regard this luxury of participating in and recording festival culture as a sacred calling, and am privileged to join my heart line with those women who first picked up a bass guitar, a stage light, a production lineup, a sound board, a soup kettle for 5,000—all those women who collectively declared, *We can do this.*

Bonnie J. Morris
1998
Washington, D.C.

Toni Armstrong Jr. and author Bonnie Morris at the 1992 Gulf Coast Womyn's Festival.

U.S. FESTIVALS, REGION, FOUNDING YEAR

Alaska Women's Music Festival; Alaska; 1989

Arizona Womyn's Music Festival; Arizona; 1981

Boston Women's Music Festival; Boston; 1975

Campfest; Maryland, Pennsylvania; 1984

East Coast Lesbian Festival; New York; 1989

Gulf Coast Womyn's Festival/Spiritfest; Mississippi; 1989

Heart of the West Festival; Las Vegas; 1994

In Gaia's Lap; Maryland; 1995

Iowa Women's Music Festival; Iowa; 1994

Lone Star Women's Festival; Texas; 1990

Michigan Womyn's Music Festival; Michigan; 1976

Midwest Autumnfest; Illinois; 1995

National Women's Music Festival; Indiana; 1974

North East Women's Music Retreat; New England, Northeast Connecticut, New York; 1981

Northampton Lesbian Festival; Western Massachusetts; 1990

Ohio Lesbian Festival; Ohio; 1989

Pacific Northwest Women's Jamboree; Washington state; 1990

Rhythmfest; Carolinas, Georgia; 1990

Sisterfire; Washington, D.C.; 1982

Sisterspace Pocono Weekend; Pennsylvania; 1974

Southern Women's Music and Comedy Festival; Georgia; 1983

Virginia Women's Music Festival/Intouch; Virginia; 1990

West Coast Lesbian Festival; California; 1992

West Coast Women's Music and Comedy Festival; Yosemite National Park; 1979

Wiminfest; New Mexico; 1981
Woman Harvest; New York; 1975
Womongathering; Pennsylvania, New York; 1988

CONTACT ADDRESSES FOR CURRENT AND ONGOING FESTIVALS, TIME OF YEAR HELD

Campfest/Womongathering: Memorial Day weekend/June
Box 559 Franklinville, NJ 98322
camfest@aol.com

Gulf Coast Womyn's Festival: Easter weekend
Camp Sister Spirit
P.O. Box 12 Ovett, MS 39464
sisterspir@aol.com

Midwest Womyn's Autumn Fest: Sunday, Labor Day weekend
217 S. 2nd Street #193
DeKalb, IL 60115

Michigan Womyn's Music Festival: mid August
P.O. Box 22
Walhalla, MI 49458

National Women's Music Festival: June
P.O. Box 1427
Indianapolis, IN 46206-1427
wia@indynet.com

North East Women's Music Retreat: Labor Day weekend
P.O. Box 597
Branford, CT 06405

Ohio Lesbian Festival: September
P.O. Box 82086
Columbus, OH 43202

Sisterspace Pocono Weekend: September
542A S. 48th Street
Philadelphia, PA 19143

Virginia Women's Music Festival: May, July, September
(July Fourth Kickback, Wild Western Women's Weekend)
InTouch R.R. 2, Box 1096
Kent's Store, VA 23084-9610

Wiminfest P.O. Box 80204: May
Albuquerque, NM 87198-0204
wimin@wiminfest.org

WOMEN'S MUSIC DISTRIBUTION COMPANIES

Ladyslipper, Inc.
P.O. Box 3124-R
Durham, NC 27715
(800) 634-6044
orders@ladyslipper.org
www.ladyslipper.org

Goldenrod Music, Inc.
1310 Turner Street
Lansing, MI 48906
(517) 484-1712
music@goldenrod.com
www.goldenrod.com

CHAPTER ONE

An Introduction to the Festival Topic

I don't think we have "women's music." I think we have a women's music audience.
—Sue Fink

When I join my picnic blanket to the patchwork of a thousand others in a women's music festival audience and write "Here I am again" on journal paper made radiant by the light spill from the stage, I'm there to hear the sound of lesbian culture. My hunger for that culture's best artistic expression, for the ingathering which women's music permits, brings me back. Summer after summer, this pilgrimage has sustained an entire generation of women, each of us exclaiming: "*This* is my tribe. And *this* is its music."

From lullabies to warrior cries, women of all cultures throughout our planet's history have raised their voices in song. In a world where most women remain poor, uneducated, and without political rights, folk songs of women's struggles for survival pass along important information—and the hope of better days ahead for their daughters. Denied the Hebrew literacy and scholarship expected of their male peers, Jewish women of 18th- and 19th-century Europe forged their own oral tradition of melodies and humor in Yiddish: the *mamaloshen,* or "mother's tongue." Throughout the 244-year history of African enslavement in North America, work songs such as "Follow the Drinking Gourd" taught enslaved women the route to freedom by following star constellations northward. Later on, urban African-American women's blues songs told of personal confrontations with men, as well as the fight for acceptance and freedom in a racially divided society. Workplace songs in a plethora of languages gave voice to immigrant women's issues in America, especially when unions excluded working women from their memberships.

The folk music renaissance of the late 1940s and 1950s drew on working class ballads that told of women's participation in union organizing and strikes. Although folk music was soon attacked by Sen. Joseph McCarthy's House Un-American Activities Committee as "subversive," resulting in restrictions on the work of outspo-

A rousing performance winds down at the Michigan Womyn's Music Festival.

ken women artists like Ronnie Gilbert, folk and protest music soon grew into a nationwide fad. The commercial success of folk music provided many women artists with a fresh medium for social change, and yet often white artists' profits and visibility came directly at the expense of black women—whose original songs went unplayed by mainstream radio stations during the segregated 1950s. It was the civil rights movement which gave national prominence to the voices of African-American women and transmitted their songs of commitment and challenge to white activists across the land.

As women of different racial and economic backgrounds met to unite on political issues such as the peace and civil rights movements, their own secondary location in a male-dominated society became more and more apparent. Thus the 1960s saw the rebirth of a national movement for the liberation of women—a "second wave" of feminism, unmatched since the suffrage campaigns of a half century before. Feminism changed forever the character of American society, awakening hitherto isolated women through street action, media debate, and consciousness-raising groups. Songs celebrating the new focus on women's self-worth emerged in a range of styles, including pop hits such as Helen Reddy's "I Am Woman" and Aretha Franklin's "Respect"—anthems we could live by.

By the early 1970s the women's movement in the United States had grown enormously, making gains in some areas of legal and economic change but still divided along the lines of race, class, and sexuality. Members of political groups such as the National Organization for Women faced off over the question of lesbian visibility— and over the question of whether to condemn male superstructures, such as organized religion and the military, or to demand women's integration into those existing halls of power. Movement leader Betty Friedan declared that lesbian rights were a "lavender herring," both a distraction from and an embarrassment for mainstream feminists. Fear of being called a lesbian kept many women away from feminist activism. But for those women who had always identified as lesbians, woman-loving was a central ethic that could not to be submerged in the waters of public relations. A literary and political subculture of lesbian feminism, which included varying levels of separation from men, attracted new followers to create woman-only spaces for work, discussion, publishing, and recreation.

In a society intolerant of homosexuality and scornful of the feminist movement, coming out as a lesbian feminist became the hallmark of a daringly visible, woman-identified lifestyle. With growing awareness that the lesbian quest for freedom was a civil rights issue like any other, some lesbians began proclaiming their right to love through song. For those women—lesbian, bi, and heterosexual—whose hearts responded to any message of woman-identified music, the next challenge was learning how to produce and market albums outside male commercial confines.

Songs that spoke of bedroom politics, reproductive-rights laws, institutionalized sexism, rape, and other issues found no mainstream radio play or promotion in the male-controlled world of album recording and distribution. Talented women discovered that few performance venues welcomed "chicks" at all, particularly if their dress and political message called for female resistance to sexual objectification. To retain control over the music and the message, women like Karen Kane and Boden Sandstrom who had no experience in the technical aspects of sound recording or concert production found it necessary to train themselves—to learn by doing—to protect the political integrity of this new product called women's music.

The last quarter of the 20th century would see the consolidation of all these earlier waves into a grassroots community of woman-identified music and comedy performers, stage technicians, event producers, workshop presenters, and craftswomen. Collectively, these women who envisioned ongoing, safe, private, and inspiring performance spaces for women's music and culture built institutions known as women's music festivals. And for nearly 25 years, in nearly every region of the United States, the familiar joy of summer "festival season" has sustained lesbian-feminist artists and audiences throughout the rest of the calendar year.

Yet in a nation where even Grateful Dead concerts, Lollapalooza events, and now the Lilith Fair command their share of media attention as music subcultures, not a whisper is heard about the contribution of annual women's music festivals, where artists such as Melissa Etheridge and Tracy Chapman won over their first fans. For every Etheridge and Chapman, there were hundreds of other talented lesbian artists who still have a devoted following and multiple albums to their credit but who are primarily supported by the women's music festival audience and remain unknown elsewhere. Despite the mainstream music industry's growing awareness of a large lesbian consumer audience, music with a specifically lesbian message is still denied a place in commercial airtime. Lesbian musicians such as k.d. lang are tolerated as long as their music is apolitical, nonthreatening.

The media's indifference to lesbian culture's most important performance institutions may be a blessing in disguise; few festivals are haunted by voyeuristic men or critical journalists or subjected to withering commentary in mainstream publications.[1] For women who rely on the anonymity of festivals for their "lesbian vacations" each summer, common public knowledge of festivals' existence might prove a real deterrent. Do we *want* to draw attention to ourselves?

It's a good question, one which haunts me as I write these words. But as we approach the millennium, the year 2000, we bring a golden era of festival culture into the 21st century's house—a legacy of work and accomplishment still lacking public acknowledgment or praise.

Why is festival history, or herstory, important? In 1992, scholar and "festiegoer" Thyme Siegel wondered at the lack of attention to the festival movement in feminist anthologies:

> Feminist historians being published today are not writing histories of the last 20 years in which I recognize my experiences. The histories are full of flattening categories and lifeless descriptions of different ideas, taken out of context of anyone's experiences. The whole move to create women's cultural community is dismissed in book after book in a few sentences.[2]

In the following chapters, I hope to fulfill Thyme Siegel's wish that the creation of a women's cultural community (at festivals) be recognized and remembered, not dismissed.

Festivals Today

There are presently over 20 women's music festivals and retreats produced each year in the United States. Primarily held as weekend or four-day events in the warm season between Easter and Labor Day but also appearing in late fall, festivals range in size from intimate gatherings of 100 to 200 women to the 5,000 to 9,000 rapt festiegoers who crowd the Michigan Womyn's Music Festival every August. Michigan and, more recently, the Gulf Coast and Virginia festivals are the only festivals attached to permanently owned private land; most festivals take place at rented summer camp facilities, state parks, or rural ranches. Three festivals—New Mexico's Wiminfest, the National Women's Music Festival in Indiana, and the no-longer-held Pacific Northwest Jamboree—have relied upon arrangements with college campuses, with more comfortable facilities but certain added restrictions (one cannot go topless in that magnificent theater at Indiana University).

Although certainly open to *all* women (and occasionally to men), the women's music festivals are produced, organized, and attended by a lesbian majority and serve as ingatherings for lesbian activists and musicians from across North America. For Canadian women and festival participants from other countries, merely mentioning Michigan (the largest and best-known festival) as one's destination can cause harassment at the border: the United States remains reluctant to issue visas to political and/or homosexual performers, so both audience and artists from abroad take certain risks in traveling to festivals. In some years Canadian performers have been denied entry. The Michigan festival's proximity to the Canadian border has made this conflict a regular topic of discussion, in particular because of the phenomenal popularity of Canadian women's music artists, including Ferron, Lucie Blue Tremblay, Heather Bishop, Faith Nolan, Lillian Allen, and the Sawagi Taiko drum ensemble.

The first festivals, held in the mid 1970s, had as their goal the transmission of a feminist message through concerts and workshops and offered the experience of woman-only jamming space as an empowering retreat for artists and audience alike. With the growth of Olivia Records as the first women's recording and distribution company, festivals also showcased performers with a product and demonstrated the range of technical and production skills women had gained access to through sheer determination. (Sexism still prevented most women from getting studio work as sound engineers or session musicians.) Musicians and comedians with a woman-identified ethic, whose work covered a range of personal and political issues, found receptive audiences at festivals, although the early years of trial-and-error financial planning and the feeding of thousands complicated the smooth operation of each "Wombstock." Egged on by rumors of safe nudity, radical rhetoric, and good guitar, many a young lesbian feminist loaded her sleeping bag, girlfriend, and djembe drum into a '71 Volkswagen bug and headed off to try a festival, thence adding her own anecdotes and memories to the culture's gradual mythology.

By the 1980s, several successful festivals had burgeoned into businesses, offering up to a week of workshops, professionally engineered performances in multiple artistic venues, crafts markets of woman-made art and books and clothing, and film series as well. This explosion in festival production throughout differing regions of the United States could be linked to five trends: (1) the intensive production and marketing of lesbian- and feminist-oriented music by Olivia Records and Redwood Records and the Goldenrod and Ladyslipper distribution companies; (2) slow but steady gains in feminist challenges to institutions once closed to women, resulting in better educational and training opportunities for women musicians and stage

Vicki Randle drumming at the 1990 Michigan Womyn's Music Festival.

Toni Armstrong Jr.

crew; (3) the choice by many women to support—with consumer dollars, volunteer hours, or other resources—the alternative culture of woman-owned businesses and services at lesbian-produced events; (4) the emergence of a second generation of performers and producers mentored by the 1970s pioneers in women's music as well as a second generation of festival audiences; (5) the visibility in the 1990s of successful lesbian "crossover" artists like Melissa Etheridge and Tracy Chapman, who began as festival performers and found artistic acceptance with mainstream audiences and record labels. (Comedians too moved from festivals to clubs to television and film in the 1990s; Lea DeLaria, Georgia Ragsdale, and Suzanne Westenhoefer are good examples.)

Change came quickly. In the late 1970s, just as America prepared to enter a long siege of moral majority and Reagan-Bush politics, there were but two or three festivals per annum, and the performer or festiegoer might attend each of these without straining her budget or vacation schedule. By the early 1990s, festivals in the U.S. included: (by calendar order) the Gulf Coast Womyn's Festival (Mississippi,

Easter), the Virginia Women's Music Festival (Virginia, Mother's Day weekend), Campfest (Maryland/Pennsylvania, Memorial Day weekend), The National Women's Music Festival (Indiana, June), Wiminfest (New Mexico, June), the Northampton Lesbian Festival (Western Massachusetts, July), the Michigan Womyn's Music Festival (Michigan, August), Rhythmfest (the Carolinas/Georgia, Labor Day weekend), the West Coast Women's Music and Comedy Festival (Yosemite National Park, Labor Day weekend), the Ohio Lesbian Festival (Ohio, September), Sisterspace Pocono Weekend (Pennsylvania, September), and the Heart of the West Festival (Las Vegas, November.) Other important regional festivals— the Southern Women's Music and Comedy Festival (Georgia, Memorial Day weekend), Sisterfire (Washington, D.C., June), the East Coast Lesbian Festival (New York, June or Labor Day weekend), the Pacific Northwest Jamboree (Washington state, July), and the New England Women's Music Retreat (Connecticut/New York, Labor Day weekend)—were temporarily or permanently suspended after successful runs of five to ten years. A host of smaller one-time or occasional festivals, some with a specific emphasis on spirituality or separatism, continue to round out the calendar.

Meg Christian strumming at Michigan in the late 1970s.

Obviously, there are now more festivals than any one woman can attend per year—although I have indeed tried and am still trying. There has been an accompanying exponential increase in the number of women's music artists who seek to perform on the festival stage; there are not, however, sufficient spaces for all artists, even within the network of multiple festivals. Seasoned artists want exposure and payment for their stage gig, and only a few "headliners" can really earn a summer's living touring the festivals. These issues of competition will be further addressed in several chapters later on.

From the pool of women who audition to perform music or comedy, festival producers must choose a lineup intentionally varied in ethnicity and music style, sufficient acts to fill several days and nights of stage shows. Audiences will typically enjoy an afternoon stage followed by an after-dinner night stage set, with up to ten acts per day (more at Michigan, which features four stages, and National, which features afternoon "sampler" concerts and theater). Many artists, including emcees, are women whose performances are considered "too feminist" or "too lesbian" for mainstream commercial venues. Nonetheless, these artists are famous and beloved within festival culture, and their albums may be bought through women's bookstores, the mail-order distribution companies, or festival sales. Ironically, it is only in festival culture that some hopefuls go unhired because they are not lesbian *enough*. (When one well-known festival producer showed me the crate of performer audition tapes she had rejected, I found yellow Post-it notes still attached: "Not lesbian enough." "*Some* dyke material." "No references to women." "Too much patriarchal God/He material!")

This selectiveness is justifiable. Many women attend festivals because of the opportunity to meet and hang out with favorite performers; some artists give workshops open to all during the festival weekend.

Simultaneous with the spirited music, theater, and comedy is a clear emphasis on political action and spiritual growth. Featured speakers and workshop presenters include writers and activists who are not musicians: Leslie Feinberg, Colonel Margarethe Cammermeyer, Mandy Carter, Dorothy Allison, and Sonia Johnson are good examples. It is quite possible to attend a festival and, if one wishes, to avoid the music stages entirely, instead immersing oneself in a nonstop series of political workshops, presentations, and debates. Many a revolutionary idea, later a national lesbian trend, came to fruition beneath festival trees. And plenty of women come to festivals just to party and girl watch.

Most interestingly, all festivals attract a mixture of veterans and newcomers, the latter routinely hazed as "festie virgins." Thus the politicization of the newcomer is a regular phenomenon. Although some women attend for purely recreational purposes or to find a girlfriend, by the end of the weekend they may also experience a political awakening to women's culture.

Toni Armstrong Jr.

Alix Dobkin performing at the 1988 Michigan Womyn's Music Festival.

Festivals are still one of the best options for thrifty lesbians. (And what lesbian isn't thrift-minded, when, according to the Women's Bureau of the U.S. Department of Labor, women still earn 73 cents to the male dollar?) A sliding scale admission price, which may be further reduced through work exchange, includes several days' worth of concerts, camping or cabin space, hot vegetarian meals, workshops, sports, and the chance to meet or study with artists in a pleasant setting. This thrill of creating a city of women, no matter how temporary or rustic, attracts both the utopian dreamer-artist and the butch carpenter, as well as a host of other recognizable archetypes.

Some in the lesbian community scoff at these idealistic summer pilgrimages, cynically noting the infamous "festival controversies"—should boy children be allowed? transsexual women? S/M activists?—that crop up each season. Evidence of misunderstandings and hostilities can detract from the utopia festiegoers expect to experience. Festival artist Alix Dobkin, however, reminds us that "part of being at festivals is being angry and frustrated and miserable because our ideals are being tested." Conflict and compromise will be thoroughly discussed in Chapter Six.

Uncomfortable festival politics are not a planned obsolescence. A welcoming atmosphere is a goal; festival organizers generally work around the clock to provide a plethora of services to Deaf, disabled, young, and non–English-speaking campers. Rather, the perennial explosions over racism, classism, and sexuality styles "on the land" more accurately stem from issues already simmering in festiegoers' home communities—issues brought to each festival as baggage, appropriately unpacked among respected peers. The political discussion one attends at Festival X may be as memorable—and as moving—as the music. Certain performers serve as highly valued arbitrators of lesbian politics. (Alix Dobkin is a good example.) Other artists hide in their tents with a sleeping bag pulled firmly over their faces during debate, preferring to express their views through music. And that's OK too.

Part of the challenge—and significance—of the lesbian political framework operating at festivals is the diversity of input. Regional, ethnic, racial, class, age, and ability differences complicate one's personal sense of "belonging." For the non-camper in her first set of thermal underwear, the adjustment to cold outhouses, impertinent insects, innovative vegan meals, and the rowdy nakedness of her neighbor can create physical and psychological discomfort. Yet women return again and again each summer, declaring that festival time is sacred. For a substantial population of lesbian feminists, 20-plus years of festival politics have helped shape career goals, artistic creativity, personal transformation, and activist strategies in no small measure. What binds us together is twofold: the collective experience of the music and the collective safety of being in woman-loving space.

The Main Event: The Women's Music Audience

How is a festival audience created and sustained? The voices of many, many festiegoers can be found in Appendix A, which features scores of festiegoers' comments collected over the past ten years. For the moment, it's first necessary to understand what a miracle festival culture is per se.

Across myriad societies, across centuries of time, male disregard for women's authentic experiences framed most public values. Work, art, and politics were all defined as masculine spheres. To this day, when women dare to forge our own institutions, our efforts are dismissed as irrelevant, as culturally unimportant.

My own good Jewish mother's first response to my immersion in women's music festivals was, "Don't you think you're limiting yourself to a narrow vision of the world?" Initially unable—or unwilling—to comprehend the appeal of women's music, many of our parents expressed dismay that we applied words like *utopia* to festival culture, where there was no male presence or input. Toni Armstrong Jr. describes this unconscious misogyny as "the idea that meeting thousands of women from every country and culture of the world, every ability and disability and talent, cannot compete with meeting one man who might marry you."

What is radical about festival culture, therefore, is not only that it dares to provide a venue for women's politics when radio, television, and Hollywood film do not, but also that festivals make possible an ingathering of artists and audiences who believe that women's voices *should* be heard—and heard daily—not just in music and the arts but in government, religion, medicine, global diplomacy, and so on. We live with the ugly knowledge that despite vague chatter about "postfeminism," most political forces are still not interested in hearing what women have to say, that women—51% of the world's people—are perceived as a "special interest" group when we speak up, despite our enormous range of concerns. We do not limit ourselves to one narrow vision of the world or one narrow application of feminist praxis, but the world certainly limits what is broadcast from our list of concerns.[3] And part of the global campaign to keep women silent and disempowered are stereotypes about women's music and art.

What are those stereotypes? You'll hear that women's music is too white but also too hostile to white *men*, too Western-identified but not an authentically American music genre like jazz or blues or country, too lesbian but not sexy, too folk-sounding and unprofessional but not analogous to the songwriting talents which emerged from male folk protest. No, women's music is "chick music," emotional, insubstantive, whiny girls with guitars—not an important enough medium for anyone to care about. Unless you're a woman, one of the 51% minority.

Since their inception, women's music festivals have of course promised a focus on women's music. But what *is* it? Artists Alix Dobkin and Kay Gardner—who released the first full-length lesbian-identified album, *Lavender Jane Loves Women,* in 1974—spent most of the 1970s educating women-only audiences about the heritage of women's indigenous musical styles. Alix, who studied folk singing and Balkan vocals with ethnomusicologist Ethel Raim, spoke passionately about the vocal heritage of European women, whose ballads and songs revealed ethnic resistance even where women were voiceless politically. Kay gave interview after interview on the concept of a circular form in women's music sound and composition, defining it as both cyclical and climactic and exploring the lost influences of female classical and sacred composers.[4] Women discovering feminism in the 1970s were hungry for the information Alix and Kay provided on female legacies in music, information seldom made available in mainstream books, concerts, or college courses. Similarly, Linda Tillery and Sweet Honey in the Rock's Bernice Johnson Reagon offered audiences insights and performances from their research on the musical heritage of African-American women. The women's music audience thus learned to expect a unique combination of original feminist songwriting from new artists and arrangements or even scholar-

With their copies of HOT WIRE *in hand, Robin Fre and Kay Gardner laugh it up at the 1990 Michigan Womyn's Music Festival.*

Toni Armstrong Jr.

ly lectures inspired by the existing legacy of "lost" female song. Not incidentally, exposure to the beauty of women's music arrangements inspired many a festiegoer to join the feminist choruses growing around the United States, such as the Los Angeles Women's Community Chorus, led by Sue Fink, or the Anna Crusis Women's Choir in Philadelphia (and later, Muse in Cincinnati), led by Cathy Roma.

Over the past quarter century, fresh questions regularly emerged about festival producers' obligations toward showcasing a diverse range of musical styles and messages. Should the women's music stage include punk and thrash and mosh pits? Women who sing tributes to male political prisoners? Women who perform music composed and arranged by men? Does "women's music" imply specifically lesbian-feminist lyrics? Who decides?

Often the audience decides ex post facto. The producers and booking agents take the risks in promoting new or unusual acts, for their sails are rigged to catch fresh trends in the wind. But the festival audience also votes its preferences by responding, writing feedback on festival evaluations, arguing, applauding, confronting. "The play is soup; the audience, art," said Lily Tomlin in her Broadway hit *The Search for Signs of Intelligent Life in the Universe,* and it's true here too. The festival audience is looking for an extension of its collective self-image on that stage.

In one of the most insightful interviews ever published in the women's music and culture journal *HOT WIRE,* composer and festival artist Sue Fink declared:

> Why not include everybody's music? It gives people more choices. Which brings me to my definition of women's music: I don't think we have "women's music"—I think we have a women's music audience. We have a group of people who want to hear music by and about women. Usually in the rest of the world you have people who like folk music, or reggae, or hip-hop; in women's music we basically have an audience of women, each one wanting to be at an event where women somehow are performing and speaking to her, and she gets to be in her community and have a night out in the company of other women, without necessarily going to a bar.[5]

Sue Fink makes several excellent points in this 1991 interview. She reminds us of the importance of music events as cultural alternatives to the bar scene, which until the mid 70s was often the only environment where lesbians might meet. Women-only spaces that did not revolve around alcohol were not just a cultural breakthrough but a blessing for women in recovery, straight feminists, young lesbians under legal bar age, and anyone else uncomfortable with the frequently smoky and depressing urban watering holes reserved for "our kind." Concerts offered a refreshing means for meeting new friends and allies, where one might hear political exhortation and/or a spiritually uplifting message, relax, and be entertained—in short, woman-loving affirmation rather than degradation.

As a new medium for female musicians in the 1970s, festivals were also entrusted with the responsibility of hiring a lineup that always reflected the sensibility of woman-loving. Festiegoers might cheerfully pay good money to sleep on tree roots in the rain, but they sure expected to hear lesbian pride affirmed from the stage by lesbian musicians at least some of the time, especially since the lesbian community

Karen Jones of the Reel World String Band at the 1991 Michigan Womyn's Music Festival. She once remarked, "There's nothing like mass media to ruin a good hometown culture."

Toni Armstrong Jr.

itself overwhelmingly provided festivals with unpaid work crews and risk-taking investors. This demand for vocally lesbian-identified stage performers often frustrated artists who identified as artists, not as *lesbian musicians*, a term as limiting to some as the antiquated term *poetess.*[6]

But Sue Fink's comments also point out that the audience is more interested in being part of a women's event than in paying for a specific music-appreciation experience. This emphasis on community ingathering and the collective moment of women's space means that audiences will respond just as pleasurably to an entertainer who is flirtatious, warm, and fun—off-key or in one key only—as they will to an artist with sophisticated musical training. Elsewhere in her *HOT WIRE* interview, Sue Fink took a risk and expressed her personal frustration with this state of affairs: "In many ways I'm disappointed that we don't have a more educated audience to tell the difference between something which is really musically and lyrically art versus something that is just fun entertainment.... I just feel that if you're going to do something, do it with art. And there's so much that *isn't*."[7]

Sue's notorious good humor, energy, and generosity have led Gulf Coast Womyn's Festival producers Wanda and Brenda Henson to establish an annual Sue Fink Award; she has earned the right to raise serious questions about artistic integrity in women's music. Has the women's music audience of which she speaks developed more cultural than musical sensitivity? Are we trained to cheer loudly at any mention of Martina Navratilova from the stage yet still unable to appreciate a composer's brilliance? Ready to affirm *any* performer who uses the word *lesbian* in a song, no matter how uninspired the rendition, but unwilling to support classical instrumentalists with our feminist dollars? Sue isn't the only one interested in this issue. Quite a few festival "divas"—including operatically trained Justina Golden, operatic satirists Barb Glenn and Susan Nivert (who perform as the Derivative Duo), and classical guitarist Leah Zicari—have expressed this reasonable desire for higher standards.

The reality is that only a few women anywhere grow up with the kind of affluence where music lessons or music appreciation classes are part of their childhood routine. The cost of a musical instrument itself can be prohibitive, and its value a constant theft risk.[8] Budget cuts in public school curricula have tragically reduced the opportunities for girls (and boys) to study music in elementary school, and sexism still prevents many women from gaining access to advanced training—or from being taken seriously as an artist if they do persevere.[9]

Without access to alternative or public radio programs which feature the occasional cut by a feminist artist, many women in small-town America grow up with radio stations that rock through an entire day without playing women's bands. And coming out as a lesbian doesn't guarantee one will find women's music in the local queer community. To this day, some lesbian bars are far more likely to play country music or male rappers than to offer lesbian-affirming dance music out of the Ladyslipper catalog. As the Kentucky lesbian band Yer Girlfriend lamented in 1991:

> Women's communities are hungry for music that is not only entertaining, but also *political*.... Believe it or not, many women's bars have nothing women-oriented on their jukeboxes or in their entertainment schedules. That was certainly the case in the male-owned lesbian bar in our hometown, which featured wet T-shirt contests and female drag shows. ("Cris who?") We figured it was time for some radical consciousness-raising![10]

That Yer Girlfriend could address this as a problem in 1991—more than 15 years after the launching of women's music festivals and concerts and Olivia Records—indicates the ongoing indifference of many lesbian clubs to independent women artists. Yet for good, sexy dance music, there are any number of lesbian rap and rock artists with a strong feminist consciousness, from Nedra Johnson and Rashida Oji and June Millington to the great Baltimore-area band Two Funkin' Heavy. There's the exciting white working-class rap of British lesbian Marilyn T. There's plenty of lesbian country-and-western satire you can two-step to and sexy jazz and world music—but women's bars seem unaware of the rich resources so popular with festival audiences. Monie Love's "Monie in the Middle," a standard cut played in Boston's lesbian bars during the early 1990s, was certainly great to dance to but also was sold in stores as a cassette single with an utterly homophobic rap ("Yo, faggot!") on its flip side. Festivals are therefore the only ongoing lesbian event where women's music is the rule, not the exception.

Festivals, however, are not just concerts but social getaways and vacations, where partying, sex, and good fun are high on the list of things to do for many women attending. A substantial percentage of the first-time audience will be women whose only exposure to lesbian culture has been The Bar, The Softball Team, and The Relationship. Women's music will seem brand new. Seeing a *woman* play bass, play drums, blow out an amplifier, bust a guitar string in mid riff, snarl "More in the monitor!" at an equally tough sound technician will be brand new. The newcomer audience, which is so important to extending and perpetuating festival culture, thus overlaps with returning festiegoers who know the herstory of women's music and have definite favorites. The challenge for the performer is to win everybody's hearts.

To give Sigmund Freud's famous complaint a lesbian-feminist twist, we might cry out, "What does a women's music festival audience want?" Sue Fink has answered that this audience wants, foremost, an intimate community event which celebrates women's space *and* personal inclusion therein. This is a given at festivals. Ranging from one to eight days, festivals create an instant majority of woman, a backdrop against which the actual concerts can assume different purposes: to radicalize, challenge, even upset the audience. Ideally, diversity in performers will guarantee that at some point each woman present will have her musical hunger satisfied. It is just as likely that with several days and evenings of entertainment provided, most women will skip or nap through a performer or two; at the Michigan Womyn's Music Festival and the National Women's Music Festivals, for instance, only Wonder Woman could muster the speed and energy to whisk about the land and see every performance scheduled between noon and 2 A.M. (New lovers, busily necking during every show, probably don't even notice the music, and I'll confess to using some of my own friends' best stage sets as background environment for important conversations or journal entries under way at the time.) Thus, at festivals, an entertainment lineup is selected to offer festiegoers an admixture of experienced touring performers, new faces, reliable crowd pleasers, provocateurs, top-quality artists from countries and/or cultures other than the United States, and good comedy and theatrics as well. Chapter Seven addresses festival humor and comedians, and there are numerous "variety" performers, such as Dos Fallopia, Lynn Thomas, and Monica Grant, whose skills in combining music and comedy defy easy categorization. Lesbian magician, comedian, juggler, and fire-eater Ann Lincoln deserves a category all her own.

What a tolerant audience asks is simply not to have its sensibilities offended, but this means very different things to different women. A boring performer or an inept newcomer with limited material never generates the disappointed and angry feedback brought on by an artist who insults women with sexist or racist comments. An artist who primarily tours among straight and/or mainstream audiences may feel justifiably terrified of the festival audience, sensing that musical mistakes may be tolerated here but political slipups less quickly forgiven.[11]

Despite the stereotype that we are political correctness police running amok, verbal hostility from a festival audience is surprisingly rare. I can recall half a dozen incidents of actual hissing or booing from my own 17 years of festival going. One incident involved a performer's joke about killing boy children, another was a performer who referred to a celebrity as a "big-toothed cunt," and *all* other incidents were responses to racially insensitive material. Humorists are more likely to take risks with offensive routines and so receive stronger reactions. In the context of festival politics, the one bad moment out of five glorious days quickly becomes legend and subject to endless discussion—often in the pages of *Lesbian Connection* magazine.

Accepting Sue Fink's point that each woman wants to feel the performer is speaking *to her*, we can better see how feelings of exclusion or insult create a shock

Sue Fink speaking at the 1992 Gulf Coast Womyn's Festival, which established an award in her name.

Toni Armstrong Jr.

wave: "This performer is not making me feel welcome here *at all*! Who hired *her*?" My own competent, woodsworthy, Jewish Camp Fire girl heart broke into two jagged halves when I heard one performer begin her routine with, "I'm a Jew, and we don't camp." Performers have the microphone power to reinforce stereotypes—or disprove them. But for all the tales of political correctness at festivals, more often the reality is that of a generous audience *not* talking back and instead trying desperately to understand the joke.

A few examples will suffice. One festival performer declared to an audience chock-full of ex-military lesbians that "people in the military aren't really people," an even more problematic insult when one takes into account the high percentage of women of color in uniform. At another festival a popular jazz artist dedicated a new piece to her male friend, explaining to confused onlookers that this friend had just been jailed for attempted political assassination. Still another festival featured a stunning South African performance group whose night stage repertoire included songs celebrating girls' circumcision rituals, a cultural issue deeply troubling to many feminists. Moments like these—and others I witnessed and tape recorded—are rare and were all let pass by audiences who really *did* like the artists' musical abilities and who tried their damnedest to understand the artists' perspectives. No one ever suggested these aforementioned performers should be silenced or banned; there was no hissing to be heard.

As members of an audience exposed to performers who are almost never reviewed or acknowledged by mainstream critics, we play two roles. We hope to be entertained, surely, but we also feel an obligation to supply critical, serious feedback where *Entertainment Weekly, Rolling Stone,* and *Spin* will not. We watch and take mental notes simultaneously—a demanding process. Perhaps the writer and humorist Jean Kerr said it best in a short story about attending endless Broadway openings with her husband, the famous critic Walter Kerr: "The critic says: This is an extremely bad play—why is that? The audience says: This is an extremely bad play—why was I born? There is a real difference."[12]

But for the festival audience, there is no difference. We are audience *and* critics for our culture. We alone see and rate our artists. And overall, we tend to be very kind and loving. We all know, to some degree, the risks a woman accepts when she finds her voice and sings out to the world.

The Collective Affirmation of Loving Women ⋙

A primary attraction for festiegoers is the freedom to walk hand in hand with another woman. This public affirmation of coupledom cannot be overestimated. Where outside in the "fake world," as Alix Dobkin says, there are very real penalties for lesbians who come out to their families and employers and schools, at festivals we have carte blanche to enjoy the normative functions our straight friends take for granted: hand holding, sweet talk, cuddling under a tree on a beach towel, watching a concert with her head on your shoulder. These simple public actions pose real dangers in homophobic society, and observing otherwise closeted lesbians experience new liberty is a bittersweet phenomenon. Some couples attending their first festival demonstrate a positive mania of public togetherness by dressing exactly alike throughout the weekend, right down to their matching fanny packs. (Of course, this does make it easier to find one's partner in a crowd.) Some couples ostentatiously make love on the ground in an open field. Some begin every sentence with "My partner and I…" or "Where *we* live…" These mannerisms may not be at all indicative of how these two live and behave all the rest of the year. Instead, they often signify the burst of relief many lesbians feel at "coming home" to festival space, where love between women wins approval and sanction, not punishment and ostracism.

Not all festival performers are lesbians, but all are counted on to embrace a pro-lesbian work ethic and to respect the sentiments of a primarily lesbian audience/fan base. How do these artists protect their sexual privacy at the same time? The audience demands to know: Is she or isn't she a dyke? And yet when a performer does speak glowingly of her woman lover—perhaps in a song about their successful long-term relationship—some audience members are curiously disappointed, preferring the brief fantasy that Favorite Performer X is single and available or, again, singing directly to *her*. The performer's real-life lover endures her share of embarrassment, invisibility, and/or audience jealousy at such times.

Two different examples may illustrate this quandary. At one festival, I listened to the very romantic Quebecois performer Lucie Blue Tremblay dedicate several songs to her new girlfriend, speaking passionately about their love and commitment. I observed Lucie's girlfriend, seated next to me in the audience, blush and squirm as jealous women throughout the audience baited Lucie with catcalls of, "So where *is* your lucky woman, huh?" In an entirely different incident,

21

years earlier, my own girlfriend was a sign language interpreter working onstage, and I was forced to listen to 8,000 spellbound fans of hers comment loudly about how good she must be with her hands, etc. These experiences do sensitize one to the privacy issues confronting women who work onstage, who are adored as our festival celebrities, but who have lives offstage as well. Probably no performer has felt these pressures more than Holly Near. Holly's celebrated com-

Holly Near in a powerful moment at the 1990 Michigan Womyn's Music Festival.

Toni Armstrong Jr.

ing-out album *Imagine My Surprise!*, released in 1978, introduced thousands of women to a lesbian music sensibility that was simultaneously political and romantic. After years of being idolized by lesbian audiences at festivals and city concerts nationwide, Holly published a 1990 autobiography making clear her involvement with a male partner. Still performing at festivals, often with Ronnie Gilbert, Holly Near has lost none of the political intelligence that made her work so nourishing to fans across two decades. Yet some festival audiences pressure her to apologize for "reverting" to heterosexual relationships. In recent years Holly rose to this challenge by commenting during her concert rap that her straight friends said they wanted to throw up when she came out as a lesbian— whereas now lesbian friends say they want to throw up at the thought of Holly with men. For all these reasons, many performers prefer never to invoke their personal lives onstage, lest today's confidences become tomorrow's gossip—undermining album sales along the way. Alison Bechdel's cartoon "Servants to the Cause" demonstrates the tension lesbian audiences feel over successful lesbian artists who don't come out:

On the other hand, many straight women who perform at festivals delight in greeting their audiences with firm statements of support for lesbian culture. Holocaust survivor and pianist Henia Goodman told the 1982 Michigan festival audience that she had "survived the concentration camps in order to play Chopin," then added, "And you are all so kind to me that I think I may try women." This gentle flirtation was a genuine "festival moment," wherein weeping and laughter, history and freedom to choose coalesced in the audience response to her candid words. Another inspiring crossover artist is comic and actress Judith Sloan, who over a 15-year era of festival performing moved from lesbian relationships to marrying a male political activist. She is uniquely able to address both lesbian and

Interpreter Sherry Hicks pays homage to the audience at the 1989 Michigan Womyn's Music Festival.

Toni Armstrong Jr.

straight feminists in her audiences today, demanding a political ethic of all and a sexual orientation of none.[13] Peggy Platt of the comedy duo Dos Fallopia puts her cards on the table about being heterosexual, and rebukes the audience for producing an inevitable groan of disappointment, then proceeds to thank everyone in festival culture for making her an "honorary lesbian."

Woman loving is the ethic, broadly interpreted but never trivialized. When I first attempted to describe festival culture to my father in 1981, he said, "Oh.

Um, a bunch of women go off in the woods and feel good about themselves for a few days?" He has certainly seen the light since then, attending Sisterfire (which was open to men) with my mother and I and proudly welcoming festival artists, including Sherry Hicks, Lynn Thomas, and Alix Dobkin, into the Morris household. Yet in 1981 he was candid about his misunderstanding of an institution based on female self-affirmation—a musical institution receiving no critical artistic attention in our woman-devaluing society.

Every day, women—and particularly poor women, women of color, and lesbians—pick up the newspaper to read that we are unwelcome in American life, our very identities pathologized, made responsible for the nation's moral decline. The problem of female poverty, the rape and battery of women by their male partners or relatives, and contempt for single mothers (not absent fathers!) has not improved, despite the best efforts of the women's movement—there is only greater *awareness* of these ongoing social issues.

Festivals provide a concentrated blast of antidote, where we are, for three to eight days, *not* the problem but the solution, *not* responsible for the sins of Eve but back in Eden ourselves, planting apple trees from whence grow women's knowledge. The visible or even excessive displays of love and partnership during festival time are one part of this journey back to feeling entitled to love—to feeling lovable.

A full generation of annually produced festivals stands as proof of success. Festivals large and small have been held in 25 of the 50 states, including Hawaii and Alaska. What is the practical structure of this ongoing subculture? Who are its sustaining returnees? And how will music trends and political change in the coming 21st century shape the future generation(s) of festival activists? Let the story begin.

1. Until 1994, even *Ms.* magazine had not sent a reporter to the Michigan Womyn's Music Festival.

2. Thyme Siegel, letter to the editor, *HOT WIRE,* May 1992: p. 6.

3. Witness, for instance, the jeering and spotty news coverage of the Fourth U.N. World Conference on Women in Beijing during September 1995. In the United States, far more attention was allocated to ballplayer Cal Ripkin on all three television networks during the most important days of the Beijing conference.

4. "Female Composition: Interview with Kay Gardner," *Women's Culture*, ed. Gayle Kimball (Scarecrow Press, 1981).

5. Sue Fink, interviewed by Toni Armstrong Jr. in *HOT WIRE*, May 1991, p. 5.

6. See, for instance, Cris Williamson's comments in *HOT WIRE*, September 1989, p. 4; Jean Fineberg's letter to the editor in *HOT WIRE*, March 1988, p. 7; and comments by Phranc and Two Nice Girls in Gillian Gaar's *She's a Rebel: The History of Women in Rock and Roll* (Seal Press, 1992), pp. 381-383.

7. Sue Fink, ibid., p. 4.

8. See Laura Post's article, "Women and Their Guitars," in *HOT WIRE*, September 1992.

9. Carol MacDonald's band Isis had the opportunity to audition for Herb Alpert (the A in A&M Records) in the 1970s. According to MacDonald, his response was: "They're great, but I think women look stupid playing horns." Gillian Gaar, *She's A Rebel*, p. 143.

10. Laura Shine and Patty O. Veranda, "Down Home With Yer Girlfriend." *HOT WIRE*, May 1991, p. 31.

11. Janis Ian, performing at the National Women's Music Festival in 1995—her first U.S. tour since coming out publicly as a lesbian—began her set by declaring how nervous she was to play for an all-woman festival audience. She was most graciously received, but regrettably went on to write several columns critical of festival culture (and the appearances of lesbian festiegoers) in the gay and lesbian magazine *The Advocate*. Interviewed by Lee Fleming for the 1996 book *Hot Licks: Lesbian Musician of Note*, Ian wrote "I don't perform at lesbian music festivals if I can help it, though. I don't participate as a performer at exclusionary festivals." (p. 53.) It should be noted that the National Festival, where Ian appeared, is open to men.

12. Jean Kerr, "I Don't Want to See the Uncut Version of Anything," in *Penny Candy* (New York: Doubleday, 1970), p. 88. Previously published in Dramatists' Guild Bulletin.

13. See Judith Sloan, "Is She or Isn't She...An Outrageous Feminist?" in *HOT WIRE*, January 1992.

CHAPTER TWO

The Early Years: Herstory and Production Stories

It's fun being a pioneer. You've just got to live long enough to enjoy it.
—Cris Williamson

I remember performing in Los Angeles in 1970 at a rally in MacArthur Park, and they didn't have sound equipment. Why? "Because," my sisters said to me, "that's men's toys, and you can't use them." And I asked, "Well, then how the heck am I going to sing?" And they presented me with two bullhorns, one for my vocals and one for the guitar. It took a few years until we had women engineers!
—Maxine Feldman

When I sat in on my first workers' meeting at Michigan, there was a real attitude about performers. The carpenters were the big shots then—still are! Those were the days when Lisa Vogel used to walk around with a carpenter belt full of cash. Someone would come up and say, "Lisa, we need $400 for lumber to build a light tower," and she'd count out $400. It was wild! There were no receipts. Nobody knew how much was going out or coming in.
—Alix Dobkin

I have a great line for National. Somebody will come up, and they'll say, "Why don't you do this?" or "Why don't you include that?" And I say, "Excellent idea! Are you going to volunteer for it next year? Would you like to coordinate that area?" That either shuts them up or puts them on the spot.
—National Women's Music Festival producer Mary Byrne

In a three-year period, 1973–1976, festival culture blossomed in lesbian America. It began in the West with Kate Millet's 1973 festival at Sacramento State University and the San Diego festival in 1975, eventually spreading the women's music spirit via the multicity Women on Wheels concert tour produced in California by Boo Price in 1976.[1] Simultaneously, festival culture emerged in the

Photographer Toni Armstrong Jr. and Lynn Siniscalchi at the HOT WIRE *booth at the 1989 National Women's Music Festival.*

Janet Ryan

Midwest with a 1974 Missouri festival and Kristin Lems's first National Women's Music Festival at Champaign-Urbana, Ill., also in 1974. And it appeared in the East with the Boston women's music festival held in September of 1975, where 18-year-old Lisa Vogel and her sister Kristie, attending from Michigan with several other interested college students, began to think about creating the first Michigan Womyn's Music Festival for 1976.

These first venues showcased the new music recorded by Cris Williamson, Meg Christian, Margie Adam, Alix Dobkin and Kay Gardner, the Chicago and New Haven Women's Liberation Rock Bands; gave Maxine Feldman a place to perform "Amazon Women Rise" for the first time; and provided the newly established women's independent label Olivia Records with a sales and performance market for its emerging lesbian artists. Several women had their big break when two mainstream performers scheduled for the first National Women's Music Festival—Yoko Ono and Roberta Flack—canceled and had to be replaced by lesser-known artists. Later festivals would be less self-consciously white, more professionally produced, yet just as politically radical: women performing for women and singing about women loving women in a decade that swept from the triumphs of Title IX and *Roe* v. *Wade* to the defeats of the Equal Rights Amendment and the election of Ronald Reagan.

The early years of festival culture were marked by trial and error, distrust of hierarchy, conflicting ideological visions, and the endless financial worry still familiar to women producing large-scale events today. But lesbian feminists in the early 1970s had two advantages: an antimodel (the rowdy and sexist male rock venues from the past decade) and a feminist organizational legacy stretching back to Rosie the Riveter's WE CAN DO IT! campaigns of World War II. American society's deeply ingrained expectation that women shoulder the load of socially redeeming volunteer work proved both blessing and curse. Few feminists expected much financial return for their efforts, and this nonprofit outlook conflicted with the high professional standards (and accompanying salaries) required for tech production. But with far less capital to invest and certainly no honored place on the social ladder, lesbian feminists also had the least to lose in constructing a new music and performance industry.

Ironically, during the early years of festival culture, some lesbian activists radiated distrust toward artists or producers who seemed too "Hollywood," too slick. The grassroots spirit of authenticity and struggle informed most stage acts and the women's music sound, and collective decision making was the order of the day. In her research on 1970s lesbian-feminist culture, historian Lillian Faderman commented on festival politics:

> At the first National Women's Music Festival in Champaign, Ill., in 1974, singers who appeared too professional, like stars, got a cold reception. The audience wanted to see their own declassed, unslick image onstage…. In fact, "professionalism" of any kind was considered undesirable hierarchical behavior: It represented artifi-

cial and destructive categories, barriers set up by the patriarchy that limited the possibilities of women "creating a vision together."[2]

It's important to conjure up these conditions. Research on "collective visions," on decisions made collectively long ago, can frustrate the historian. Who really inspired, drafted, wrote which speech? idea? song? The blurring of accountability is a by-product of consensus; it can mask leaders. Frustrated feminist Jo Freeman addressed this problem in her landmark article "The Tyranny of Structurelessness," first published under the name Joreen in the early 1970s and later reprinted in the 1973 text *Radical Feminism*. Of course, the consensus-based community ethic wasn't brand-new or invented by lesbian feminists; the Society of Friends, or Quakers, are one religious group who have long operated by such methods. But the identification of hierarchy with patriarchy meant that lesbian feminists engaged in festival work could be tough on women with real leadership skills. Though their money, ability, and organizational know-how were sorely needed, producers who had to make the final decisions were routinely scrutinized for their "control issues"—meaning their loyalty to feminist consensus and antihierarchy.

Toni Armstrong Jr.

Michigan Womyn's Music Festival producer Lisa Vogel in 1997.

If the producer happened to be Jewish, words like *pushy* might be applied in unconscious or overt anti-Semitism; this was Robin Tyler's experience during her years with festival and comedy production.

These producers, who undertook the greatest risks in launching new festivals, are living texts themselves: Lisa and Kristie Vogel, Boo Price, Robin Tyler, Wanda and

Brenda Henson, Lee Glanton, Kristin Lems and Mary Byrne, Tam Martin, Michelle Crone, Maile Klein and Marina Hodgini, Lin Daniels and Myriam Fougere, Chris Patie and Kim Kimber, Amy Horowitz and the women of Roadwork in Washington, D.C. Most of these women have been profiled repeatedly in the lesbian press, in some instances giving classic interviews that cannot be improved upon here. (For an excellent interview with National Women's Music Festival producer Mary Byrne and a splendid overview of Lisa Vogel's role in the Michigan festival's development, see Loraine Edwalds's and Midge Stocker's 1995 anthology *The Woman-Centered Economy.*) For this chapter, I sought oral narratives from five women who have (temporarily, perhaps) retired from festival production after years or decades of success. I was curious to see how separation from active festival work might color reflections on years past.

Included here are narratives from four producers and with pioneer festival sound technician Boden Sandstrom, one of many women to break into the formerly all-male arena of stage production. What is most remarkable is their open candor in noting how they learned from one another. As the baton was passed across 15 years or more, proven methods and standards of excellence paved the way for regional festival expansion. Where Boo Price recalls sneaking in men to fix rain-soaked sound equipment at the second Michigan festival in 1977, Tam Martin's decision to start her own festival in 1989 seems a leisurely magic trick, the title scrawled down on a bar napkin and a site picked by the following week. Boo Price—who inspired Robin Tyler, who inspired Tam Martin—began festival work training other women to take themselves seriously in production.

BOO (BARBARA) PRICE

Coproducer of the Michigan Womyn's Music Festival (1976–1994)
Producer, main stage, West Coast Women's Music and Comedy Festival (1979)

The first outdoor lesbian event of a festival nature that I went to was the San Diego Women's Festival in 1974. We all kind of got there by accident. There was very little; it was very rough—a little platform for sound—but we were totally excited. There were so many downpours—this was in the desert hills outside San Diego—that most of it got washed out. It started me thinking about the possibilities of outdoor production. At that point I'd only done indoor production.

In those early days I think I was perceived as the producer who was always pushing for better quality production. And there weren't very many of us as producers to begin with! But that was part of my role. I was certainly criticized for it at the time—for going from basements into theaters, getting "overground" press. I got the first regular newspaper coverage of concerts in [California's Bay Area, including Berkeley, Oakland, and San Francisco]. Also, I was determined to work with women technicians, and there were almost none. I looked for anybody with the slightest inclination! We were at the very early stages of building the sense of community that underpinned festival culture; there was almost a hysteria about getting together as lesbians in large groups for concerts that validated the new wave of feminist identity.

Toni Armstrong Jr.

Dr. Ruth Simkin "in the mix" at the 1991 Michigan Womyn's Music Festival.

This was the background I brought to festivals. I was managing Margie Adam, and we went to the Boston Women's Music Festival in 1975. A group of college students drove there from Mt. Pleasant in central Michigan because they couldn't get this music in Michigan. So they went to where the music was, and this later led to the name the "We Want the Music Collective." That was Lisa Vogel, her sister Kristie, Mary Kindig [who is the only original Collective member still active as a festival coordinator], and others. Lisa was perceived to be too young to represent the group, so they didn't let her talk to us, but Kristie came forward to talk to Margie and me. They said they would see us again in Chicago at a concert Margie was doing at The Second City theater in four weeks. They were like so many excited young women we met on the road; we didn't think much about seeing them again. When we got to Chicago and saw them, they said they wanted to bring Margie to Michigan the following summer to do an outdoor concert. I told them, "Sure, we'll talk about it. Call me."

Well, by the time they called, they had the idea to do two or three sets in this day, outside. I said, "I have a lot of thoughts about outside festivals. Because right before we saw you, we'd just come from San Diego. So I'm really interested to work with you, and I can collaborate." Now, this was still supposedly a one-day concert with three sets—that's it. The next time we talked with them, it was going to be a whole weekend.

A few of us talked among ourselves. Ginny Berson [at Olivia Records] called me. "Who are these kids in Michigan? Do they know enough about what they're doing? They're trying to book Meg Christian. What do you think?" I said, "We're going to work with them. They seem really inexperienced, but let's give them a chance."

The next thing we hear, they're having internal problems because there's a question about whether it should be all women or mixed, men and women. I said, "It can be mixed if it's *one day*. If it's over the weekend and people are going to be sleeping out, it has to be women only, or we won't be there." Eventually, that issue broke up their committee of producers. The people who really wanted it to be mixed left.

That's how I got there to begin with—and I went as Margie's manager. Then I asked, "Who's doing the sound?" They had a man and a woman, sister and brother, though it was his company. I said, "You *have* to have a woman engineer." Well, at that point there was almost nobody, just Marilyn Ries. Nobody had done outside stuff. I was just starting to work with Margot McFedries—that's a whole other story. I bought her first sound mixer for her, a little baby board. I said, "You've gotta keep learning because I've got to have a woman engineer." So I said, "Bring Margot to Michigan," and they agreed. She worked with the sister of the team they'd hired, and that was our technical crew!

No stage production to speak of. One potato out of an oil drum for dinner. We were all so excited that it almost didn't matter. Lisa was finally allowed to come forward and talk with me; she had just turned 19, and I was almost 32. That's a huge difference. But I said, "If you're thinking of doing this again, I'd love to talk with you about production." And the first thing I said was, "You need better graphics." And I recommended Sally Piano, a talented songwriter and pianist out of the Washington, D.C., area who had performed at that festival and a *great* graphic designer. She had just moved to Chicago. She designed the now-famous Michigan piano-tree logo, and for a while, she and Lisa became lovers. Meanwhile, I said, "There needs to be a production company and a producer. I'll produce the stage and bring my own people." Lisa was into it and convinced the Collective that they could bring in this group of five or six women from California.

So from the second festival on, I was producing the stage. When did we get sign-language interpreters? Oh, that would be Susan Freundlich, beginning in 1980. Honey, at this point we barely had sound engineers! I brought in the values I had about production. I also said, "You have to have lights," and I brought in Leni Schwendinger, who I had met when she was working as a clown and who reluctantly started working as a lighting tech because we needed one. She quickly became a brilliant lighting designer and worked with me for many years. And Jennifer James, a friend of Margie's from Santa Barbara, Calif., was our first stage manager; so many women now in the field ended up being trained by Jennifer James.

It was a big step, having a production crew. And schedules! And sound checks! All of that. In Hesperia [the Michigan festival site until 1982] we did three concerts in the afternoon, three concerts at night. Lisa was trying to buy a sound system from this guy, and it was being kind of built and tweaked on the spot. And there was torrential rain, and everything flooded. We'd have to stop and take the whole system apart. This man was working child care for boys at the other end of the land, and we'd bring him in in the middle of the night to put the equipment together. We'd dry everything off, lay it out. It was nuts. Therese Edell would stand onstage, performing without amplification when the system wasn't working.

We were making it up as we went along. Like Lisa laid out snow fencing to accommodate women in wheelchairs; it was rough going to try to roll over, but it represented an attempt to provide accessibility. And so much of it was fighting the elements. The second two years were heavy rain years: 1977 had a series of the worst thunderstorms they'd ever had continuously in Oceana County, and '78 saw a tornado.

When we were in Hesperia, even though I was doing producing, I would run a workshop on production at least once or twice during each festival. And so women producers would come—whoever was there—and we'd share information. That was how we brought in crew, and it was the beginning of our awareness of a network of production people. Later, volunteers would just come to us. Here's a story of a woman who just walked up at the second or third festival and said, "I'll help": She looked like a good worker, and she helped as a stage hand that whole time. This was Muffin Spencer-Devlin. She told us, "I'm going to start playing professional golf this fall!" She was just barely on the tour then.

The year I took Robin Tyler was 1978; we were having a little fling. She came from television—she was waiting on a contract with ABC then—and although she had all the best feminist politics in her act, I had to help her get over her feeling that the women's music scene was just kids in basements. And she was so fascinated by what she saw, by the huge audiences we had even then, that she went home and began to think about creating her own festival.

I had a very significant role in launching festivals where none had been before because I was a collaborator and consultant with Kristie and Kindig before the start and then, by the second festival, with Lisa. I took a production team to produce the stage from the second Michigan festival on. I encouraged Chris Patie to become a concert producer in Hartford, Conn., and then to come to Michigan to look over my shoulder, then go back to Connecticut to start the North East Women's Music Retreat. I took a production team to the first NEWMR to get them started and to train local women to continue. I took Robin Tyler to her first festival in 1978 and then later produced the main stage for her in California in 1982, when she was getting started with the West Coast festival.

Lisa and I worked closely together to create the concert production of the Michigan stage from the start, but it was she and Kristie and the women of the WWTM Collective who launched the Michigan festival. I would say that from 1983 on, Lisa and I developed the festival beyond the monofocus of the performance stages, into the form that is now recognized as "The Festival." The early years are significant because they were the organic creation of festival culture. The largest factor was that feminist women—mostly lesbian—would go to great lengths to get together in large groups, brought by the excuse of their new "women's music" but driven by a desire to affirm an identity as independent women forging a revolution.

There was an ecstatic quality to these first years of gatherings, punctuated by acts of social defiance: letting menstrual blood flow freely, throwing off shirts or all clothing, taking on male-identified jobs such as trench digging, tent stake sledging, stage rigging, tractor driving. Most of festival culture in the early days was the result of doing it all ourselves. The principle activity was sitting in front of the stage and waiting for or watching the concerts.

By 1982 the Michigan festival had been in operation for seven years, and it seemed to be running its course. The Collective wasn't willing to take on real financial debt of buying property; there was so much internal dissent that little joy was apparent among festival workers. The leadership was putting far more of its energy in conflict than in creativity. Large audiences began to dwindle, and festival debt was mounting.

When Lisa and I agreed to pool our skills and experience and see what we could do as coproducers, I believed that the future of the festival lay in the ability to create a much more conscious community for both the workers and the campers. We began to build much more of a staff village and to actively seek women from other countries to join the working staff. Expanding the Signz area from Mitzi's lone drawing table to a whole artistic complex had the same effect that valuing art in any community has. Creating a meal area for all workers that was attractive and comforting rather than segregating the staff by those who could eat with the performers and those who couldn't was essential in building worker-family esteem.

On the camper side, my personal determination was to create more and more opportunities for women to create and participate in festival programs and traditions. The tenth festival was the first year we ever had the international welcome or an opening ceremony, and both had a huge effect in creating a sense of festival community and shared culture. The creation of the community center, One World tent and workshop program, open reel video showings, Women Over 40 and Women of Color tents, festival dance classes, quilting, and the festival band, chorus, and choir transformed the definition of festival culture. Women returned year after year to create their own performances, to share their work, to find affinity groups with structures for networking. The printed program itself was important to the development of festival culture because it documented what we were all doing there together, the richness and diversity of who we were together. It gave words and context to what we created and elaborated on year after year.

I believe the festival would have foundered beyond repair in the early '80s if there hadn't been a major shift in the priorities by creating a cultural expansion. What became known as "festival culture" was then replicated in many of the regional festivals—even carrying over festival names, jargon, customs—with individual variations and distinctions. It created a common tribe of women who recognized one another across national borders, language barriers, ethnic backgrounds, and all the differences that so readily define and separate us.

❖❖❖❖❖❖❖❖❖❖❖❖❖❖❖

Within two years of experiencing her first time at Michigan, veteran comedy performer Robin Tyler was determined to produce an event of her own. Despite the San Diego, Sacramento, and concert tour events that established women's music in California during the early to mid 1970s, the bulk of festival action took root in the Midwest and remained there. Those who scratched their heads at the success of the Michigan festival and the National festival in Illinois/Indiana might be forgiven for associating all things liberal and feminist with the California coast or the Northeast. Yet it's important to recall that the Midwest has often broken social codes to offer women opportunities: the World War II–era All-American Girls' Baseball League, of course, attracted huge crowds and located its teams squarely in small-town Wisconsin, Michigan, Illinois, and Indiana. The Midwest drew on the tradition of strong, capable farm women and wartime industrial workers, black and white: Why couldn't the same state that built the Motown empire host the largest festival of woman-identified sound? It took producer Robin Tyler to bring a festival back to the California hills.

ROBIN TYLER

Producer: West Coast Women's Music and Comedy Festival (1980–1992);
Southern Women's Music and Comedy Festival (1983–1992);
main stage, March on Washington (1979, 1987, 1993, 2000)

Boo Price and I were dating when she took me to Michigan. At first Lisa [Vogel] did not want me to emcee, as this was a music festival and, she felt, should be emceed by musicians. It was still the mid '70s; I was the first and, at the time, the only openly lesbian comic. I had just done four television pilots, costarred on ABC's Krofft Comedy Hour, and had produced three comedy albums; so although Lisa wasn't sure that comedy was a part of "women's culture," Boo convinced her to let me go on. The response to me was fantastic. However, I was very controversial because I wore a tux, said I was a butch—remember when butch/femme was politically incorrect?—and I was considered "too Hollywood" because I came out of show business. I also made fun of vegetarianism and declared the stage a "crystal-free zone." The majority of the audience loved the material; a small minority did not. Since 80% of stand-up monologuists had been Jewish, I felt badly; I was just too polished, slick, butch, Jewish for Michigan.

The next year, Lisa invited me back to line produce the stage. I remember there was a rainstorm, and I tried to get the women running around on the water-soaked stage to put on their shoes, as they could have been electrocuted by the wiring. They refused, saying the stage was run by a "collective." The other thing that happened that year was that Canadian women—I'm originally from Winnipeg—were being held illegally by immigration at the border. Some Canadians at the festival tried to reach Ginny Apuzzo, then director of the National Gay Task Force. But because both women and men belonged to the NGTF, they would not announce it from the main stage. I finally walked out to the mike on the main stage, surrounded by threatening Michigan security, and made the announcement. Ginny, who is now one of President Bill Clinton's top aides in the White House, did come to the rescue. I do not know who she called, but those women were let out.

Then and there, I decided to start another festival. Unbendable rules made by a few for the majority—in the name of what is "politically correct"—were unacceptable to me. What some women saw as "rules and regulations for women's space," I saw as the equivalent of fundamentalism. Intolerance of others' choices was not acceptable. I was a feminist, and to me feminism meant the right to choose.

Robin Tyler and Boo Price, two happy producers in a candid moment, August 1978.

I spoke to my lover, Torie Osborn. We decided to do a festival. I would put up the money and produce/own the festival, and Torie would be the "director." I had just won an $18,000 settlement from a car accident. This was all the money I had in the world, but I put it up. I loved the dream of a women's festival on the West Coast. I admitted up front that this was a women-owned small business. (So was Michigan, hidden behind the word *collective*.) I did not know that telling the truth was a high crime in the women's community. We were supposed to embrace downward mobility. But downward mobility is a middle-class ethic. Any of us—myself included—coming from poverty did not see the nobility of remaining poor. I had never heard of any revolution fighting for *less*!

So in 1980 I produced the first West Coast Women's Music and Comedy Festival. Two thousand women came; by the second year there were 3,500 at the festival. I was thrilled the week before that second festival. However, at the beginning of it—and this is still painful for me to talk about—a small group of women of color came to me and said that I had to give one third of the festival to women of color, as I was a rich Jew, and Jews were responsible for slavery. I couldn't believe what I was hear-

Robin Tyler with her partner, Lisa Ulrich, at the 1983 West Coast Women's Music and Comedy Festival.

ing! I immediately said that I was from Canada, but they said that it didn't matter, that I had hired "all black women" in the kitchen. Actually, I hadn't. We had hired two African-American coordinators, and they had hired all their friends because the kitchen was the best-paid position on the land—$500. But they said that I was just a rich Jew trying to get rich off the backs of the women's community. They told me I had to give them one third of the business or they would organize a march against the festival. And I said no, that I wouldn't give in to this form of extortion.

That night, over 200 women marched on me while I was on the main stage. A group of women even came with torches—Yosemite had a "no fire" rule because the fire hazard was enormous—and they threatened to burn down the cabin I was in. I was in shock. The Michigan festival, with many more attendees, was not attacked for living off the backs of women. But I was called a rich Jew. At the time, no one was discussing the split between people of color and the Jewish community—the anti-Semitism was rampant. Women held meetings in which I was put on trial for being a racist; of course, I was not allowed at these "trials," never allowed to defend myself, and the press carried their stories.

I had a nervous breakdown. Actually, for the next 12 years I not only disassociated, but to ease my anxieties and nightmares, I also became a periodic alcoholic. The next year the West Coast festival was boycotted, and I lost $50,000—that I didn't have. I managed to persuade the people I owed money to give me one more year.

The reason I write about this is that so many individual women have been attacked by various mobs in the name of oppression at these festivals. To have large groups attack individuals is a form of abuse. It is not actually enlightening or educational. We now know that the cycle of abuse is continuous. Abused people who are not treated batter and abuse others, and being a victim is not an excuse to make other people your victim. Once again, I must thank Boo Price, who took me to the only community meeting where some women admitted they had lied about me. But by that time I was condemned in the gay press, and not one of them carried the story of that community meeting that absolved me of my "crimes." I believe to this day that my only crime was that I was Jewish. I did not write another line of comedy for 12 years, and because I was boycotted, I performed very little for the next five years. The laughter had left my life.

During those next 12 years, the festival was thrown off various campgrounds. Even the city of San Francisco threw us off our original, wonderful land. We went to Boy Scout land in Willits, Calif., but after one year they said we couldn't come back. The Boy Scouts were—and still are—allowed to discriminate based on sexual preference. We finally ended up at a Jewish summer camp near Yosemite National Park and stayed there for the next ten years. And after the fifth year of the West Coast festival, I decided to start one in the South. My lover, Lisa Ulrich, was from Florida, and she said the women of the South really needed their own festival. The Southern Women's Music and Comedy Festival in Georgia was born!

We were in the middle of some of the most red-necked Ku Klux Klan country. We used a Jewish camp in Georgia, but this county made *Deliverance* look liberal.

We were 2,000 strong but still had armed security at our borders because we knew how dangerous it was. That festival lasted for eight years on that land owned by the United Association of Hebrew Congregations—most gay and lesbian synagogues are UAHC members. One Baptist reporter wrote about our being there, and then a handful of people started to threaten UAHC. Did UAHC stand up to them? No, they tried putting us off the land. We fought them for several years. The last year we were there, they doubled our rent. Finally they just told us not to come back. And their leader, Rabbi Alexander Schindler, was at that time going around making speeches about the inclusion of gays and lesbians. They threw us off the land because they were cowards. We moved and lasted one year in North Carolina, but I did not have the heart to continue with that festival.

I have been asked what I think about some of the controversial festival subjects. Leather is fine, as long as it's matching. Actually, I truly believe women have the right to choose, whether I agree with their choices on a personal level or not. At one festival an artist sang, "Meet me in the woods." However, a group of about 20 women came to me and insisted that the artist sang, "*Beat* me in the woods." They wanted, as a group, to confront and "deal with" that artist. They also yelled at me for not censoring her material. I refused to let this group meet with her; I said if they had any criticism, they needed to put it in a letter, not threaten the artist in person (I've never forgotten what happened to me.) And I told them the lyrics *were* "Meet me in the woods." But they insisted this artist was into leather and sang "beat me"; the women said they were going to boycott her forever and were also going to tell all of their friends never to go see her. I'm sure they did. But it didn't matter. The name of the artist was Melissa Etheridge.

Transsexuals? Our fire captain—California law required us to have one on the land—was a transsexual, Captain Michelle. We not only did not have any backlash accepting her on the crew, but we were grateful because without her, we would not have been able to have the festival. I see the transsexual issue and the issue of gender identity as a lesbian and gay issue. And I support their movement toward full equality in this country.

I am constantly asked if I remember any one particular thing from the 25 festivals I produced, but there are so many things. I remember the great Yosemite fire of 1987 (at that time, the largest forest fire in American history). I vividly remember 156 of us workers being trapped at the camp and coming very close to dying. For several days we had no electricity, our water was running out, and the fire surrounded us. I remember how we all started to cry when we finally made it off the mountain. The eighth West Coast festival was the only festival of ours ever to be canceled.

I remember singing "Over the Rainbow" and telling the women that I would stop when we raised $10,000 to fight an initiative that was to put people with HIV into "camps" in California. We raised the $10,000 in about four minutes, but I kept on singing until we raised $18,000. We also raised $13,000 at the Southern festival for the second March on Washington in 1987 and $10,000 at the West Coast festival so that Wanda and Brenda Henson could put up an electric gate on their property in Mississippi to give them some element of safety. At one festival we raised $10,000 for Redwood Records to help them stay afloat.

I remember doing a written survey asking women if they were survivors of physical or sexual abuse and being stunned when 80% of the respondents said they were. I remember the true safety of women's space, where women shared their concerns but were not allowed to attack each other over "issues." We learned to communicate.

I will always be grateful for the festivals. Now that I am clean and sober and have gone to therapy for several years, I can even forgive the women who attacked me. I had always blamed them for taking away 12 years of my life. But they didn't. It just took me that long to seek help and sobriety.

When I think of the festivals, what I miss most are the workers. Many were with me throughout the years. Our sense of community and family is something that we as a generation of women loving women were privileged to experience. Our culture, our commitment, our growth, and our love for each other will sustain me throughout the rest of my years.

〰〰〰〰〰〰〰〰〰〰〰〰〰〰〰〰

The political ugliness Robin experienced personally threatened many a festival's moral cohesion. But Boo Price, Lisa Vogel, Robin Tyler, and all the other producers primarily struggled with endless problems concerning land, weather, and reliable production quality. These became the trinity of challenges familiar to every festival producer. Those women who eagerly volunteered to train as sound engineers ultimately became some of the most respected professionals in women's music. It pained many sound women to run a less-than-perfect show, to observe audiences applauding sound they believed could have been crisper and cleaner, yet the rain conditions or constant change of venue wreaked havoc even with the best intentions, skills, and equipment. For a unique perspective on the early days of festival work, nothing beats a sound engineer's memories of the danger and exhaustion involved in creating great concerts for 5,000.

BODEN SANDSTROM

Sound engineer: National Women's Music Festival, Michigan Womyn's Music Festival, West Coast Women's Music and Comedy Festival, Sisterfire, Southern Women's Music and Comedy Festival

I started Woman Sound with Casse Culver in 1975 in Washington, D.C. I used to be a librarian, and I loved that, but after graduate school I had stopped playing the French horn and was missing music desperately. I really wanted to find a career that involved music, and I had just discovered *women's* music. I came out in Boston in 1972, and I was an ardent feminist involved in left-wing politics and the abortion struggle.

I discovered that if you wanted to find lesbians somewhere other than in bars, you went to women's music concerts. One of the very first concerts I went to was put on by Olivia Records in 1974; the performers were Casse Culver, Willie Tyson, and Meg Christian. And of course it blew my mind. I fell in love with Casse Culver that night, and later she became my girlfriend. All of her lyrics were specifically about women and loving women; the others' seemed couched in euphemisms and code language. That particular night I saw Judy Dlugacz mixing sound. She was right on the stage because she had a high impedance mix board; that means you can only get about 20 feet away from the microphones or you lose sound levels. It was almost like hi-fi rather than professional equipment. She was virtually mixing on the stage. I saw who she was, and it totally struck me that *this* was something I'd love to do. It moved me. And I went up and talked to her after the concert. I remember that I said to her, "How do you get to do that?"

Judy told me they were leaving town. They had already formed the Olivia Collective, and they were moving to Los Angeles to become a record company. But she said that [local performer] Casse Culver had her own little PA system and was looking for someone to teach how to mix because she was getting tired of setting up her PA and trying to sing. It took me a year to get Casse to actually talk to me, but I was persistent. She agreed to teach me, and that's how I started to learn. Her little production company, Sweet Alliance, was with Mary Spottswood Pugh, and I started doing their concerts. This was at a lesbian bar—or a bar with a lesbian night—in Southeast Washington, D.C.; they had a series of concerts every Thursday night. That's when I started to meet all the women's musicians I'd soon get to know; they all came through that circuit. I got to mix them all, every Thursday night at this bar. I remember Maxine Feldman came through town, and others—tons of people!

Boden Sandstrom in a reflective moment at the 1986 West Coast Women's Music and Comedy Festival.

Deborah Jenkins

Very quickly, Casse and I decided we should start a sound company, and we started looking around to buy our own gear. We named our company Woman Sound. I remember we had long discussions about what to name it. Casse wanted to call it D.C. Sound (Dyke City Sound). I wanted it to be a bit more user-friendly. Soon, different women who came to the club or heard me mix started hiring me for other things. And my other big link to community was through my left-wing politics, so

I got asked to mix all the political rallies. I met Holly Near at those events, when she was singing on the same stage with Pete Seeger.

But even my first church rally required a bigger PA than we had access to. Now, Casse had taught me everything she knew about how to run her little eight-channel system, and she knew a fair amount—her father was in electronics and radio. I

Toni Armstrong Jr.

systematically went to all the male sound companies in town. Nobody had any time for me, and it was very frustrating. I tried to get hired, to get some experience, to figure out what to rent. I would end up at gigs with systems that didn't work or were missing parts because men would just throw me out the door with this stuff. Finally, this one company, National Sound—actually one of the biggest ones in Washington, D.C.—whose owners were really unusual guys, kind of took me under their wing. The blind man who ran the company and his partner told me everything I needed to know; they took the trouble to talk to me. I learned on the job by trial and error, and since Judy Dlugacz had left, I didn't have any women mentors at all.

Someone told me about the National Women's Music Festival. That was the year I was just learning from Casse, but I really thought I should be mixing there; I was a little cocky. I just went out there to Illinois and introduced myself to Kristin Lems, told her I wanted to work, wanted to mix. See, there was a political controversy because it turned out that the person they had mixing sound was her boyfriend, and I was just horrified. I really convinced her to let me work with him. And all of this was during the first or second festival!

Stage-crew techie Lauren Heller at the 1992 Michigan Womyn's Music Festival.

This was also how I met Amy Horowitz of Roadwork. I hitched a ride with her the next time I went to National. I knew more by then, and she looked to me a bit to answer all her questions about the political struggles that were going on at festivals—debates about lesbian separatism, about men being allowed there. Our friendship began in that car ride and continued. As soon as Amy formed Roadwork, she hired Woman Sound and gave us the opportunity to work, which is how I came to do sound for Sisterfire every year. Sisterfire and the West Coast festival were where I really got to do it all.

I don't know how Lisa Vogel knew I existed, but she called me to do the very first Michigan festival in 1976. I was amazed, but at the last minute I couldn't go because I couldn't get away from working on Casse's album as second engineer with Marilyn Ries. We were recording up in Deer Isle, Maine. I felt terrible that I bagged out on Lisa, but fortunately, she asked me to do the next one, and I was really thankful. However, throughout all those years I did sound for Michigan, there were problems because Lisa kept control over hiring the sound company. We were always working on somebody else's system. We had a lot of problems with the PA—I was much more passive in those days. I didn't suggest that there might be another way.

But mixing at Michigan was a fabulous experience—the music was wonderful, with so much variety. It was an engineer's dream: working all day, outside with the music and musicians that you love. It was here that I met two of my best friends today, Margot McFedries, another great sound engineer, and Jennifer James, who was the stage manager through many of those first years. We definitely had hilarious experiences with certain performers. There were performers we didn't want to work with because they were so awful to the sound people. And then there were others who were always a lot of fun—Rhiannon and Alive were great to work with. And I want to mention Sue Fink. Although I'm not sure she was at Michigan when I was, she was fabulous at other festivals and everywhere I worked with her. She signed on the back of my T-shirt, "I will always love to sing through you." But what always comes to mind when I think about doing sound at Michigan is the weather. That second year? Amazing tornadoes. And we had virtually nothing to eat; it was all salads. It was so cold and wet. We'd come home at night and find everything we owned floating in our tents. We worked all the time; we never stopped working. All night long we'd be trying to make the PA work. Morning would come, and we'd do the sound checks. Then the shows. Then everything would fall apart again. That one year when there were tornadoes—there were several, but during the worst one, we were literally onstage. I remember being up on top of the speaker stacks, trying to keep the tent from knocking over the whole stack. The lightning crashing, everyone trying to hold the tent up. I remember making a choice between letting the equipment come down or dying. I thought I should protect the equipment! Those years were very hard and scary. But I worked the first 11 years at Michigan.

I worked for Robin Tyler while her festival was still at Yosemite; she called me to do the sound, and that was music to my ears because I really appreciated Robin's approach. She said, "I want you to do all the sound *and* get all the equipment." I wanted that control, to be responsible for all the arrangements. At Michigan, in the early years, we were still using whatever showed up! I picked out the PA for Robin by bidding from Washington, D.C. with a sound company in San Francisco. There were four stages at Yosemite, several of them small. But I'll never forget that feeling of setting up every single PA, and they *all worked.* They all sounded great. What a sense of accomplishment! Especially because back in Washington, D.C., I was still fighting to be recognized in a male-dominated field. Then when Robin started doing the Southern festival, she hired me. And that was great for us. It was close enough for us to take the Woman Sound system. So for several years we'd do Sisterfire, then take the system to Southern, then drive to National. This would be all in one month, May to June.

And it was fabulous. But Southern was very scary sometimes. There were two years in particular when there were threats from local men. I always feared for my equipment; it was like my life. I watched it like a hawk; I was very uptight. I was very particular about stage security. They had to show up at a certain time. I wouldn't leave my gear until I had security there, and then I'd show up in the middle of the night to make sure they weren't sleeping. Yeah, I was demanding and overly protective. But I was the most concerned because it was my personal equipment at stake. My feeling was that anyone could steal at any time, and I helped train the rain crew efficiently. I brought the experience of doing sound from doing all those rallies on the Mall in Washington, D.C., where I'd be out in the rain with my equipment for a week.

My last year at several festivals was 1987, and I ended up selling my company soon afterward—although I continued to do sound and technical production, including work at Southern and then the million-strong 1993 March on Washington. And I'm currently the sound engineer for Washington, D.C.'s RFK Stadium, going on my 12th year. But I remember 1987 particularly because at the end of that summer, Robin Tyler's festival at Yosemite burned—*while I was there.*

It was the scariest thing. Unbelievable. I went early, to do the setup. When the fire started, it quickly became clear that it was out of control. There were a couple of women on the land who were firefighters, and that was really helpful, but the 40 of us who were there lost radio contact with the forest rangers. It was mind-boggling; we thought we were going to die. The line that had been fed to us by the rangers throughout all the years we'd done the festival there was that if there were ever a big fire, all we had to do was get into the camp's swimming pool. But as soon as the ashes and the smoke started coming in, we realized that we were choking. The gas would kill us before the fire did. We would all suffocate, in or out of the pool, and the sprinklers wouldn't work because the electricity would go out. The whole scenario we'd been given was a total, ridiculous lie. We'd all die in this valley!

They couldn't take us out. We got into a paranoid, conspiratorial fear that they'd never rescue us because they knew we were 40 lesbians. The sky was yellow and gray. On that last morning, huge ashes were coming down, and we could see flames up on a ridge. They still had no plan for getting us out. We'd had no communication for two days. We stopped all work, loaded our cars, and finally the word came to go *now,* and Robin had decided that I was to lead everyone down the hill! I felt really, really important, I can tell you.

At every turn down that mountain there were firefighters holding back the fire so we wouldn't get burned. It was that close. I didn't feel safe for an hour or more. We could feel the heat. It was so warm I was afraid the gas in my car would explode—or my tires. We finally made it safely to Robin's house in Southern California and then had to call all the festiegoers and cancel and help Robin deal with the politics of whether they'd get their money back.

That's not all. One year the West Coast festival met in Willits [Calif.], where we nearly froze to death. Boo Price was there with Robin, and we had another mini-tornado there. I was up on the stage lighting truss, and I turned to the left and just happened to see out of the corner of my eye this little tornado coming down the hill. It was coming right at me. My mix platform started to blow. I grabbed the microphone and screamed for help, screamed that there was a tornado coming. This was in the middle of a sound check. Everyone dove off the stage. The tornado tore up the lighting truss—it fell on the stage—but because I had yelled, everybody was off the stage. The lighting truss came down, and it missed the piano and the harp and didn't hit anybody. I felt the Goddess had come through me.

In my career I've trained many women. At Michigan this past year [1997], three of the sound engineers there were women I'd trained: Kris Koth, Moira Shea, and Marion Colbeck. And they were all at the same table eating hamburgers in that bar where we all go after the festival when I walked in. It was very gratifying to me to have helped these women along in their dreams.

⇸⇔⇷⇔⇷⇔⇷⇔⇷⇔⇷⇔⇷⇔⇷⇔⇷⇔

In its first decade (1974–1984), festival culture exploded like popcorn in all directions. Lesbians freshened their camping gear and loaded their car trunks at the start of summer because now June meant the National festival; August, the Michigan festival; Labor Day weekend, Robin Tyler's West Coast festival; and late fall, the Sisterspace Pocono Weekend or Woman Harvest. Shorter, regional festivals established by 1983 included Sisterfire, Arizona Womyn's Festival, Wiminfest, NEWMR (first referred to as the New England Women's Music Retreat, later North East), and eventually the Southern festival and Lee Glanton's Campfest. To accommodate working women, most festivals met over weekends, three-day holiday weekends in particular. This soon meant that consumers had their choice of several festivals vying to attract women for Memorial Day or Labor Day. Some artists doubled their opportunities for exposure and income by playing at two or more festivals scheduled for these popular calendar dates. By the mid 1980s it was common to hear a dazed performer explain that she was flying from Connecticut to California or vice versa to play both West Coast and NEWMR over airport-clogged Labor Day weekend. The expansion of festivals also meant new opportunities for producers to forge different approaches, perhaps applying skills learned at the "big" festivals. After many years organizing workers at Michigan, political activist Michelle Crone decided she wanted to produce what she envisioned as a workers' festival.

MICHELLE CRONE

Producer, Rhythmfest (1990–1995)

I began as a worker at Michigan in 1979, later helping to set up the political tent and "Rumor Control." At a certain point while I was there, Lisa Vogel and her sister announced that the festival was no longer going to be a collective; it moved from collective to cooperative, cooperative to partnership, partnership to ownership. And we workers divided into groups—the "Lunts" (land union negotiating team) and the "Cunts" (coordinators' union negotiating team) to process festival issues versus business issues. We believed that business issues shouldn't dictate festival philosophy. But the year the festival lost money, all of us in the union kicked back our salaries, and the Cunts raised $12,000 so that a percentage of the new land purchased could be owned by workers and festiegoers. In the rush to pay off land debts, Lisa Vogel approached us for the money, and despite some moral dilemma, we gave it. And the following year many of us got fired—about 30 or 40 of the most *political* people.

It was difficult. We wanted to go back and have an open forum about what happened instead of all the character assassination. I felt that if all that hadn't happened at Michigan in '84, the festival would have been the most revolutionary social change movement ever to hit Lesbian Nation.

Instead, I left and went to work for Robin Tyler. She'd had her stage stormed by the women of color and had no internal process for dealing with conflict like that. Working for Robin, I had no illusions about being in a "cooperative." She was up-front and honest—if you didn't like the rules, you didn't have to be there. But it was different from sisterhood.

And then one night there were four of us sitting on a porch in Tennessee in Feb-

51

ruary 1990. We'd done a festival called Full Circle in Massachusetts, open to men and women, during Hurricane Hugo, unfortunately. It was a bust. We decided to go forward with a land search, and that night in Tennessee we were brainstorming at the house. It took us forever to hash out a vision statement. We vowed that we would never turn anyone away, never say no to any idea before asking, "How do you make it happen?" We vowed that everyone would eat the same food, get paid the same amount, and that there would be no distinguishing wristbands or armbands; we organized Rhythmfest as a cooperative, everyone equal across the board. Although organizing would prove difficult because we all lived in different cities, Rhythmfest became known as the workers' festival.

Barbara Savage had remembered a woman who owned a horse ranch in Cloud-

Festival producer and emcee Michelle Crone. Her "worker's festival," Rhythmfest, shook up the Southeast in the early 1990s.

Joan E. Biren

land, Ga. There wasn't anything in the Deep South at that point. We made a conscious choice to keep the festival in the Southeast. And the majority of our workers were leather women and women from the rural South, who would sit down and have dialogues about nudity and S/M. Some of those women had never seen a dildo, let alone discussed the theories of public sexuality. All of this took place on a horse farm! In a barn! Surrounded by mice and horse shit!

The craftswomen were also considered workers and were always very grateful, going out of their way to help out. And the musicians were wonderful: We insisted that our performers give workshops, that we were more than music. Melissa [Etheridge] said she'd help. She performed at the first or second Rhythmfest and did pickups at the airport. The Indigo Girls came too—as festiegoers, not as performers. Coproducer Kathleen Mahoney, who worked as artist liaison, booked Edwina Lee Tyler in a hotel off land because we didn't have enough cabins, but Edwina refused, saying, "I need to eat with the people, touch the people." We canceled the hotel. Our performers were like that.

I remember walking across the field in 1992 and hearing Pyramid read her erotica, her voice rising out of the dense fog. It was surreal. And we always had a problem with fire ants and had to decide what to do by consensus. There was a Native American way of dealing with them, and then two workers tried to burn 'em out with gasoline, and then we spent thousands of dollars to ship "organic poison" in from Oregon. I remember one woman who was an actress from Los Angeles riding around on a golf cart at midnight, flicking lighters at fire ants.

I did a lot of emceeing at every festival. We did worker meetings twice a day, and it was like a performance for 200. Kate Clinton told me, "You're good, Crone; you should be up onstage!" Sure, I used cutting-edge humor to achieve consensus, to go to the next step without anyone having to feel they'd "lost" something. Festival culture is the only arena lesbians have for processing our issues, for building a village together. You have to have everyone's safety in mind—like *Where do you have sex at a festival? Is that a prude mentality? A concern with kids?*

Festivals are still *the* places—especially as our other institutions are closing, like so many of the women's bookstores. If it wasn't for the far right, we'd still be operating. One year we had gunshots at 2 A.M., we had busloads of kids going by shouting antilesbian epithets, the local sheriff may or may not have been a Klan member—it was ugly. Our lawyer said to me, "Crone, the way you do things drives me nuts." She came out of Wall Street and entertainment law. But by the end of five years, her life partner was my head of security.

Our search for land to restart Rhythmfest continues. But you know, the Seneca Women's Peace Camp, the Gay Games, the Marches on Washington events—all benefited greatly from women who learned their skills or had training that came out of festival work, because logistically there was no other training ground for women but festivals.

TAM MARTIN

Producer, Pacific Northwest Jamboree (1990-1994)

It was 1989, and I was in Southern California. Friends were visiting me from Seattle, and we were out dancing Saturday night when they said, "Why do we have to go all the way to Yosemite for a women's festival? Why don't we have anything local?" I scribbled the idea down on a napkin that night, made some calls on Monday, and by the end of the week had a site and a budget.

What made me feel I could do this? You know that Robin Tyler's Yosemite festival burned out in 1987. She hired me to handle all of the incoming calls about refunds and the bookings for the [1987] March on Washington. Throughout all of 1988, I worked in her office in Los Angeles as a subcontractor, her assistant for the 1988 Southern and West Coast festivals. I booked entertainers and hired workers. When I thought about doing more, I knew I could do it. I had experienced all those challenges when helping Robin.

So there I was, living in Long Beach, Calif., but I wanted my festival to be in the Northwest—Evergreen State College in Olympia, Wash., was my first choice. I sent my proposals both to Evergreen and to Western Washington University in Bellingham. The person at Western Washington University called me up, very enthusiastic—a married lady who had no idea what women's music and culture were. But a dean named Marie Eatin, who sang in the group Mother Lode, had seen my press kits and cassettes in the office that day. I flew up a couple weeks later, talked about facilities, and signed the papers.

I wanted to make sure the festival title had Pacific Northwest and women in it, and *jamboree* is such a Girl Scout word. As a former Girl Scout, I called all my Girl Scout friends. All five years they helped. Mom and Dad did registration the first year; attorney pals sold coffee. The performers were my friends, and I needed them to take the risk with me—which they did. Though I did everything that first year on credit cards, I was able to make money and hand out bonuses!

It worked because there were less rules. I knew I did not want it to be the deal where certain people ate in certain places; my performers were really accessible, and I didn't have security. See, I was 31, and I didn't want to be underground in the rain. I wanted a festival *I* would go to: on a college campus with flush toilets, a real piano, and a roster of workshops *I* would go to. How to buy your own house. How to start your own business. And every year I did a workshop to show women how to bring women's music production to their area, training producers on site and following up on them. I was able to get work for a lot of performers, and I introduced women like Suede, Melanie DeMore, and Susan Herrick to a new audience.

I made sure that I did four shows, each with three acts. We'd have 12 to 15 acts and an emcee. There would be at least one local Northwest act, one nationally known, and one woman of color for each show. And because 10% or more of the audience came from Canada every year, at least two Canadian performers. And a comedy night, a country-and-western dance…

Wester Washington University really begged me to hold my festival there, thinking it would diversify their campus. For a state school, they sure weren't set up for disabilities. As a result of my festival, they added several accessible rest rooms and elevators, and they created a handbook based on my brochure! I brought to their attention the need for a shuttle service and other things, and now it's all been implemented on that campus. I eventually received a letter from the Association of Students with Disabilities, and when I'm down, I read that letter. Yeah, for such a little fest, we had 16 Deaf women, 11 women in wheelchairs, and an older audience in their 40s and 50s who'd never seen anything like it. *High* from the whole weekend!

I announced at the festival in 1994 that it was the last. The audience has so many choices now. But it took me two years to pay my debts, and that last year of festival I only had 360 prepaid people. Women will say, "Oh, I don't know; we'll go next year." But to break even, the numbers have to be there—even with loyal friends like Suzanne Westenhoefer telling me she wouldn't take a check. Now I'm brainstorming about a one-day festival. I'm still a registered Girl Scout, and because I was a counselor for five summers, my five years of festival were real similar to planning a weekend camp out. It came very naturally. I did it all myself.

〰〰〰〰〰〰〰〰〰〰〰〰〰〰

Oral herstory is a compelling medium. But for the serious scholar of 1970s festival culture, there is indeed a literature predating *HOT WIRE:* Published from 1975 to 1980, *Paid My Dues* was the first women's music and culture journal. *PMD* featured valuable articles by women's music artists such as Susan Abod, Margie Adam, Ginni Clemmens, Robin Flower, Kay Gardner, Kristin Lems, and Linda Tillery and interviews with Alix Dobkin, Therese Edell, Sue Fink, Cathy Roma, and Cris Williamson. Boden Sandstrom contributed articles on sound production, Leni Schwendinger on lighting, and the National Women's Music Festival and the Michigan collective voluntarily published financial breakdowns of their festival spending in one Autumn 1977 issue. Reading back volumes of *PMD*, one finds a mix of song lyrics and music lessons, feminist analysis and festival ads— the same mix that would later dominate *HOT WIRE*, which Toni Armstrong Jr., a *PMD* contributor, began editing in 1984. With only a few years' gap, women's music and festival culture thus produced two decades of journalism and accompanying photography. (*HOT WIRE* itself was also famous for including a music sound sheet in each issue.)

Marcy Hochberg

Retts Scauzillo, now the stage manager for Campfest, works the day stage at the 1989 Michigan Womyn's Music Festival.

Neither publication ever attained a huge circulation—although Toni ultimately received *HOT WIRE* reader mail from as far away as South Africa. Both *HOT WIRE* and *Paid My Dues* were careful to promote artists and production skills without taking an editorial stance on festival controversies or issues divisive to the fragile production community. The featured artists were just as diplomatic. Therese Edell, interviewed in the spring 1978 issue of *Paid My Dues,* was asked to define women's music. Her response: "Women's music is…Let's see. Damn. Music made

Shelley Jennings and Myrna Johnston at the 1990 Michigan Womyn's Music Festival. Note Myrna's multiple wristbands for backstage access.

Toni Armstrong Jr.

by women that makes other women feel like they are strong human beings in their own right. How's that? We'll take that one for now."[3]

Within festival culture, the spider web of established work roles slowly grew to include the many strands taken for granted today: producers and booking agents, artist liaisons, security, sign-language interpreters and disability access coordinators, photographers and the lesbian press, kitchen and stage crews, box office and budget, and of course the performers themselves. The roster of trained sound and stage engineers continued to draw from the Boston area: Myrna Johnston and Shelley Jennings, Moira Shea and Darby Smotherman, lighting designer Linda O'Brien, and also in Boston but later from Toronto, legendary recording engineer Karen Kane. From Long Island, a stage production crew soon beloved to many festiegoers featured Retts Scauzillo and lighting engineer Karen "K.C." Cohen; they were joined at many festivals by Kathy Belge, Coni Robinson, and Janice Jackson. Other important women in stage production included Connie Lane, Kris Koth, Jeanette Buck, and Tia Watts. One concern during the early years was the evident drug use by some techies; a worker confided in me that a rival crew was always faster than her own but that this dazzling efficiency was actually because "they were all on speed." On the other hand, veteran crews now know better than to party too hard before a long day of stage work: "Time to go to sleep, everybody!" Retts Scauzillo orders her Campfest crew, breaking up the gazebo party gathering well before midnight.

Although festival programs routinely credit each worker and explain work areas, audiences may not be aware of the cooperative efforts and vindictive squabbles unfolding backstage. The structure of rules and hierarchy, however, do interest festiegoers, who are affected by the end-product decisions of all that worker processing. The next chapter explores daily life in the matriarchy that is festival week.

1. Boo Price produced the San Francisco Bay Area concerts of "Women on Wheels"; these attracted 4,000 women, the largest women's music gatherings for that place and time. For an excellent description of the 1975 San Diego Women's Festival, see Holly Near's autobiography, *Fire in the Rain...Singer in the Storm* (William Morrow, 1990), pp. 107-8.

2. Lillian Faderman, *Odd Girls and Twilight Lovers* (New York: Penguin, 1991), p. 222.

3. Therese Edell, interviewed by Karen Corti. *Paid My Dues*, volume II, n. 3, spring 1978; p. 18.

CHAPTER THREE

Eden Built By Eves: Matriarchal Structure

Imagine a city where women rule. Where all the roads, all the buildings, the plumbing, the hospitals, the restaurants, the stores are run by women. Imagine a city where all the arts and all the crafts, the dance, the movies, the theatre, the poetry are created by women. Imagine a city where women and children feel free to walk anywhere, day or night, in total safety. Imagine a city where it doesn't matter what we wear, where we're not judged by our clothes, where clothing is optional and our bodies are sacred. Imagine a city of thousands of women, where there's no violence and no weapons, no criminals and no jails, no oppression and no fear. This city has existed in only one place in the history of the earth. We are in that city now. Welcome to Michigan!
—Jean Fineberg, musician

I was at the very first Michigan festival. And you cannot imagine what it was like. Because you turned off a two-lane highway onto a one-lane highway and then onto a road and then up a dirt road, and then suddenly you were on a driveway, and there at the entrance stood a woman in coveralls and no shirt. That was what I had heard about and what I had come to see.
—an anonymous professor, Northern Kentucky University

All festivals are life changing, but Michigan is unique due to its enormity (nearly 10,000 women in its most crowded year) and its aura of mystery (privately owned land, womyn born womyn only). This festival, ongoing since 1976, is in itself a political action. It is proof that women can perform every job required in the construction and administration of a city.

Jean Fineberg speaks for many women in her tribute to the exuberant sense of safety at Michigan. An entire city run by and for lesbian feminists. Utopia revealed. An Eden—built by Eves. Yet some women find the matriarchal separatism stifling at best. For every festiegoer who sighs, "If only the real world were like this!" there is usually a critic who replies, "God *forbid*!"[1]

Lesbians who have never attended any of the available festivals nonetheless loudly debate their merits. The fantasy of an alternative, futuristic, women-only dreamland has long stimulated the lesbian imagination. The birth of festival culture in the 1970s dovetailed with an emerging literature of lesbian-feminist science fiction clas-

Rhiannon with interpreter Sherry Hicks at the 1990 Michigan Womyn's Music Festival.

Toni Armstrong Jr.

sics that particularly emphasized the idea of utopias for women: Sally Miller Gearhart's *The Wanderground*, Marion Zimmer Bradley's *The Mists of Avalon*, Joanna Russ's *The Female Man*, Ursula K. LeGuin's *The Left Hand of Darkness*, Marge Piercy's *Woman on the Edge of Time*, and Katherine V. Forrest's *Daughters of a Coral Dawn*. What happens at Michigan and at other large festivals matters very much to the the armchair visionaries and theorists at home.

Are festivals merely weeklong vacations from patriarchy or serious models of the alternative society women might create on earth? Festival controversies exacerbate this debate. One aspect of Michigan's women-only policy is an age restriction on boy children (boys over age 3 stay in their own weeklong camp near the gate but not in the festival proper). Recently the women-only issue has exploded over whether or not transgendered folk (male to female transsexuals) are welcome (officially, they are not). These issues will be explored in Chapter Six. Potential festiegoers do consider whether festival policies represent "temporary" or "utopian" ideals. For mothers of boys, the inner debate goes like this: *It's not such a big deal to plan four personal vacation days away from my sons. But will I be spending those days among women who would never accept my sons in their vision of utopia?*

The lack of crime at Michigan—aside from the occasional mistaken-identity theft of underwear, flashlights, chairs, and canteens—suggests that thousands of women can live together peaceably, creating a harmonious structure where men have failed. This is not a new concept: Charlotte Perkins Gilman, who wrote the utopian feminist novel *Herland* in 1915, envisioned a women-only country where maternal love fostered a natural emphasis on caregiving and education. At Michigan and other festivals, there is safety from rape and from mugging. A crying child may readily find solace in the arms of anyone nearby. But is safety utopia? The white majority does not spell utopia for women of color. And the predominance of women over 35, as the original, perpetually returning first festiegoers go grey, does not spell utopia to the young women attending, especially when those aging Amazons are the ones who set and enforce the rules.

Whose Eden? Whose utopia? What does Eve look like here? And is it simply our socialized hostility to female rule enforcers that creates the backlash against a "politically correct" heaven?

Newcomers can be easily overwhelmed by a festival's organic layout. Some first-timers (more commonly called "festie virgins," an unavoidable rite of passage) turn frustration over unmarked paths and collapsed tents into attacks on festival politics, often in the pages of the grassroots publication *Lesbian Connection*. In this chapter I suggest that we remember how women-only events demand a dramatic, psychic shift of focus: the total separation from male authority and input of any kind. This can be a wake-up call for first-timers who suddenly realize how many feminists still depend on men to perform certain tasks and services or to make crucial decisions. Here in this Eden, we do it all.

The Shock of Arriving

Welcome to women-only space. An enormous amount of work has been done behind the scenes before you arrive, and the Amazons committed to making the festival a success are buzzing importantly about the land. The worker driving the tractor, the stage technician climbing the lighting tower, and the carpenter drilling the ground to lay cable lines are all female, their collective expertise unsullied by old objections that women cannot do these jobs. With their walkie-talkies, tool belts, partially unlaced work boots, and heavy clipboards, the land army of crew workers and coordinators are ready to tackle whatever needs doing to keep the audience safe, fed, and well-entertained.

For the festival to run smoothly, everyone must work: staff crews and work-exchange folk in predetermined job areas, as well as general festiegoers in the one work shift they are customarily asked to select for the weekend. All capabilities are welcomed and valued here; volunteers are needed 'round the clock in areas as diverse as child care, backstage security, garbage removal, massage, lost and found, sign-language interpretation, and of course, the kitchen. Being asked to sign up for a work shift (ranging from two to four hours, depending on the festival) is the first responsibility greeting most women after they have parked their cars and dragged their gear to the registration area. An important point is made here: to minimize the number of men brought on and off the land as plumbers, garbage and sewage patrol, delivery service, et cetera, women with these skills must step in and assume responsibility for the shit work.[2]

The work shift component startles some campers who feel the ticket price implies a total vacation. Other women raise important questions about class differences. The expectation of unpaid labor offends certain working-class festiegoers and women of color. Regrettably, even in this climate of heroic egalitarianism, we cannot help but reproduce the symbols of hierarchy from the "real world": black women serving food to white women or taking out their garbage are not experiencing cultural revolution—although some affluent white women lacking the historic heritage of bonded servitude find it a fun challenge to do "butch" work shifts, like parking cars or using walkie-talkies.

RUMOR CONTROL: Rumor Control is designed to be a channel available for input and output of information of Retreat happenings. You can go there if you have questions or want updates on "Retreat news."

SWIMMING: Swimming hours are 8:00 A.M. to 6:00 P.M. Bathing suits must be worn at all times because of the public boat launch across the lake. Lifeguards will be on duty during designated hours. Please do not swim under the influence of alcohol or drugs. No flotation devices except those used by women with disabilities will be allowed. Swimming will be allowed within designated areas only and at specified times. There will be a long distance swim once Saturday and Sunday afternoons at 4:00. All rules will be strictly enforced and it is important that they are respected—an accident could ruin everything that the women of NEWMR have worked for.

PICTURES: Photographers, please be sensitive that many women do not want their pictures taken. For many women this is an invasion of their personal space. For women who do not want their pictures taken, stickers stating this are available at Rumor Control.

PLEASE STAY WITH US: Due to the parking limitations, please do not plan on leaving the land during the Retreat. Connecticut liquor stores are closed on Sunday and Monday. A public telephone is located at registration.

GARBAGE: We have provided you with a garbage bag. Please use it to bring your personal garbage from your campsite to the collection sites. Smokers, remember to dispose of your butts properly; the woods are extremely dry. Let's all try not to trash the land.

BOTTLES AND CANS: Connecticut has a bottle bill. This means that all bottles and cans are recyclable, and that there is a five cent or twenty cent return on each container. There will be separate canisters around the land for returnable containers—if you don't want them, we do. The money we receive from returning the empties helps to keep the cost of the festival tickets within reason.

LOST AND FOUND: Many camping and personal items were found during the clean up last year. These items will be displayed in the registration office. If you lost anything last year, please check to see if we have it.

WE NEED WOMEN to stay on after the festival to help us tear it down and clean up. If you can stay for a while, please let us know during the weekend.

THANKS: Hugs to all of you for coming here to share with us. Thanks for your support during the planning stages, thanks for caring and being. Enjoy....

Excerpt from the program for the 1988 North East Women's Music Retreat.

Overall, however, most festiegoers agree the short work shift is one of the most rewarding aspects of the weekend—an occasion for meeting a cross section of new friends, learning new skills, making an appreciated contribution. Whether she ends up spooning out granola to thousands of sleepy-faced women at breakfast or driving a shuttle to pick up a famous performer at the regional airport, each woman will go home with amusing memories from her work role.

For one week or weekend, festiegoers will experience living in a city of women at work and play, where each individual's part is acknowledged gratefully. The Michi-

Ramona Galindez, emcee for Deaf performers, at the 1992 Michigan Womyn's Music Festival.

Toni Armstrong Jr.

gan festival attracts women from all over the world; the global representation is acknowledged in an international language greeting during each year's opening ceremonies.[3] Presumably, despite our national and cultural differences, we all share this sense of a feminist "homecoming." Yet that cannot always appease the intense dislocation some campers feel upon entering a matriarchal superstructure, with its accompanying policies and expectations, for the first time.

As one teenage woman declared at the National Women's Music Festival in 1995, "I have enough difficulty with my own mother; here I enter a system of a thousand mothers making the rules." Even in the gay and lesbian community there is a typically American ambivalence toward mother-aged women activists. Public service ads for the 1997 AIDS Ride, for example, shown repeatedly in Washington, D.C. movie theatres, introduced one gay male volunteer who remarked, "A friend of mine told me that not only was *he* doing it, but his mother was also doing it. And I figured, if your *mom* can do it, well, *I* can do it." In the same film clip, audiences heard a white-haired woman announce that she raised over $3,000 for AIDS research, yet the first speaker was allowed to dismiss mother figures as questionable athletes, weak, and with little expected from them. Psychiatrists blame domineering mothers for male homosexuality; the Promise Keepers movement urges Christian men to take back the leadership role in the family. Female leadership and initiative, in short, are customarily presented to us as a form of social pathology.

What is astonishing is not merely gay and lesbian America's casual disrespect for older feminist activists, who founded, among other institutions, the radical festival movement and continue to provide it with unpaid labor. The real mindblower is the common sexist and ageist notion that all women of *mother age* are restrictive and oppressive toward youth—in a word, *unhip*. How is it possible that the thousands of lesbians who opted *out* of motherhood have, by virtue of turning 40 in our youth-obsessed society, have been recast as irrelevant mamas by the incoming generation?

While matriarchal images are everywhere at festivals, from the arts and crafts to songs invoking foremothers, the reality of mother mistrusting is part of what we must unlearn. Into this experiment of collective living, this radical festival culture, we bring our society's stereotypes: women are the worst bosses to work for, mothers the most oppressive moralists, feminists politically correct dictators. Indeed, these images were powerful arguments against extending the vote to women in the late 19th and early 20th centuries: Antisuffrage men feared zealously moral women would use the ballot box to ban alcohol. Later, in the 1940s, Philip Wylie's viciously misogynist text *Generation of Vipers* insisted that "smotherlove" had weakened America's sons and that the power of maternal energy sapped male competence. Twenty years later, Philip Roth's novel *Portnoy's Complaint* would vilify the image of the Jewish mother as an intrusive castrator. And beginning with the Moynihan report in the early 1960s, a series of racist and sexist edicts by white *and* black men have continually blamed African-American women—who are workers and heads of families—for emasculating the black male.

No era or ethnic group of women has been safe from these attacks on female independence and empowerment. While women are held to a higher moral standard than men (as anyone who was ever called a "slut" knows), we are also feared for our potential to impose good-girl standards on those around us. In the traditionally female—and traditionally underpaid—professions of nursing and school teaching, the image of the uptight, prudish disciplinarian keeping good order has been viewed as a necessary evil. Miss Grundy of *Archie* comics fame symbolizes the old-fashioned schoolmarm of previous eras who, forbidden by law to marry, enjoys flunking or punishing bad boys. Fear or hatred of men characterizes the spinster: Think of the evil Big Nurse in *One Flew Over the Cuckoo's Nest* or how, in *It's a Wonderful Life,* the angel Clarence shows Jimmy Stewart that if he hadn't been born, his lovely wife would have turned out an "old maid"—worse, a man-fearing, glasses-wearing librarian.

Both Wylie and Moynihan were obsessed with the ideal of military service for young men as a crucial breakaway from the female sphere at home. Athletic competition in adolescence has also served to initiate boys into masculine hierarchies, replacing Mom's control with Coach's role modeling. Continuing to take orders from adult women signifies being "pussy-whipped" for the growing male; to reinforce his desire for independence from home, the image of the overprotective, busybody mother is set up as adversarial to attaining manhood.

Ultimately, lesbian feminists have been saddled with the worst combination of stereotypes: We are moralistic busybodies who want to spoil men's frat binges and Tailhook parties, but we are not credited with maternal qualities though we fight to protect the world's daughters. Women who fight for human freedoms (men's rights) are noble mothers; women who fight for women's freedoms are cranks.[4]

Many women come into festival culture with these internalized notions, fearful of self-government, eagle-eyed for any behaviors that suggest, Yes, we *are* strict, humorless, moralizing. The idea of matriarchy is terrifying because until we create it during the festival week, we have only negative images of what it might look like.

But the blueprint for a woman-identified community can actually mean doing away with many uptight rules we live with elsewhere. At most festivals this freedom is symbolized visually—by the vast numbers of bare-breasted women.

Forget structure and hierarchy for a moment; the first shock for festival virgins is the plethora of *breasts*. This is women-only space, folks—which means the freedom and safety to go without a shirt in the soft summer air. It means for many a woman the first day of being at home in her body and the first sensation of sun on her bare back since babyhood. There is no need to cover up here; there is no need for shame.

Matriarchy here is a physical embodiment of primarily adult women, in their prime at every age, breast after breast in infinite variety reminding us of the folly of body competition. There are white-haired women with creased faces and strong hands, toddling girl children beaming through smeared finger paint, women of fine bulk and women of thin sinew, Deaf women and interpreters signing their conversations in urgent grace. There are black, brown, tan, golden, red, pink, and white skins glistening in folds and ripples, the sheens of skin spiraling outward from the central configuration of breasts and bellies. There are enormous breasts like full and intricate baggage; smaller breasts, erect and goose-pimpled by wind; breasts marked or altered by cancer surgeries; breasts stretched from lactation or swollen with milk for the nourishment of a dangling girl child. Muscles and veins run strong beneath the rolling flesh. Here and there sunburned white women ruefully atone for the unplanned nudity, rubbing lotion onto one another's chests with glad palms.[5]

Many women see what they have been taught cannot exist: women who are sexy in wheelchairs, women who are sexy at 260 pounds, women who are sexy at age 70, long-term interracial romances, young women in charge of complex light and sound technology, poor women who speak with eloquent brilliance—and all the rest of womankind that television will not show us or will tell us does not count. And it can be a shock, a shock so profound it may take the entire festival for some women to adjust. The essential philosophy of "political correctness" on the land is that while women are adjusting, internalizing what it means to work alongside women of difference, we are held accountable for stereotypes we bring in and are invited to unlearn them.

Hierarchy ⌇⌇

Plenty of festiegoers discuss and even protest the hierarchies they observe in festival culture. While no woman is ascribed a higher value than another, roles on the land do carry differing privileges. The producer—or producers—rule. Just below are the trusted office managers, area coordinators, stage and land crew. The artists, of course, are catered to and admired, but no one depends on them for manual labor or problem solving. At the Michigan Womyn's Music Festival, which annually juggles some 600 workers plus 5,000 to 9,000 festiegoers plus performers, plastic hospital wristbands indicate status; different colors or stripes indicate a festiegoer, worker, stage artist, craftswoman, and so on. Only workers and performers are permitted backstage, and this is generally arranged to protect the privacy of the artists and to allow the workers to do their jobs in the performance venue. Flashing a wristband to the security staff indicates that the woman rushing backstage is not a drunken fan (these do exist in festival culture) but a musician or technician arriving to do her job. Likewise, craftswomen, who keep their valuable stock set out in sales booths throughout the festival weekend, have separate wristbands for their own campground near the crafts area. After the booths close each evening, no one is permitted to go into the roped-off crafts area without wristband identification; this is a theft precaution, although most festiegoers are honest.

Workers and performers at Michigan live in a backstage compound with a more extensive eating schedule and rehearsal spaces that festiegoers do not have. This is because security, stage, and land crews have round-the-clock shifts, and some women will always be eating or sleeping, despite the hour of day or night. To keep the work crews fed, undisturbed, and happy, the worker community is also off-limits to regular festiegoers. Although most Michigan festiegoers could not care less what goes on "back there" and are quite satiated with other interests on the land, the thriving worker colony at Michigan is an anthropological wonderland unto itself. It is perhaps the greatest numerical concentration of movers and shakers in women's music and culture per square foot of primitive camping space. And the mutual respect between artists and work crews in this backstage community debunks most hierarchical tension: Here the first-time young worker from Ireland, stumbling to her tent at 2 A.M., notices her most admired performance artist weeing into a slop jar behind a tree. Each woman begins with, then loses, then reestablishes her dignity throughout the week.

In contrast to Michigan, most smaller festivals do not use wristbands.[6] The National Women's Music Festival uses plastic conference name tags—an excellent way to get to know new friends—and the name tag is possible in that National is held at an indoor university site where participants cannot go shirtless. While artists and festiegoers usually eat together in the dining areas of festivals such as National, Campfest, the East Coast Lesbian Festival, Rhythmfest, NEWMR, and so on, some of these festivals have also had a hospitality room or food line just for performers, and performers usually camp separately. Again, these measures are typically about privacy: Artists are indeed celebrities in the festival community and subject

A crowd shot from the early years of Michigan. Note the rain covers on the stage and sound tower.

Joan E.Biren

to the same kinds of fawning excesses which characterize devoted fans everywhere. Women's music fans are not above behavior that is out of line; I have seen women bodily hurtle themselves on beloved performers at festivals and know of at least one case where a woman was accused of stalking a popular artist. During the 1991–1992 period when I first became a festival performer myself, I had at least two "fans" mailing me rambling letters and tapes or inappropriately sending flowers to my workplace. One young woman had surreptitiously obtained my home telephone number from a festival's business office.

Despite reasonable boundaries, festival artists are the most accessible performers in the entertainment world. Whether she is strolling on the land with her girl-friend, eating lunch, or offering an intensive workshop, the festival artist is available to her audience much of the day. This approachability goes a long way toward reducing the star system that exaggerated distance creates. At one Michigan festival, Bay Area vocalist Rhiannon gave a workshop to several hundred women while enjoying the sun on her own bare breasts. When someone in the audience raised a camera to snap a candid shot of Rhiannon so revealed, this always honest artist said, "Please—let *me* just be here too," and was supported by vocal agreement from all others present. The vulnerable humanity of the performer increases at a festival like Michigan, where one is likely to encounter one's music heroine coming out of a Porta-Jane or bleary-eyed in the open showers. (I own a popular pin that leers I SAW YOU NAKED AT MICHIGAN.)

Some festival artists do not sign autographs on principle; others enjoy the attention and respond lovingly to fans' demands. Alix Dobkin is an example of a long-time performer and lesbian cultural worker who deliberately seeks out contact with new women from different lesbian communities for good workshop discussion. Alix is about as *heimish* (Yiddish for home-style, informal, unpretentious) a performer one may find. A majority of stage artists give workshops on music skills, production, comedy, or lesbian issues, and the festiegoer gradually realizes her ticket price includes the opportunity to vocalize with Rhiannon, circle sing with Kay Gardner, drum with Ubaka Hill, laugh with Jamie Anderson, or practice daily in choirs led by Melanie DeMore or Justina Golden.

A fascinating discussion centers around whether artists—and certain workers—enjoy too many privileges at festivals, and often this is a question of menu. Robin Tyler served delicacies such as caviar or lobster to artists at her festivals (Southern and West Coast); the National Women's Music Festival has a buffet backstage for artists in its main theatre; the workers' kitchen at Michigan offers 24-hour bagels, cream cheese, hot chocolate—and an extra midnight meal for the performers, usually along an ethnic theme (Cajun, Caribbean, Latin, or Asian food). Meanwhile, hungry festiegoers eating tofu and melon in the twice-daily food lines hear rumors of backstage bounty and feel ripped off.[7]

"That's ridiculous," says Toni Armstrong Jr. "When an artist like Lynn

Lavner or Vicki Randle plays in New York cabarets or clubs, she gets picked up in a limo, she stays in a hotel with room service, she has a contract rider indicating the meals she'll need. At festivals, though, the artists camp like everyone else, have no special shelter from the rain, heat, bugs, chill, and are expected to muster that burst of performance energy for all of us—so yeah, they get an extra serving of food! What's the issue?"

The issue is finding class distinction here in Egalitaria. There is an idealistic expectation that no one will receive preferential treatment during an event which celebrates the struggle against racism, sexism, and so on—and the performers are alternately revered as goddesses or watched like hawks for any suggestion of prima donna behavior. Many festiegoers don't realize that touring performers may play two or even three venues in one weekend (this was particularly true in the late 1980s, when multiple festivals met over Memorial Day and Labor Day weekends). Rushing across the country by plane, arriving late at night, performing jet-lagged or ill, artists rely on that 1 A.M. protein meal or that dry cabin bedding to remain in good voice. Festivals pose unusual hazards for musicians: Pianos and guitars go gaily out of tune in the damp outdoor air, and handling complex instrumental riffs with swollen mosquito-bitten fingers isn't fun either. Perennially poor, the lesbian community simply isn't in a position to offer its artists the kind of limo-and-hotel treatment we might like to provide; the easiest area of compensation is the wider range of food performers enjoy at festivals.

Robin Tyler adds, "Sure, I brought trunks of pâté to my festivals. I love activist Flo Kennedy, who said that if you take away people's food, you control their culture, no matter how well-meaning you are. Forcing the vegetarian ethic on everyone is a form of abuse. Please don't tell *me*, as a Jewish woman, what's good for me. That's not enlightenment—that's control."

An oft-overlooked figure is the performer's lover, who typically receives a wristband and backstage privileges on a par with those of her famous partner. Children also accompany some stage artists, sometimes even performing with their famous moms (see Chapter Five). The result is that any number of folk living and eating in the backstage area are support people or loved ones without a clearly defined work role, who occasionally get the belligerent festiegoer's query, "*You're* not performing.

You don't look like a techie. How come *you* get to go backstage?"

But this attitude is rare. While festiegoers may peek at or gossip about the women and girls who make up a performer's entourage, there is genuine support for the women who make the music—and the women at their sides.

Occasionally there have been demonstrations against the wristbanding system at Michigan, along the idealistic but financially hopeless principle that all women

Mimi Fox performing at the 1990 Michigan Womyn's Music Festival.

Toni Armstrong Jr.

should be admitted free upon request. In certain years festiegoers who paid full fare refused to wear or show their wristbands, in support of women who had driven to the festival hoping to get in free. Michigan is not Woodstock; the sliding scale, and donations, make possible a generous spectrum of arrangements for lower-income women to attend. But it is expected that such negotiations will have occurred before the women in need show up with their tents on opening day. Some misguided festiegoers have wreaked havoc by sneaking in nonpaying friends and then blaming the wristband system itself for causing a problem. Because festivals depend on committed worker volunteers in all areas, work exchange is open to any interested woman who cannot afford a ticket, and it remains the best way to experience a festival's "inner circle" while providing a needed service. The only hurdle lies in knowing the work-exchange option exists and applying far enough in advance.

A number of workers are in fact paid beyond receiving a free festival pass. Sign-language interpreters, some stage technicians, longtime coordinators, and others are compensated for the skills they bring to the festival; Campfest producer Lee Glanton calculated that for her 1991 festival she paid out $20,000 in staff salaries alone. Almost no women, however, earn their yearly living from festival work alone, regardless of the high quality of their skills as women's music artists or workers. There simply isn't enough of a year-round festival economy to support more than a handful of producers, and while some workers are renowned for their summertime positions at the top of the festival hierarchy, their "day jobs" back home are rarely noted. Festival stage coordinator Retts Scauzillo has two Master's degrees in special education and for years worked with developmentally disabled children, a fact which might surprise those who only know her as a spandex-clad techie. Brilliant pianist Adrienne Torf is a banker. Mississippi blues guitarist Pam Hall is a fourth-grade teacher; country line-dance instructor Maile Klein is a fire-fighter; composer Lynn Thomas coaches a sixth grade parochial schoolgirls' basketball team. Margie Adam is a substance abuse counselor; comedian Nancy Norton is a nurse; sound crew worker Laurie Bennett is a federal cartographer; Ronnie Gilbert spent ten years working as a clinical therapist. Former East Coast Lesbian Festival producer Lin Daniels is now a dynamic caterer for Marriott; Michigan techie Jeanette Buck recently completed film school and in 1997 directed her first feature-length release, *Out of Season.*

Not surprisingly, many festival workers (and festiegoers) are teachers—a traditionally female occupation. The academic calendar with summer months off is perfect for festival work and touring. However, the same American school system that once required its teachers to be unmarried "spinsters" now attacks lesbians in the classroom; right-wing religious campaigns to fire homosexual teachers have spanned the same decades as festival culture. From the 1978 Briggs Initiative in California to the proposed Family Protection Act of the Reagan years to the ongoing repression of gay and lesbian students and teachers in Utah's public schools, the past 20 years have seen continual homophobic pressure on school boards. The resultant stress for good teachers attempting to hang onto their jobs can be unbearable. But again, festivals offer a protected space for dialogue and strategy: Daylong intensive workshops for lesbian teachers—complete with year-round newsletter—have long been a staple at Michigan, and in recent years many teachers have joined the Gay, Lesbian, and Straight Educators Network.

Festivals honor volunteer workers and coordinators in a range of ways. At Campfest, workers completing their fifth or tenth Memorial Day weekend of service receive coveted Five Year or Ten Year Jackets, which are presented onstage in a formal evening ceremony. All workers at Campfest and Michigan also receive free staff T-shirts. The Gulf Coast festival selects a different staff member each year to win the Sue Fink Award, which acknowledges outstanding contributions of time and support.

Perhaps no role is more demanding than that of craftswoman. Competing for the limited booth spaces at any given festival, paying a rental fee if granted a booth space, and spending the entire weekend seated in the booth in hope of making a sale can tax even the most heroic woman's patience. Festiegoers flock to festivals to shop, finding goods and services offered nowhere else: tarot readings, fun "lesbian haircuts," woman-affirming sculptures and jewelry, even (before health concerns eliminated this service) tattooing. Craftswomen's specific concerns are often unheard by festiegoers; one excellent source of the craftswoman perspective is Kady Van Deurs's 1989 collection *The Panhandling Papers*. At one 1993 mass meeting about the Michigan festival's policy of holding a lottery for booth space, craftswomen spoke out: "On what basis do I compete every year to be a member of my community?" "This is a large part of my income, although my income is not large." These laments illustrate the problem of too many talented craftswomen seeking to sell their wares per festival and the painful but necessary elimination of many from the competing pool.

After paying for their own crafts materials, transportation to the festival, booth-space rent, meals, and so on, few craftswomen turn a real profit. Yet their art is in many ways the soul of the festival, and it is in the thriving crafts area that the performers' music tapes and CDs are sold. Not quite festiegoer, not quite worker, not quite performer—craftswomen represent the question mark in the hierarchy: lesbian business agents whose products cannot readily be sold in too many other venues. But most longtime festiegoers have their personal favorite craftswomen whom they matronize each summer. Blanche Jackson and Amoja Three Rivers of Market Wimmin, Carolyn Whitehorn of Feminist Forge, Sara McIntosh of Sara's Shoes, and many other women are legends on the land. Festiegoers grin when, "off land," they spot women about town wearing tie-dyed T-shirts from Snake and Snake or Willow Moon Designs. Products—art or clothing or music—become part of the lesbian code.

In this village of bright skins, work is just one part of a truly organic schedule in which all aspects of personhood are exercised. What eases the demanding work experience is knowing its immediate value. Women in particular have been greatly affected by the past century-and-a-half shift into a postindustrial workplace, which separated waged work from the home and isolated housewives as nonproducers. Historian Alice Clark, who wrote *Working Life of Women in the Seventeenth Century,* suggested that in the past many women enjoyed higher status in their communities because their work in the extended household had immediate benefit and value to the family. It is quite recent in Western history that the male has gone *out* to work; when home production was the rule and husband and wife labored together in the home, men had far more appreciation for "women's work." All of us have been changed by the modern dichotomy of public work and private household. If women's work at home is not waged, like the public work of men, how can it be important—or skilled?

In festival culture, however, we return to village life, where the work site is also the home, however temporary, and where we see the woman who takes out the garbage, the woman who chops the onions as a valued contributor to the community. And the kitchen worker—like Gretchen Phillips or Kay Turner or Katrina Curtiss or Kady Van Deurs—is also likely to be an artist.

Rita Mae Brown commented in her 1997 autobiography, *Rita Will,* that "America contains strange contradictions.... We pride ourselves on being a democracy, but we create few safe public places where people can practice the mixing that is so important to democracy. Europe abounds in beautiful public squares where people promenade, eat, talk politics, and flirt. By contrast, the American, hermetically sealed in his/her car, drives home."[8] Perhaps festivals are an answer to that longing for a safe public square, a promenade for women to talk and flirt.

Life in the Village ⪢

As we meld into this matriarchy, we need structure and schedule to ease our adjustment. Most festivals offer an activities menu—summer camp for grown-up girls. In between pleasant periods of eating communally and sleeping, exploring the woods, or socializing, there are workshops and presentations to choose from and, of course, concert performances throughout the late afternoon and evening. One invents one's own curriculum here, changing interests by the hour, dabbling in art, politics, sports, sexuality, spirituality. From the Gulf Coast festival to Campfest to Wiminfest to Michigan and NEWMR, there are workshops on every conceivable subject: car repair and crystal healing, daughters of Holocaust survivors and daughters of preachers, journal keeping and flag football, stage production and cancer recovery, mobilizing against the Christian right and building a better compost heap, mask making and biracial identity.

Festiegoer A wants to try everything. She chooses a physical challenge first, completing an intensive training session in stilt walking, then heads off with her daughter to a workshop for lesbian families. Later she will sit in on a discussion about Deaf culture, led by Deaf women, with interpreters; she'll come away with her first basic vocabulary in American Sign Language. She concludes the "learning" portion of her day by offering her own workshop for writers interested in self-publishing and then rushes to place her chair in a good vantage point for all the afternoon and evening concerts. By nightfall she's exhilarated and exhausted.

Festiegoer B begins her day at a goddess ceremony. She has intentionally come to this festival because of the opportunity to attend a series of workshops on Wiccan and pagan spirituality. She spends a good deal of time meditating with other like-minded women and is not particularly involved with the entertainment schedule, preferring to network with other women who identify as witches. But when Kay Gardner or Ruth Barrett go onstage, Festiegoer B sits in the front row, glowing.

Festiegoer C is seen about the land with her drum constantly at her side. For her, a festival is its music, and drumming workshops drew her here. She gravitates toward the workshops and activities with an Afrocentric focus, but because her own lover recently became disabled, she also seeks out workshops on disability issues.

There she speaks up about connections between health care and environmental racism in her home community, where she works with children.

Festiegoer D is here to find a girlfriend. She attends any workshop with the word *sex* in its title and finds herself being pursued by a cute cowgirl. She hides in her RV while figuring out her next move, reading literature on safe sex that she purchased at the crafts-area bookstall. Later she eats at the "singles" table in the dining hall, where she is shocked to run into her own eighth-grade English teacher from 1971.

Festiegoer E is trembling from the excitement of meeting her all-time favorite women's music artist in a songwriting workshop. She doesn't want to seem too much like a groupie, but the informal proximity is so gratifying after all the years spent "coming out" to this artist's recordings. She really wants the performer's autograph. She

Country line-dance instructors Marina Hodgini and Maile Klein at the 1991 Michigan Womyn's Music Festival. Tush-push, anyone?

can't believe how easy it is to meet and speak with the stage artists here. She goes back to her tent, writes in her journal about the encounter, and makes love to herself, knocking over a box of Pop-Tarts; these will unfortunately attract raccoons in the middle of the night.

And Festiegoer F? Watch her writing it all down, interviewing women, taking pictures of touching moments that move her, tape-recording stage announcements and producers' speeches for posterity. Her feet ache, ink splotches cover her bare skin, but she only slows down to debate with trusted friends the meaning of this or that incident on the land. Festiegoer F is me.

The point of these contrasting samples is that each woman arrives with a dis-

American Sign Language interpreter Joy Duskin signing at the 1992 East Coast Lesbian Festival.

Toni Armstrong Jr.

tinctive emotional, political, or recreational agenda—often with all three. We bring personal sorrows or losses to the festival, commitment to relationships and to community activism, an eagerness to learn and to socialize with old or new friends. The festival schedule offers a flexible means for engaging all these interests and permits some women to enjoy an in-depth focus on one particular art or subject. But as with the beloved television series *Cagney and Lacey,* there are always emotional subplots overlaying the planned storyline. At festivals we attend the scheduled workshops and concerts but, after a few days, begin to mark the hours in different terms. We go home remembering the internal diary—the friendships, flirtations, insights—the massage under the trees or the encounter with a performer we admire.

Festivals do evoke a powerful range of high and low emotions over a few packed days. For many women, however, this freedom to experience all of one's strengths, joys, passions, and beliefs at once is a cause for praising the festival schedule. At festivals we experience total personhood, whereas the rest of the year we and most lesbians are compelled to compartmentalize our personal, professional, and political lives. Festivals exercise all parts of the human body and spirit, permit an integrated personality, and—most importantly in our industrialized world—briefly reverse the modern trend where the working environment and the home/family environment are separated.

The Festival Guidelines

For practical reasons of safety and liability and in fairness to participants' needs and beliefs, festivals cannot indulge a purely "anything goes" atmosphere. There are indeed rules—often hotly contested rules. When each woman arrives at a festival, she will receive a festival program listing these guidelines. She may also be asked to sign a release form absolving the festival from liability in case of injury (an insurance precaution) or a statement permitting her photograph to be taken. As she reads through her festival program, eyeing the workshop and performance schedules, she will find what we might call the festival's statement of purpose, a paragraph or so of welcome which includes the philosophy and ethics for this event as well as complex lists of rules and information.

Culled from a 15-year period, differing programs show a common commitment to festiegoers' safety and comfort. Fire and garbage safety, respect for chemical-free and differently-abled spaces, and restrictions on flash photography (or taking photos sans permission) are key points. Different campgrounds are reserved for corresponding needs: quiet camping, chem-free (no drugs, alcohol, perfume, smoke, or incense), meditation. Shower and eating schedules are noted so that women may plan ahead, and health tips receive emphasis. Michigan, the largest festival, now includes in its guidelines a plea from the health-care staff that women not go off important medication—there have indeed been women who assume that a festival's healing energy can resolve all ills.

At many festivals, meals are strictly vegetarian. Not so at Campfest, with its superb turkey dinners and kitchen services overseen by Chris Geschwantner, or the Gulf Coast festival, where freshly caught Gulf shrimp rule the party. Experienced campers, knowing that meal lines can be long and time-consuming, bring their own snacks and food coolers to supplement festival chow. Increasingly, festivals have added snack concessions as a fund-raising enterprise; this service is greatly appreciated by festiegoers. Whereas in 1981 the only munchies sold at Michigan were bags of popcorn—labeled "mamacorn"—now Michigan's Cuntree Store sells everything from Ben & Jerry's gourmet ice-cream pints to tampons, folding chairs, mugs, film, rain gear, batteries, cookies, and even—oy!—cigarettes. Permission for festiegoers to cook at their own campsites over fires or gas stoves varies according to region; the West Coast festival— its Yosemite site devastated by fire one year—was certainly the strictest in this regard.

One set of rules that is constantly misunderstood or made fun of is the seating arrangement at concerts. Simply put, women with disabilities are up front, Deaf women are also up front where they can observe the sign language interpreter, and behind these front rows the rest of the audience is split into "chem" and "chem-free." In some instances chem means drinkers only, and all smokers have to step to the rear or outside if the festival is indoors. Craftswoman Susan Baylies's popular cartoon at the end of this chapter shows a good-natured satire of the seating hierarchy. Most women comply with the guidelines, although new arrangements and compromises crop up every era and can be challenging to plan—for instance, How to have a mosh pit at the foot of the stage while simultaneously respecting the space for women in wheelchairs?

These blueprints for matriarchy are sufficiently flexible to permit nearly every woman the freedom she desires during festival time. What is *not* permitted—abusive behavior, racist or ableist humor, blocking another's view by setting up a high-backed lawn chair, loud partying or music in the wee hours (except in remote and purposely marked areas)—is that which we might assume to come under the heading of common courtesy. However, some women also arrive at festivals believing they will be able to sample every activity and find that this is not so. The Women of Color tent at most festivals is intended for women of color, period, although certain activities, workshops, and browsing tables with informational materials are usually advertised as open to all. It is remarkable how many white women pursue the right of entry to this one sanctuary of space. (The politics of racial and ethnic dialogue within festival culture will be further addressed in Chapter Six.) In terms of land guidelines, what many white festiegoers learn is that being in the majority does

Faith Nolan and Masa jamming at the 1991 East Coast Lesbian Festival.

not entitle them to enter or be the center of all scheduled events.

It can take the entire festival to learn one's way around, to adjust to camping and Porta-Janes, to memorize mealtimes and concert schedules, to figure out the best seating options, to understand the ethics of difference and respect. Some festivals offer support meetings for festie virgins to expedite the process. Other women return again and again with increasing smugness that they, as veterans, know the deal and become involved in extending a helping hand to newcomers. There is nothing a lesbian likes better than demonstrating her capability and know-how, and it can be amusing to hear seasoned festiegoers and festival workers conduct conversations in their butchest Festivalese dialects[9]:

"We need 15 workers up at the Womb right now."

"When's the next DART shuttle? Does it go to Treeline or just Downtown?"

"This tofu's vegan, that tofu's dairy."

"Day-stage raffle tickets are being sold at the Goldenrod booth!"

"We have a 'terp here who needs some deep Swedish work—send her to the massage tent before sound check, OK?"

And so on.

When a festival runs smoothly, without incident—neither mishap of weather nor illness nor political gaffe nor technical snafu—the festiegoers will barely think about the plethora of work specialists buzzing around them or the land rules everyone must internalize for maximum harmony. There will instead be a sense of heaven, of ease, of perfect choreography—the magic of the diver who practices for years, only to have onlookers declare, "She makes it look so easy." We sigh, "Why can't the 'real world' be like this?"

Jeanette Buck, a stage technician at Michigan for many years, reminds us: "But in the 'real world' we don't have the festival producers as mothers to us all, taking such good care of the workers and keeping it flowing behind the scenes." She pauses, then adds, "And thus the festivals themselves aren't really matriarchies. Certainly Michigan isn't. Because the producers make the final decisions; they have to. And so, really, Michigan is more like a benign dictatorship."

1. See a disappointed first-timer's anti-Michigan letter in *Lesbian Connection,* v. 20, issue 4, for example.

2. However, at festivals using "Porta-Janes" rather than flush toilets, male cleaning service crews are usually brought in one or two nights of the festival to clean the outhouses. This delights many festiegoers, who take great satisfaction in seeing men clean up women's shit for once.

3. This does, alas, create, or rather reveal, certain divisions. As each language is represented in turn onstage, there is partisan applause from the audience, some obvious nationalism. Competition for visibility led one Jewish woman to shout "We've hit big time!" when two Yiddish greetings from a mother and daughter were heard onstage at Michigan 1996.

4. See Sonia Johnson's chapter "They Needed to Lose Weight Anyway" in *Going Out of Our Minds* (Crossing Press, 1987).

5. This paragraph was first published as part of my short story "The Festival Virgin" in the 1997 Alyson Publications anthology *Hot Ticket* (edited by Linnea Due).

6. Loyal workers leaving Michigan at the end of the festival sometimes leave their bands on for as long as possible, dreading the return to "outside" society. Three weeks after the 1997 Michigan festival had ended, I ran into another Michigan staff worker, Judith Treesburg, on the streets of Washington, D.C., and noticed that she had yet to remove her wristband.

7. After financial losses at the 1996 Michigan festival, however, producer Lisa Vogel mailed returning crew workers a letter warning of cutbacks in backstage bagel expenditures.

8. Rita Mae Brown, *Rita Will: Memoir of a Literary Rabble-Rouser* (Bantam, 1997), p. 225.

9. Marcy Hochberg, a longtime festival photographer and stage techie now conducting research on butch-femme identity, commented that the "butch look" at festivals is deceptive: All those flannel shirts and Swiss Army knives are there partly because we're camping out.

by Susan Baylies

⌐⌐⌐⌐⌐⌐⌐⌐⌐⌐⌐⌐⌐⌐⌐⌐⌐⌐⌐⌐⌐⌐⌐⌐⌐⌐⌐⌐⌐⌐⌐⌐⌐⌐⌐⌐⌐⌐⌐

CHAPTER FOUR

In Their Own Voices: Self-Portraits of Festival Performers

Music marks time in lesbian herstory. For those women coming out of the closet after 1974, an independent women's music industry provided the sound track for self-discovery. To this day, the sounds of those early albums, those specific tracks on specific recordings, remind many of us of where we were when we realized we loved women; one need only look at the dreamy faces of women over 35 attending a Ferron concert to feel the emotional legacy "our" artists provide.

Rarely promoted on radio or television, our favorite artists achieve their most visible status as lesbian celebrities during festival season. If they no longer tour—or do tour but bypass our towns—we wait all year to see them live, onstage at festivals. This chapter offers authentic reflections from eight artists who have been consistent festival performers and who openly embrace festival work and culture.

Typically, overviews of lesbian-feminist music begin with the "Big Four" of the 1970s: Holly Near, Cris Williamson, Meg Christian, and Margie Adam. However, the first women to record and perform openly lesbian music in the very early 1970s, prior to the founding of Olivia Records or Holly's coming out, were Alix Dobkin and Maxine Feldman; let's not forget that both the feminist movement and women's music and entertainment owe a great deal to Jewish foremothers. As the festival circuit grew after the mid 70s, popular headliners included more women of color (June Millington, Linda Tillery, Vicki Randle, lesbian reggae duo Casselberry-Dupree, Mary Watkins, Women of the Calabash, Edwina Lee Tyler, Nydia Mata, the Washington Sisters), artists from Canada (Ferron, Heather Bishop, Faith Nolan, Lucie Blue Tremblay), and occasional guests from England, New Zealand, and Australia

(Ova, Marilyn T., Judy Small, and later the Topp Twins). Popular and consistent festival performers throughout the late '70s and '80s included Sue Fink, Ginni Clemmens, Therese Edell, Betsy Rose, Nancy Vogl, Kristin Lems, Robin Flower, and blues-country artists Teresa Trull and Barbara Higbie. From the Bay Area, jazz vocalist Rhiannon and the group Alive! contributed creative vocal imagery and percussion to festivals. And ensemble groups, including Sweet Honey in the Rock,

HOT WIRE
THE JOURNAL OF WOMEN'S MUSIC AND CULTURE

JAMIE ANDERSON

DC in '93

CHICAGO
BIG MAMAS
GULF COAST
FESTIVAL
OUTWRITE '92
BLACK FILMMAKERS
DEL MARTIN &
PHYLLIS LYON
WOMEN and
THEIR GUITARS
JUSTINA & JOYCE
SCARY VIDEOS
MONICA GRANT
JUDY FJELL
ELLYN FLEMING
HUMOR BOOKS
MARKETWIMMIN
7th ANNUAL
READERS' CHOICE
AWARDS

STEREO RECORDING INSIDE

VOLUME 8, NUMBER 3 · SEPTEMBER 1992 $6.00

Libana, and the Reel World String Band, featured new arrangements of traditional songs and introduced festival audiences to a continuum of women's music from different cultures. Nonmusicians also made their mark as festival artists, beginning with the groundbreaking political comedy performances of Robin Tyler, Judith Sloan, Kate Clinton, and Lynn Lavner.

Over 20 years ago, readers were introduced to both Maxine Feldman and Cris Williamson in Rita Mae Brown's second novel, *In Her Day*, and several other women's music artists published perspectives on lesbian identity in books during the 1970s and '80s. More recently, artists' reflections on festival performance and festival networking have appeared as a new genre of writing. The voices of festival artists may be found in a variety of sources today, including Holly Near's own autobiography, *Fire in the Rain...Singer in the Storm*, Gillian Gaar's book *She's A Rebel: The Untold Story of Women in Rock and Roll*, and the anthology edited by Bernice Johnson Reagon, *We Who Believe in Freedom: Sweet Honey in the Rock*. Compelling profiles of lesbian musicians may further be located in Lee Fleming's *Hot Licks: Lesbian Musicians of Note* (though not all of Fleming's subjects work the festival circuit.) Alix Dobkin, whose 1973 album *Lavender Jane Loves Women* launched a longtime career in festival work both for herself and Kay Gardner, serialized her memoirs in Chicago's lesbian periodical *Outlines*, and

Kay Gardner has published her own musical perspective, *Sounding the Inner Landscape.* Women's music journalist Laura Post recently published her collected interviews as *Backstage Pass;* festival sound engineer Boden Sandstrom and filmmaker Dee Mosbacher are now collaborating on a book and video history of women's music. And so the coming years should see a cornucopia of women's music biographies and autobiographies—plus documentary filmmaking.

In this book I quote, interview, cite, mention, or otherwise profile over 200 festival performers, approximately one third of whom are women of color and/or Jews. Comedians receive special attention in Chapter Seven, and other chapters include extra focus on certain artists such as Ubaka Hill, Deidre McCalla, Dianne Davidson, Sue Fink, Gretchen Phillips, and Tribe 8. But in these next pages, to capture the feel of festival work from artists' perspectives, I chose to profile eight women who are proven veterans of festival networking—and who, as articulate speakers, have important stream-of-consciousness perspectives on where festival performing fits into their lifelong political or artistic outlook:

Maxine Feldman, whose beloved composition "Amazon Women Rise" opens the Michigan festival each year; Alix Dobkin, the outspoken troubadour who remains a tireless symbol of Lesbian cultural commitment;[1] June Millington, the pioneering rock guitarist whose 1970s band Fanny was the first all-female rock group to chart in the Top 40 and who now runs the Institute for Musical Arts recording studio in Bodega Bay, Calif.; Jean Fineberg, of the duo Deuce (with Ellen Seeling), who speaks eloquently of sexism in the mainstream music industry; Margie Adam, one of the first women's music composers in the early 1970s, who went off the road for a seven-year sabbatical and returned to festivals of the '90s with plenty to say; Linda Tillery, the Bay Area jazz vocalist who is also a scholar of traditional African-American women's songs and arrangements; Ronnie Gilbert, best known for her years as a member of the red-baited 1950s folk group The Weavers, who came out as a lesbian in the mid 1980s and began performing at festivals with Holly Near; Jamie Anderson, a true second-generation artist nurtured by the festivals of the late '70s and early '80s, who has played nearly every festival as an out lesbian folksinger and humorist of the 1990s.

I turned on my tape recorder, and these friends spoke to me.

MAXINE FELDMAN

I've been a dyke all my life. Let's start with that. And I'll be honest—I was very male-identified. I was a very butch girl; I could do anything a guy could do except produce sperm. But there was only so far a girl could go. I always felt that something was unfair, wasn't right. I didn't understand that the problem was sexism.

I was completely involved in civil rights work, even in high school. Our energies were focused on civil rights, and before that, on not having the bomb dropped. Children were dying because of the Cold War. You marched, you registered people to vote. Then the focus went to Vietnam; protesters were being killed in the streets. Women were writing songs about the times, certainly—Joan Baez, Judy Collins—but at age 20, I didn't know the influences of previous women. Remember, I was born in World War II, when women had barely had the right to vote for a generation. I could see what was wrong. I grew up in a very political household, but it took a long time for women in the protest movements to realize we were the ones making coffee.

I was thrown out of the Boston folk circuit for being queer. I refused to sleep with this radio producer who plugged folk coffeehouses. He said, "What are you, a queer?" And I responded, "Yeah!" So he put out the word that I brought the so-called wrong element to folk shows. And I was banned in Boston.

I went to California and wrote my first lesbian song, "Angry Atthis," in May 1969, one month before the Stonewall Riots. I wrote it in about three minutes, in a bar in L.A. Before Stonewall we had Mafia-run bars where you were a fourth- or fifth-class person. It was the only place for dykes to meet; we didn't have festivals. Or women's bookstores. At these bars, if you were in butch drag you could be arrested; you had to wear three "female" items *by law*. And be prepared for bar raids. I didn't like the way it made me feel—like we were all useless and sick. I felt we were worth a lot more. Stonewall proved I was not alone. It was a time for all our protests. Nothing happens in a vacuum.

"Angry Atthis," of course, is a play on words. I was "angry at this" lesbian oppression. My brainy girl side wanted to call my piece "Sappho's Song," but then I read that Atthis was the name of one of Sappho's lovers. And "Atthis" began to appear to me as a better statement of all I felt. Yeah, angry at this—that's how the final title came to me. And then of course the song took two seconds to write; it spewed out of me.

I was so excited by the Stonewall Riots that the very next day I went to a gay lib meeting in Los Angeles; I still have the button. But the guys—I didn't even know the word then—were so *chauvinistic.* Then, when I was singing on a college cam-

Maxine Feldman and Saraswate, interpreter for the Deaf, performing at a 1977 Washington, D.C., concert.

Joan E.Biren

pus, a copy of *Sisterhood is Powerful* fell into my hands and forever changed my life. And then someone sent me *Patience and Sarah*—I couldn't believe it, a lesbian love story where the women didn't end up getting killed, maimed, or married. Remember, the lesbian movies in 1968-69 were homophobic tragedies: *The Fox, The Killing of Sister George.* Through reading new lesbian and feminist writing, I started to examine my own sexism.

In 1971 I played "Angry Atthis" for Robin Tyler at a college gig, and she loved it. She was performing with Patty Harrison—they did the first feminist comedy—and they dragged me everywhere for a year as their opening act. In 1972 we recorded "Angry Atthis" on some extra tape in a studio at 20th Century Fox. Naomi Littlebear and Robin Flower, who were in a group called Sisterhood, recorded "Angry Atthis" with me in this enormous cavern of a Hollywood studio. We were there for maybe an hour and a half, recorded my song "Bar One" on the B side. Then we tried to sell this 45, and you couldn't give it away.

At that point the writers were the big muckety-mucks. At feminist events, performers sort of did a little song in between *their* lectures. And I said I'd stop talking about lesbian music the day there were as many albums as books.

But then women's groups started to split—from men, from each other. Separatists began to put me down because I played on college campuses where there were men in the audience. But it was very important to me to play campuses. My optimistic view was "Fine, more audiences, more places for me to play." First of all, it was safe to be out; I was sponsored by the school. And performing was like breathing; there was no question of *not* doing it. I'd also give classroom lectures. I'd start with "Angry Atthis" and then say, "I'm not here to describe what I do in bed. Let's talk." I'd stun 'em into silence, but it raised their consciousness—they weren't as frightened after I left. I was a real live person who made them laugh, cry, and think.

Ironically, I frightened my *own* kind. Dykes asked, "Could you tone it down? Why do you have to be so blatant?" I'd say, "Why do you have to be so closeted?" And the Jew-baiting! One lesbian performer I shared a stage with called me a "filthy rich Jew." I had death threats from the KKK; I needed Secret Service protection at one show. I walked a fine line because I did comedy and music. I told stories—something very Jewish, an ethnic tradition. No one knew how to categorize me. Comedians didn't understand my music, musicians didn't understand my comedy. I was an *entertainer.* And some producers preferred the women's music artists who were, you know, two slices of white bread with American cheese.

I began to play festivals—West Coast in 1973 and Boston in 1975, where Lisa Vogel heard me, and National, 1976. I had no manager. I was alone and had to be very tenacious. The National Women's Music Festival in 1976 is a favorite memory. It was the first year I performed there, and I wasn't even a scheduled artist. I just asked for a little time. Casse Culver and Willie Tyson gave me time from their sets, and that's where I introduced "Amazon."

And then I became a festival emcee. The first year the Michigan festival had a separate day stage, I said to my accompanist, Dovida Goodwomon (now Dovida Ishatova), "We're going to make day stage the hottest spot in town." There were 7,000 women, and unlike a nighttime performance with stage lights, you could *see* the audience. What a connection of the heart! To get right in someone's face—it was magical.

As a festival emcee, I'm not there to do Maxine Feldman. I'm there to introduce the act, to set up the audience, and to demystify the stage. In the early days I didn't know all the performers—they were *all* new faces—and I had to get their bios. And some artists had never worked with an emcee—like Orquesta Sabrosita. But after I introduced them, they thanked me, saying, "You made the audience so ready for us. They embraced us!" And Toshi Reagon told me, "My mom said that if I had Maxine as my emcee, I'd be all right."

I opened the Michigan festival singing "Amazon" until 1989. I had ruined my vocal chords doing drugs, although I got sober in October 1976, and I had to have polyps removed. So Rhiannon began singing "Amazon" because I could no longer trust my voice; I was terrified. But as long as "Amazon" is sung at Michigan, I'm there. And I got to select the artist to give my baby to. I talked to Rhiannon, we cried, I wrote the lyrics down for her, and she took off. Yeah, I cried for another 24 hours without stopping. But once Rhiannon opened that first note, I felt a burden lift.

As an emcee, I'm handed announcements that are funny in and of themselves, like reminders about the world's strangest workshops or workshop time changes. I have to tell the audience to please get out their pencils, and they're all sitting there naked. Not like me, who can carry a briefcase under her breasts.

The 1990 opening night of the East Coast Lesbian Festival was one of the nights it's all about. It flowed. Kay Gardner followed June Millington's incredible performance, so I went out into the audience and told stories from the old days, preparing the transition, readying everyone's buzzing ears for an acoustic coffeehouse kind of space. And I had them ready.

"Angry Atthis" is still a blatant, powerful song. The Kentucky band Yer Girlfriend asked if they could record it in 1992. I cannot tell you how excited and honored I am that women young enough to be my daughters chose my music for their very political band. Today there's a lot of self-hatred among young lesbians, a "so what" attitude. But it's not a "so what" issue, no matter how decorated your closet is.

I get furious when a talk show features Suzanne Westenhoefer or Lea Delaria and the host tells the audience, "There were no lesbian role models before them." What am I, chopped liver? And Melissa Etheridge and k.d. lang—these girls wouldn't be doing what they're doing if we hadn't raised the consciousness of the music industry. It was my white tails before k.d. lang's suit. Still, I think women need to create their own coming-out experience. And let's face it, rock and roll is one of the world's biggest consumer markets. The expansion of women's music into the mainstream should have been happening 25 years ago. I want more mainstream artists to come out in their prime, not after they've retired. Come out and say who you are while you're peaking—don't lie to us all these years.

I wouldn't trade any of it—the death threats, the struggles. I'm not a star, I'm a festival worker. Today I'm mainly working to stay alive. I've been in and out of the hospital many times, and I'm well past 50—a crone! But when I hear Yer Girl-friend playing "Angry Atthis," I realize how far the community has come. In some ways it's moved away from feminism. In other ways feminism is a continual issue. As I age, my awareness *behind me* grows.

ALIX DOBKIN

I have been at the right place at the right time all my life, starting with my parents wheeling me to the waterfront in New York City to organize for the National Maritime Union. They would give out union literature, holding little me in their arms so that the thugs wouldn't beat them up. That's how I started—at the right place. The unions were organizing, there was all this energy in that kind of progressive movement for social change.

I was in New York when the Brooklyn Dodgers were the team that *Field of Dreams* is about. I saw Jackie Robinson steal home; I was at Ebbets Field. I was in Kansas City listening to rhythm and blues when rock and roll was first invented—I was there for that. I was in Philadelphia in the late '50s, in Greenwich Village in the early '60s, when folk music was just beginning to change popular culture as we know it. I was in New York City in the early '70s, in a consciousness-raising group, 1971. Like Forrest Gump.

That's why I started writing my memoirs—because this is history that's gone from contemporary consciousness. I walked around New York in 1949 when I was nine years old, a New York that doesn't exist any more, but I was there, and I remember. I remember seeing Marlene Dietrich's legs as they disappeared around the corner at Radio City Music Hall.

I was raised in a Yiddish culture where education and culture are inseparable, where you don't have a show unless you teach something and you teach with songs, with stories. That's how I was raised—to find a way to perform this function. We need festivals to do this, but we need *more*. What I'm writing in my memoirs is not for Lesbians only; I want everybody to be educated.

My first album was *Lavender Jane Loves Women,* in 1973, with Kay Gardner. And I recorded that when I was 33⅓ years old. My first festival? The second Michigan, in 1977, is what I remember—going out there to Hesperia. I wore a nightgown, and people were so shocked to see me in what they thought was a *gown*. Somebody took

Adrian Hood sharing a moment of affection with her mother, Alix Dobkin, at the 1989 Michigan Womyn's Music Festival.

Toni Armstrong Jr.

a picture, and it wound up in *Off Our Backs,* blowing everybody's minds. In those days Lesbians didn't do that.

As the festivals came into being they all generally invited me because I was a very prominent figure and a symbol and, oh, yeah, a *performer*. I sat in on worker meetings at Michigan before I ever became a worker; I thought it was all so interesting. How did these women do this? And in those early days, Michigan's postfest wrap-up meeting had maybe a dozen women sitting around a campfire and calculating the total number of garbage pickups. I found all of that much more fascinating than the stage showbiz stuff. And so I became a worker.

When Lesbians get together, you never know what they "do" in the fake world, who's the corporate executive. I'll never forget one experience I had at the Women's Motorcycle Festival, where I performed several times. A couple hundred motorcyclists—Lesbians, of course. Some women were so awestruck by me—I get that a lot, but here it was really touching. We slept in a dormitory, and one evening I was in the one bathroom everyone used at night. I had just been in my room, thinking, *These women appreciate me so much. They think so highly of me. But if I were put out in the woods, I wouldn't know how to survive; I wouldn't last a day out on my own in nature.* I was thinking of this as I brushed my teeth, and a little butch older woman came up to me and said, "Oh, Alix, I love you so much. I'm so thrilled to be here with you." We talked, and after she left someone said, "Do you know what she does? She teaches the Navy Outward Bound course on survival skills."

That woman made such an impression on me—it was exactly what I'd been thinking about! You don't know what skills and knowledge so many of these Lesbians have. They are really accomplished. And I remember one worker talent show at Michigan where a crew counted how many teachers, social workers, mothers they had. It was an amazing statistical analysis.

How do I deal with being a symbol? I like it. I like being a role model. I have a lot of opinions, as you know; I've had *experiences* with so many issues, and have come to distill and refine my responses to situations. The lesson I learned working at Michigan for so many years was that certain issues appear again and again. Some will never be solved. What has changed is not the solution to these more persistent challenges but rather how we deal with each other, the process. And so I've decided that any issue can be dealt with if we treat each other with respect— even when we don't respect each other. Out there in the fake world and in our Lesbian community, it comes down to treating each other with respect, being honest and real, not enabling each other to be abusive assholes.

A TYPICAL ALIX RAP,
LIVE AT THE GULF COAST FESTIVAL

I've prepared all my life for this job. Because being a Jew and being a Lesbian are very similar. That's why I look so much alike. I have so much in common: It's OK to be a Jew, it's OK to be a lesbian—as long as you don't mention it. And what we also have in common is that we were never supposed to survive, yet here we are. And you know the old saying "For every Jew there are six opinions"? With Lesbians, it's eight.

For me it was easier to come out as a Lesbian than it was to come out as a Jew. But when I came out as a Lesbian, I gave myself permission to claim all the different parts of myself that maybe I wasn't so comfortable with before. That's one of the great things about being a Lesbian—that we must invent ourselves, and that organic process is ongoing. But it's very important for us to know where we come from.

Every country, every culture has Lesbians—wherever there are women. And my vision of international, indigenous, global Lesbian culture is that each of us has the responsibility to look to our past, to our own heritage, whatever we bring forward from our traditions. We sort through it, and we select the best. I don't want the junk. I want the best from you, and I want to give you the best from my Jewish-Yiddish culture. That's my vision of Norah's Ark.

And that's why I include a little piece of Yiddish in every performance I do because Yiddish is such a fabulous culture. It's a women's language. How many of you have never seen me in concert before, never seen me live? OK, I'll explain. The rest of you are veterans, my varsity Lesbian audience.

Yiddish is a women's language. Hebrew was the scholarly language, was reserved for the men, because only men could be scholars. So Hebrew is tremendously male-identified. Yiddish, on the other hand, was spoken universally by two thirds of the world's Jews before the Holocaust—in most Jewish homes and in family life of Eastern Europe, right through the 1930s. So, as the "language of women and fools," it's a great language for gossip, for expressing feelings; it's very emotional. And it also has more words to insult men than any other language in the world.

JUNE MILLINGTON

This is really ironic. I'm a person who came into women's music and festival culture through the back door. I mean, I started out in rock and roll. I hadn't the slightest interest in being "feminized." I just wanted to kick butt. And, certainly, to rise above the status to which I felt I was relegated simply by being of mixed race and a woman. But now I'm explaining to people what the essence of festival energy is: number one, a safe space where we gather together in large numbers and build the event. We need that so badly that I just can't see it *not* happening in the future. I know change is the name of the game, and the music is already changing. But the context in which it is presented is so comfortable. Festivals give everybody in the audience some way to speak their mind too, in some capacity, whether at a workshop or in an open forum.

Cris Williamson was the first person I went on the road with in women's music; it was her first national tour, in 1976. And the *feelings* at those performances were the same feelings that you get at festivals. Today you still really feel that at the festivals and not so much at women's concerts. And that could partly be attributed to the fact that women feel more safe at festivals now, whereas in the beginning, everything about women's music was so separatist. Just by definition, attending a women's concert, women felt safe, felt protected. Nowadays, concerts, for the most part, aren't separatist, aren't women-only space. But most festivals still are.

The first festival I attended myself was on the East Coast: a Long Island women's festival that didn't continue for many more years. It was held at a college, and I have to separate that from a women's festival where there's camping, where the women have the land to themselves. Let's set that as a criterion. So that would make my first big experience the West Coast festival, where I played at Yosemite in 1980 or '81. I certainly remember that it was the year when women of color rushed the stage because they said the kitchen was so racist, that the black women were the ones doing all the menial work. I wasn't there for all the commotion—I was practicing in my trailer because I'd been asked to sit in with Teresa Trull.

In a way, one could say I was happy to be in oblivion, to have my head deep in my work. I remember once when I was processing with Holly Near during the making of her album *Fire in the Rain*—well, it was a confrontation, really—and she said something like, "I wish you wouldn't internalize that." I didn't even know what internalize meant. I mean, my pain was so deep from all the racism first, then sexism I'd encountered, I couldn't even deal with the whole on any level. I had to shut down and plow on, get by, in 1980, when I was 32. It was probably another two to four years before the facade could begin to crack, and then the real work began.

But that first festival was also memorable because my mom came. We were driving up into the mountains, to Yosemite, and got stuck behind this car. Of course it had to be a Volkswagen van with a women's symbol on the bumper, and my mom asked, "What's *that*?" It was the first of many questions. But she loved it. Whenev-

June Millington getting down at the 1990 Michigan Womyn's Music Festival.

Toni Armstrong Jr.

er people *like* me, she has a good time. It didn't bother her that there were all these women loving women. She might have been slightly shocked that most of the women weren't wearing any clothes.

I find festivals tremendously interesting. I don't categorize festival culture into what I like or don't like. One of the first things I discovered during all the separatism that we created in the beginning to keep us apart from men was that we also divided *ourselves* into subcategories. Different types of separation, different camps—just within festivals themselves! I spent quite a bit of time thinking about this, about the amount of fighting that went on. Well, about ten years ago at a Buddhist retreat, my teacher, Ruth Dennison, went over the Four Divine Abodes, and one of them is

"Join the joy of others." I've been concentrating on that for a decade, actually. It's been tremendously helpful in my life, certainly as an antidote to, let's say, jealousy.

It's meant that on a practical level, for me, the idea of going to a women's gathering or a women's space where there is so much potential joy—well, I personally question women who go in there with a need to *vent*. Of course, we've all heard the reason that's posited: that it's a "safe space" to let it all out, to let internalized stuff come out. But that makes me question the work people do on themselves individually. As a unit of force in the world, we can affect change much more quickly if we move forward together. We fall right into the hands of the enemy if we fight each other. I don't mean that we shouldn't get together to discuss our different views on separatism or whatever. But when we walk away, it would be great to have the sense that we'd had a *dialogue*. When we get two, 50, 100 women together, we don't have to batter each other emotionally. Battery is what goes on in the world we're trying to change.

I'll tell you about the time I was most uncomfortable with rhetoric: This was when my first solo album came out. I was interviewed in Washington, D.C., and this woman suggested I'd be criticized as racist for my song "Coconut Mentality," where I say, "What's good for the monkey got to be good enough for me." I'm thinking, *This woman has never lived in the tropics. She totally did not get what I was talking about yet wanted to point a finger at me and call me racist.* I grew up in Manila [Philippines]. I encountered racism every single fucking day of my life and still deal with its effects. Don't tell me what it's like in the tropics. Don't tell me I can't call myself *oriental*—I like that connotation because I'm *from* the Orient; I'm part Chinese. I find people projecting an idea of prejudice, and their idea contains the seeds of that which they're speaking against. Now, a song is something that just naturally brings people together, where everybody disappears into the mood of the moment. That really is wonderful. And it's wonderful when performers bring guests onstage and you see the interplay happen, back and forth jamming, women sharing their skills in that way. That giving and taking is beautiful. *Powerful.* A really big change I've seen is that in the beginning, the 1970s and early '80s, there weren't that many women of color on the stage. I immediately noticed that. But this has changed, and it's really heartwarming. I like having that company.

I love performing the song "Brown Like Me," but there have to be women of color in the audience for that song to go over. I noticed that if it's mostly white women, there's no place for it to go. There isn't the cultural experience to absorb it. My audiences seem to respond more to "All That You Need (I Got)." They seem able to sink into the deepness of that, really feel it with their bodies. And that's one thing I realized about some of my message-type songs—people weren't really hearing the words, I felt, as much as they were receiving something from the rhythm. That's really what I am, a rhythm-based instrumentalist songwriter, and my messages are really kind of subtle. *Oriental*, if you will.

After that first year, 1976, I don't think I performed at any of the major festivals with Cris. But so much of that first year I played with her was the pure essence of what everyone's trying to touch base with now. I consider myself really lucky; just the fact that I played with her that first year cancels out much other stuff, disappointments I may have had. When I think back to everything that women's music and feminism has given me to come home to myself, I feel nothing but grateful. And I'm very loyal to the essence of it all. Beyond that, I've really enjoyed playing with Vicki Randle, Linda Tillery, Bernice Brooks; sitting in with Teresa Trull; jamming with Toshi Reagon; playing with Adrienne Torf. And Mary Watkins—boy, when she and I play together, there's just something that happens between us that's magical. Nonverbal. And when I see her little butt start to wag, I know she's having a good time. I've had plenty of good moments with Sue Fink, onstage and off. I think she's one of the bravest performers I've ever seen. The best times I've ever had playing at women's festivals would have to be those first couple of East Coast Lesbian Festivals, when they were small and unknown; they were smaller, kind of a family feeling, and lots of women of color. Boy, I loved that. And now, playing with the [Slammin'] Babes is so incredibly fun—it's me and Jean [Millington] playing with the energy of our first all-girl band in high school, the Svelts, but with the wisdom to back it up. And we're playing with younger women who had the advantages and opportunities that came after us—they actually took music lessons. Our drummer, Janelle, was 6 when Jean and I first went to Hollywood to cut a record. Imagine that. And last year, there we were, all together at [the Institute for Musical Arts] working on Cris and Tret's latest album, *Between the Covers*. That's deep. That's uncanny. It's so full circle that I hardly know whom to thank.

And to top it off, I get to be involved with the Institute for Musical Arts, which in a fundamental way is bridging the gap—some would say, abyss—between women's music and women in music. There I was in September 1997 at the first IMA festival that featured both the "older" musicians and the "youngsters" who, you know, are cutting their teeth on Ani DiFranco and Alanis Morrissette records. But every one of them had eaten at our kitchen table, performed at IMA, hung, brainstormed, really connected. Mary Watkins. Barbara Higbie, Teresa Trull. Ferron. India Cooke. Sharon Burch. June and Jean Millington and the Slammin' Babes. And Megan McElroy, Copper Wimmin, and Amy Simpson—all "youngsters" recording their albums at the same place we cut *Between the Covers*. How can you beat that? You can't tell me that anything's dying. We're here!

When I go to a festival now, I know that 90% of my needs are going to be taken care of. I may not like all the food all the time, but I know I'm going to be fed. I know that I'm going to meet a diversity of people. I know that the security and stage crews are going to be *excellent*—if a little bit anal. The crews do their best to be professional; they take great pride. In the old days, the expectations of the level of musicianship or songwriting ability were pretty low. As long as it was a woman up there, it was thrilling. I think people's expectations are much higher now, and that's good. I don't think just anybody should get up there—that's what day stage or Monday night is for, whatever is set up in terms of new talent discovery. I believe in giving people a chance to shine, to do their thing, but in terms of the main stage presentation, we need high standards.

What I look forward to at festivals is the unexpected. For example, when there was that huge storm at Michigan in 1987, there was a jam that went on in the backstage tent during that storm. It was the *real* show, far better than anything that went on onstage. And I have almost all of that on video.

I'm having a much better time as I get older, across the board. I want to spread the word to younger women that it just gets better as long as you keep your nose to the spiritual grindstone. Accumulate good karma, continually fine-tune your motivation. Ask yourself, Why am I performing? Why do I write a particular song? Why do I want to try and make a lot of money—if I do, What's going to happen? And I personally have been asking myself, *How can I try to spread that which I'm learning as I get older?* Because experience is just so much of the picture. So much of the picture!

MARGIE ADAM

I.

I am a product of the festival open-mike show. The very first time I ever sang in public was at Kate Millet's women's music festival at Sacramento State University in 1973. I just walked up to her in this small music room—she was sitting at a school desk taking names, and I gave her mine, and I sat there in this room and waited for my turn. I remember thinking, *I'm going to have diarrhea any second. I'm not going to make it through this.* Then, of course, I watched the women in the audience support the women who went before me, and I listened to the music, and I thought, *I can do this. I don't know how to use a microphone, I've never performed in public before, but I can do this.*

That's really the story of my career—being surrounded by women who lifted me up so I could feel, *I can do this.* That is the message of the women's liberation movement, the message of feminism, the best message of the women's music movement. Now and forever. Women, *we* can do this.

In 1974 I came to the first National Women's Music Festival, in Champaign-Urbana, Ill. I didn't have the slightest idea what I was doing there. Something about women and music. All the unknown performers played early in the week, while Saturday night was reserved for the two big names, Yoko Ono and Roberta Flack. Now, as the Goddess would have it, both Roberta and Yoko cancelled. So as the concert approached, the organizers went to these unknown performers and asked us to "save" the Saturday night show. We got together and talked about what individual songs we would sing and then decided we'd learn some of each other's songs. On Saturday night at the first National Women's Music Festival, Cris Williamson, Meg Christian, Vicki Randle, and Margie Adam sang together for the first time. The rest is history.

Many things I remember about the five days at that first festival, but two in particular are significant to me personally. The first memory is of Kay Gardner taking over the stage with her flute and 75 women on Sunday to teach all of us at the very birthing of this glorious women's music movement that women's music is not just in the lyrics. It's also in the music itself.

The other moment for me, which changed my life forever, was when I had the opportunity for the first time to hear Meg Christian sing. I listened to her music,

Margie Adam at the piano: photographer Irene Young captures beautiful hands in action.

Irene Young

and I put my head down on my hands and began to cry. Quite simply, I felt to my soul's center, *This woman is singing my life.*

In that moment my life was forever changed. I knew clearly and absolutely that I was not alone any more.

II.

I came off the road in 1984. The last two performances I did were at the tenth anniversary of the National Women's Music Festival and the first Southern Women's Music and Comedy Festival. In a sweet bit of closure, Meg sat in on both sets and sang "Beautiful Soul" with me. I think those two events were emblematic of the time: a new festival starting in the South and a very hearty sense of festival culture ongoing in the Midwest. There were a lot of festivals sprouting up regionally at that time. However, simultaneously, production companies were going out of business in city after city.

When I came off the road in May 1984, the women's music industry was committing itself to *mainstreaming*. There was a very strong push from both the major women's record labels; some artists had two press kits, one for the women's community, one for "mainstream" media and producers. Several artists who had been closely associated with "women's music" began to move away from the phrase. At the same time, there were those of us who felt that part of our work was to be in the mainstream, even as we identified our work as women's music. As early as 1975, Boo Price, who was my business partner and manager at the time, and I had been doing mainstream overground media work with major newspapers, radio, and TV. We both felt that it was extremely important to get the concept and reality of women's music as far out into the world as possible. It never occurred to me that "women's music" and "mainstream" might be mutually exclusive.

By the time I came off the road, I felt uneasy about the shift in focus away from the woman identification in the music and some artists. The kind of issues that began to take center stage changed to the nuclear freeze movement and the liberation struggles in Central America and the Middle East. I felt it was absolutely essential that the focus on women's lives and concerns not be lost, even as we addressed other progressive issues.

The balance changed. The audience began to say, "What kind of event am I going to? Is this a lefty event or a women's event?" An audience that had been absolutely loyal and essential to women's music began to complain: "She hardly talked about women's stuff at all—the whole show!" Around this time, audience support for women's music began to decline.

The Ronald Reagan years had a huge impact on the social and political atmosphere in which women's music and culture took place. Certainly by 1984 all outspoken feminists were being marginalized and ridiculed. It was far less popular to stand up and say that you were a feminist or even an activist working for women's rights—almost as unpopular as it had been in 1970. It was a really hard time for women artists, who felt that they weren't being backed up when they made statements, and while certain people in America were enjoying economic benefits, a whole bunch of Americans didn't get to take that ride. That ended up specifically affecting women's music producers. Many of them had risked losing money in the

1970s; by the mid '80s they could no longer afford to do so. These were the individual women producers across America who had said at some point, "I'm willing to put my money where my heart is," and had brought women's music they loved to their community.

The political-economic shift in the '80s was part of the "middle age" of women's music, from the halcyon days of "Everything's possible!" to "We need to get serious, need to get professional, want to go *overground*." Of course, some of us had been operating out of these premises from 1975.

When I came back in 1991-92, I found myself singing into the faces of an audience that seemed to be asleep, no longer politically turned-on. Many women who came out to see me in 1992-93 hadn't been to a woman-identified event in eight years. As a political activist who had stepped back *in*, it seemed to me that lesbians had taken their feminist energies into the gay male political arena to work on AIDS. I'm sure they expected to feminize the men. But I feel that an unintended consequence is that it shifted the energy of radical feminists away from the ongoing struggle for women's liberation in this country and around the world.

Back on the road, I met women who wished me luck but clearly felt detached from feminist activism—as though they felt awkward that I was bringing back memories of a certain woman-identified music. I stood backstage at Michigan, and an overwhelming number of the musicians didn't identify with women's music, thought of it as a kind of retro concept, something that didn't have anything to do with them. It is both breathtaking and horrifying that our herstory, our story, is getting lost while it's still going on.

I liken it to the civil rights movement. People think of the civil rights movement as happening in just ten years, the '60s, when in fact it's still going on. The same is true of women's music. You could argue that it exists in a period of history, 1975-1985, but since the struggle for women's liberation is not over, there continues to be a need for strong, independent women's music to raise a joyful noise. There were strong women before us, women singing strong music about their lives. Barbara Dane, Betty Carter, Bessie Smith, Elizabeth Cotten, Marylou Williams, Malvina Reynolds—all out there way before the first National Women's Music Festival, in 1974. I never want to forget I am a part of an historical and ongoing movement of women making music to save and celebrate our lives.

Ellen DeGeneres stands on the shoulders of all the women who built and supported the women's music movement. Just look at that last scene of her coming-out episode on television: women together in a coffeehouse space, singing women's music. Sure, it was a stereotype—a folksinger in rainbow suspenders and '70s dyke haircut. I was proud, though, and felt it was an affectionate acknowledgement. And hey, some of us looked like that! I don't think it's by accident that when Ellen DeGeneres chose to honor her lesbian sisters, she chose two musicians, k.d. lang and Melissa Etheridge—the Melissa who started out at festivals of women's music. She opened for me at the West Coast festival one year. I don't need Melissa to acknowledge where she comes from in her media interviews; I *know* she comes from us. In a touching, sweet way, that's what that last scene in *Ellen* was all about—a broad tribute to us, which went right over "straight" America's head.

JEAN FINEBERG

Sure, I specifically remember Herb Alpert saying, "They're great, but women look stupid playing horns," when ISIS auditioned for A&M records. That attitude is very pervasive. I know exactly where he's coming from: They need to keep it an all-male club.

Musicians are so tied in with their egos. A lot of men feel they have to keep women out of their bands because as soon as there's a woman in the band, that band is perceived as being not as good, as *weaker.* They certainly don't want to have a band that's perceived as weak, so they have to say to themselves, well, women don't look right playing the horn.

It's a way to keep out a lot of competition. If you can eliminate half your competition with one stroke—well, Alpert can't eliminate the men competing with him, but he can sure as hell eliminate the entire other half of the population. So why not do it? I see that all the time. A lot of my male saxophone player friends will be real friendly with me, but they won't call me to sub for them. Some of them have actually come out and verbalized this: They think I'm a great player, but "I couldn't send you in the band because the other guys would object." The

Deuce members Jean Fineberg and Ellen Seeling performing at the 1989 Michigan Womyn's Music Festival.

Toni Armstrong Jr.

whole "I'm not prejudiced, but since they are" kind of deal. And they're afraid that they will be seen as weak by sending me in. "Couldn't you find a *guy* to sub?" It actually affects their reputation.

What you see changes what you hear. If you look at a woman playing, what you hear is different from when you look at a man and hear the same thing. All your senses contribute to what you're hearing. *We have to be better.* That's why, thank goodness, orchestras have "blind" auditions—they audition people behind screens, so you can't see who the musicians are. Except, of course, there are still orchestras like the Vienna Symphony, that won't audition women at all. But even there, men audition behind a screen so the good-looking man isn't perceived as a better player. It's just human to have all your senses affect your perception; there's posture, of course there's grooming; everything about you affects the overall perception.

Men have actually convinced themselves that women have an advantage, that there's reverse discrimination, that women and blacks and other minorities have an advantage. But in reality, a festival like Michigan is the only place we can get on a stage and just be like everyone else, starting with a clean slate, being seen just as a musician. Here you're just a musician, not a "woman musician." In the real world—or rather, the outside world—you're always that "woman musician"; you'll never be anything but a "woman musician." Here, only here, you can breathe a sigh of relief—and finally relax.

LINDA TILLERY

I played at the first Michigan festival, if I'm not mistaken, and I went with Meg Christian, Holly Near, and Teresa Trull. Three of the four of us were involved with Olivia Records, two were involved with each other, and Holly was in charge of her own label, Redwood Records. We went together from Los Angeles, and that was basically my debut into the women's music network.

Prior to that, I had no idea—no concept, really—what women's music was. What I did know was that I was going with my friends to play for a bunch of women. And I have to say that for me, my work within the women's community as a musician has been very challenging. Because what I brought to the table was the cultural aesthetic of an African-American woman who was raised in a primarily black neighborhood in the inner city of San Francisco.

My musical background's based in jazz, rhythm and blues, and some gospel, with a very heavy dose of the blues. In the beginning I wondered, *What on earth am I going to do for these women? How do I present who I really am to this audience, which may or may not have had exposure to the kind of music that is important to me?*

It was a matter of the artist wondering about how to reach her audience without compromising herself. That was a challenge. I think the audiences I've performed for within the women's music circuit were being educated just by virtue of being exposed to what I've had to offer. If there had been a plethora of black blues singers, black R&B singers, black gospel singers throughout "women's culture," then my experience would not have been unique.

What emerged as a blessing for me is that one of the producers of the Michigan Womyn's Music Festival made it possible for me to present some programs that were really kind of groundbreaking. I would get an idea, Boo Price would hear it, and we'd toss it around. She would say, "Well, why don't you do it if you think you can pull it together?"

One of these projects was called A Tribute to Black Women and the Blues. The scope of that project itself was so overwhelming and so powerful that it became much larger than the people involved. And that unfolded during the performance. I actually stood backstage and watched in awe this artistic expression of respect and gratitude paid to some women who might have been otherwise ignored. And it was one of the most satisfying moments of my life.

I also had the opportunity to bring my version of a Motown band to Michigan and had the opportunity to bring the Cultural Heritage Choir to Michigan. So I can say that I was one of the women who was instrumental in exposing women's audiences to African-American music. And that too is a very satisfying thing for me.

Toni Armstrong Jr.

Linda Tillery performing at the Michigan Womyn's Music Festival in the mid 1980s.

In the 1980s I went to the North East Women's Music Retreat every year. I always felt at home, loved, and taken care of. I would shake my head in wonder. It was the largest group of adoring fans I ever met. The audience would sing "Happy Birthday" to me. I certainly felt that giving 100% was the least I could do. Maybe I should give 150%, 200%! I gave my time as well as my talent; I walked through the grounds and spoke to clumps of people and formed many long-lasting friendships. We all want people to say, "Come back again." We want people to say, "You are welcome here. We respect your work." And we want people to say, "We love you." I got all of that from NEWMR and was very sad when that festival was no longer around.

We also change with time. And what we look for as expressions of gratitude and admiration becomes real different. I am in a period now [1996] where what I want is to see clearly what my goals are in life for the next, say, 20 years. I know how I want to live my life, and I know what I need to do in order to live it that way. It certainly doesn't include gratuitous sexual admiration, as in former years. So, as we change, our audiences change as well. Since my life now involves a good deal of time spent on research and reflection, that's what I'm radiating—I've become Professor Tillery, and that's that.

When I came to women's music and festivals, I was straddling two sides of the fence. I've always had one foot in mainstream music and one foot in women's music. Really, each side had to deal with the effects of the other. I was 27 when I did my first women's music concert, and I'm now 47. Twenty years! My career started when I was 19.

But festivals—it's pretty doggone unique in a society such as ours that a group as small as ours can do such amazing things. I have witnessed things at women's music festivals that I'd never seen before, like creating a city. Years ago I learned the importance of making friends with the tech crews. The crew is another subculture, a whole different world. If you want to eat well, you need to make friends with someone who's on the tech crew; I discovered *that* right away. But also, if you want to see another aspect of festival life that as performers we took for granted, you can hang out with the crew and see how they build and then take the city apart. I did that one year and it blew me away to see them dismantle everything. To see women drive a tractor-trailer, erect speaker towers, build a stage, use chain saws and drills—and the *tattoos*.

One successful festival makes it possible for another to emerge. There were very few festivals in the 1970s. Then it became a major thing on the continent—by the 80s we had National in Indiana, the Southern festival in Georgia, the West Coast festival, NEWMR, Rhythmfest in North Carolina, the Gulf Coast festival in Mississippi, and now Las Vegas.

I'm a middle-aged woman now. And while I'm not ready to step aside, I do have to allow for the generations of younger musicians who are emerging—women, in this instance, who have different ideas about how they want to make music and how they want to perform—just as I was at 22 and 23 years old, finding my way. These young folks have to do the same.

What do we, the baby boomers, do with ourselves now? Well, we're the largest age group in the United States, and we still want to hang on to our heroes and heroines: James Taylor, Carole King, Aretha Franklin, Jackie Wilson, James Brown, etc. Women's culture is not exempt. We're going to have to go through the same stuff. For me, solid musicianship is first and foremost—more important than emotionality. Quality is important to me, and I hope I have communicated that to my audiences.

There are still some areas of music that have not been explored as they should be.

Classical music, for example, has been all but ignored in festival culture. Choral music, oratorios, solo recitals, instrumental soloists. There are large parts of the musical spectrum we've missed, and I wish the door were open a bit wider. Therefore, I maintain that this is primarily a popular music network. It's not a network where all genres of music are well-received. For a long time, women's culture was dominated by European-derived folk music. And it was defined in that way for a real long time.

But do I look forward to festival season? Sure. Preparing for Michigan, I always say to myself, "You have to rest. You can't do too much. Don't stay up late every night and then try to get up early that next morning. Try to pace yourself." You can burn yourself out at Michigan very easily.

What I look forward to, most of all, is the networking. There are women I see once a year, every August. I count on it, look forward to it. And as a woman who appreciates and respects New York culture, I look forward to the women from New York like you can't believe. I get into conversations—if I want to know what's going on in Latin music, I pull aside one of the New York women and say, "Who's playing?" And they don't just talk to me about the women, they talk to me about the Latin *music*—what's new from Cuba, who just put out the hottest record from Puerto Rico or the Dominican Republic. If I want to know what's happening in African drumming or theater arts, who's been at the Met lately—all of that I can get without going there. I look forward to the networking; interacting with other working women.

RONNIE GILBERT

It must have been the late '70s when I had my first look at a women's festival, almost in spite of myself. I was visiting Berkeley, Calif., from eastern British Columbia, my home at the time. A new friend, Holly Near, suggested that I check out "women's music" at a festival in Portland, Ore., "on your way home." She wasn't going to be there, she said, but her sister Laurel would, also so-and-so, and she listed some names unknown to me.

Driving north, I thought, *Women's music? What is that supposed to be? Something like "women's movies"—sappy enough for only women to like?* Really, I was 50 years old, and except for singers with guitars and Phil Somebody's novelty All-Girl Band on the radio, I'd hardly ever run into a professional female musician in all those years of recording studios, concert halls, and the rest. I pictured the festival: many girls with guitars. And I wasn't crazy about milling about in crowds either. That's how I was thinking, so why did I detour and steer myself to Portland and the first Northwest Women's Music Festival? I don't know. I must have been very curious to see another one of the Near sisters in action.

Anyone who suddenly acquires an open mind about anything at all knows the feeling: Gusts of cold air blow through the skull, shattering preconceptions—painful at first. All day I was in a state, listening to lyrics that made me smile or rage, voices that thrilled. I can't remember now who the performers were, only that they were very good. Listening to a woman's clean, exciting guitar work, I found myself wondering why I had always taken it for granted that studio musicians and pit bands would be exclusively male.

At a poetry session a woman read something loving, delicate, deeply moving— about a cave and a jewel. Suddenly, it came to me: *My God, is she talking about her* [gasp] *clitoris? In public?* Why, yes, she was.

Laurel Near, it turned out, was a gorgeous dancer in an amazing dance collective called the Wallflower Order. Their piece was passionate, accessible, political, calling up images of Vietnam and Nicaragua, beautifully choreographed, powerfully danced. I found it hard to recover from the impact.

Where had all these remarkable artists sprung from? Where was I all the time it was happening? My brain swam with impressions of the day that didn't fit into any available context. And I realized I really couldn't take in any more.

I needed badly to talk, to compare notes with other newcomers, especially some older women. I looked around for gray heads, but the one or two there seemed to be in comfortable conversation with young friends. I should have been more assertive. I wasn't and left after one day of a two-day festival.

For a few years I watched for a second Northwest Women's Music Festival. It didn't happen again, but the effect of that one day lasted. My sense of myself as "one of the boys" and, therefore, privileged began to crack—although I didn't get it yet.

By the mid 80s, having teamed up musically with Holly Near, I came to know the festivals as a performer, at first with her, then solo. One of the first and best festivals

I went to was Sisterfire, held at a public school near Washington, D.C. Another was the more venerable, beautifully produced National Women's Music Festival in Bloomington, Ind., at which concert producers, artist managers, booking agents, technicians, and performers meet together to "focus on the process."

Sweet Honey in the Rock was the cornerstone of the Sisterfire festival. The producers were committed to Sweet Honey's approach: diverse woman-made music,

Ronnie Gilbert and Holly Near performing a duet at the 1997 Michigan Womyn's Music Festival.

Toni Armstrong Jr.

dance, and crafts in an accessible urban setting, for an inclusive audience. Sisterfire drew old, young, black, white, gay, straight, female, and male to its concerts, as Sweet Honey does to theirs—my idea of an ideal audience.

Then I was invited to sing at the women-only Michigan Womyn's Music Festival. There, I had been told, nudity is the norm. My nervous reaction was, "I'm not taking off even my shirt—take it or leave it!" As it happened, Kate Clinton's was the first familiar performer's face I saw, and below it she was [*whew*] fully clothed. In fact, unobserved and unharassed by men, everyone clothes or unclothes herself to please her own sense of comfort and aesthetic. There are some great getups—or get-downs.

As for me, Michigan was a true eye-opener. All my life I have been a small fat person, except for short-lived times of severe self-starvation. I had always felt sorry for myself to be such a departure from the female norm. On the land at Michigan, I'm suddenly surrounded by thousands of visible bodies, not one in four resembling that longed-for "norm." Compared to the grand diversity of the vast majority—short, tall, fat, skinny, half-and-half, thighs, stomachs, bosoms, rumps, all marvelous shapes and sizes—the "average" seemed fine but not really so inspiring.

I don't know what Michigan's onstage atmosphere was like while the women were learning the challenges of huge open-air stage production, but by the time I came into it, the whole operation moved like ballet. In the hands of a tough, highly skilled stage crew and brilliant sound technicians, I felt a level of care as a performer, of understanding and support that was—*womanly* is the word for it, I think.

Looking out into the night at an audience of several thousand people is a trip and a half anywhere. I had done this many times with The Weavers and on my own, decades earlier, but this was a new time, a new audience. At one concert I chose to read a poem that I loved, Oriethyia's "Mother's Day," the poet's tribute to her mom's unfaltering support of her through many life changes and choices. It's a long, personal piece. Would it hold an audience that size? What exactly would I do if I began to hear the restless rustle of 6,000 women?

I started to read. It was as if the words were birds fanning out over the field, settling down, finding every bittersweet, mother-daughter seed in that vast crowd—which came back to me in the audience's deep silence and, finally, in their applause. It was a real communion. I think it could only have happened in the company of an audience exclusively of women.

I came late to women's (or womyn's) music. Better late than never. At 60 and now 70, I have been proud to be counted one of the girls among women like Linda Tillery, Barbara Higbie, Alix Dobkin, Sabia, Ady Torf, Ferron, the Washington Sisters, Women of the Calabash, Holly Near, Sweet Honey in the Rock, Teresa Trull, Casselberry and Dupree, Heather Bishop, Edwina Lee Tyler, Toshi Reagon, Janet Hood, etc., etc., etc.—to mention only a very few of the magnificent musical artists with whom I've snared a stage at festivals. It's been an honor I couldn't have anticipated at 50.

JAMIE ANDERSON

Jamie is unique because she launched her career as a very popular festival performer after more than a decade of being a festiegoer. She also came out at a relatively young age. Hence, festival culture and lesbian pride were already comfortable themes for her when she made the transition from audience to stage.

I met my first lover when I was 15 and came out as a lesbian at 18—when I could finally say the words. And the year after I came out is when I discovered women's music. Women's music was very important to my becoming a feminist and my learning about lesbian culture—learning, in short, about who I was. To me, having women's music was a great advantage: It made me real strong right away. I didn't have to go through what a lot of women go through—getting married, having kids, taking ten years to find their first feminist book. I never had to do that.

The first time I was hired to play at a festival was in 1990. But I'd been going to festivals since 1979, at least one every year. My very first festival was Michigan, of course, the fourth Michigan festival, in 1979—when they were still getting used to moving so many women around. I remember that we couldn't park very close to our campsites. I'd been on the road for four days with five women in a little pickup; it's a wonder we didn't kill each other. We arrived ragged out, so tired we couldn't think straight, so to speak, but I was so energized by being there that I felt like an Amazon. We had these two huge ice chests, and I carried them by myself to our campsite. I carried our stuff, set up the tent—I was sore for days, but I felt like, *I can do it all.*

I always had my guitar with me, always signed up for open mike. In fact, in the early days at Michigan there were great jam tents. I have this good memory of being in a jam tent at Michigan. A group of us started this song that had a reoccurring chorus. Women who walked by kept joining us until we had a whole crowd, and people thought we were a choir. The line we kept singing was "That's the way it is at Michigan," and then we'd add another line about the festival. It was really, really fun.

What came from the stages really excited me too. But making my own music was so important. I really envied those performers who were hired there and at the other festivals. Meg Christian, to me, had it all. A fabulous guitar player, a skilled songwriter, and she had a wonderful voice and a warm, engaging stage presence. I always want a performer to feel friendly and accessible to me. Not accessible in that I need to know details about their life but rather to feel that I'm with a friend.

I bought every one of Meg's albums. I knew the words to every song. I would have learned to play every song too, except I thought that she was a far better guitar player than I was. I remember going to the National Women's Music Festival in 1980, and Meg taught a workshop on playing guitar. There I was, in the same room with my idol, and she taught us to play "Sweet Darling Woman" just like she plays it. And I remember thinking at the time, *Oh, that's not as hard as I thought it would be.* I left the room—and completely forgot everything because I was so enthralled at being with her. To this day, I can't even remember what key that song is in.

So it's not like I had an epiphany any one day at a festival and said, "I want to do this." It was a gradual thing, from the time that I learned to play the guitar in high school. I knew that I liked playing music, and I knew that I liked performing, but I didn't actually start applying to perform at festivals until 1989 because I would

Jamie Anderson takes a laugh break at the National Women's Music Festival in 1993; humor plays a key role in her political message.

compare myself to someone like Meg Christian and think, *I'll never be that good. Obviously they won't want me on the main stage.* I'd usually apply for the showcases.

I was also inspired by straight folksingers like Steve Goodman, who successfully combined comedy and music in his work. Comedy and music are how I live my life. My family is very much into humor, especially when we get together. In normal conversation, I love to make people laugh. So that naturally translated to the stage; I could never be one of those stately, very serious performers. Not that I can't do serious numbers, but I like to lighten it up so people can get up out of their seats at the end of a concert.

I didn't start writing music until 1984 or 1985. It wasn't a conscious decision, but because I was listening to women's music when I started writing music myself, it was natural for me to start with the kind of lyrics that I was hearing. It seemed silly to even try to be in the closet. I saw no purpose to that. And when I figured out how healthy it was, how freeing it was for me to be out, I just wanted to encourage everyone else—"Look how great this can be!" I'm really proud of who I am. And I thought that through my music I could encourage women and empower them.

I still maintain a distance, though. There are some things I don't sing about because I've chosen to protect myself or my friends. There have been a few songs that I've written that delved into something I felt was too personal. Also, there are songs that I have to sing to myself for a few months, until I get used to them.

Breast cancer is a topic I sing about in "One Out of Three." When I first wrote it, I still had the lump in my breast and was really worried. And my cousin was diagnosed with cancer. I couldn't get through the whole song without crying, without feeling too close to it. Originally I had thought, *OK. This will be a song for me.* I do have a few songs that I never perform. I learned to realize songs serve all sorts of purposes and to rest with that. But after I felt stronger about the song, and after my cousin went through treatment and was feeling good again, I started thinking that maybe this is a good song to bring out to women. Because the most powerful songs of change are those written in the first person, about personal experience. There were women in my life who were worried about lumps in their breasts. And my cousin, who became a survivor of breast cancer, liked the song.

I started doing it in performance and got to the point where I stopped breaking down—I never wanted to do that onstage. I never want the audience to feel like they're taking care of me; I simply want to sing my story. I've been performing the song for a couple of years now. I've met lots of survivors, I've met people who have lost loved ones to breast cancer, and I've heard their stories.

The first festival I was booked at was the Gulf Coast festival in Mississippi in 1990. I was so thrilled to get a spot on the night stage at this brand-new festival. It was only their second year. By 1992 or 1993 I was playing at a lot of festivals. In one season I played nine festivals. Now, a lot of that was day stage, and in the hierarchy of festivals, the better-known performers and the bands—with a bigger sound—usually do night stage. I'm not a band, and I wasn't really well-known. Also, I was a "girl with guitar," which is a definite drawback at festivals because there are so many of us. Being picked out of the crowd was quite an honor, but I still felt like Jamie Anderson, "the folksinger."

At the time I felt happy, felt good that so many festivals wanted to book me, but like I said, it was mostly day stage. I wasn't getting paid very much and was often paying my own transportation. I'd do a signing at the Goldenrod booth, and no one would show up. Things like that reminded me that I was "on my way up." 1993 was very exciting because I got to play at National on the main stage and with a band. That was the same year that I sang at the national March on Washington [for gay and lesbian rights], in front of hundreds of thousands of people. That was *the* high point. I kept feeling like, *OK.* Now *I'm going to make it.*

Looking back on it now, as a woman talking to you in 1996, I'm thinking, *Well, that was great—but I don't feel like I got there.* I don't have the draw that someone like Holly Near does—not that I'm comparing myself to her, certainly. But the ascent of the popularity of women's music didn't quite coincide with my career. I came onto the scene kind of late. And one of the main reasons I was able to keep on doing it was because my partner was so supportive. If it hadn't been for her being so financially and emotionally supportive, I would have quit because I just don't have the audience base that I need. And now, in this day and age, even the bigger names are having a tough time. I feel fortunate that I continue this work.

I did work really hard at all those festivals. And I really, really enjoyed them. I remember the year I did nine festivals, thinking, *My God, I'm getting paid to do this. I've been a festiegoer for 13 years, and all of a sudden I can go to* all *the festivals and get paid for it? A dream!* And I happily went to all the workshops and stages that I could. By the ninth festival that year, I was babbling. But I got to know a lot of the craftswomen, I got to know the techies, and I liked that familiarity, that feeling of home.

Oh, and the things you have to deal with! Mostly because the festivals are outdoors. It always rains on me. That's why I really enjoy National because it's held inside. And as I get older, I get crankier about sleeping on the ground. I don't want to do that anymore. I still really enjoy festivals, especially the crafts area and the music, but by 1990 I stopped going to festivals I wasn't booked at. When I get booked at so many, I don't want to go to others. People often ask if I'm going to

Michigan, and I say, "I'm booked at these other festivals, so I won't go."

Because I do original music, I can't stay in my home state and make enough money. Even though I won a Tucson Area Music Award, I can't make my living in Arizona. My audience remains largely lesbian, though straight folks do come out to hear me. So I tour a lot, and it can be real frustrating out on the road. Sometimes I go to an area of the country that doesn't have a women's music producer or a gay bar or someplace where I can play that I would not have to explain myself to.

Straight folks have been very, very hard to break through to. There are a couple of venues that have had women's music for a while, but they're the minority. Nobody thinks they're homophobic; they simply think they're being "protective of their audience." You know, "Well, we have a *family* coffeehouse." Or, "We don't think our audience would understand what you're doing." Or, "Could you tone it down, *if* we booked you?" All sorts of crap, rude things that they tell me.

There's one straight coffeehouse in Illinois I've worked at a couple of times. From the beginning they realized that their regular audience was not going to enjoy what I do. The first time I played there, they had the event sponsored by a bookstore that carries a lot of feminist and lesbian titles. The store helped with the publicity and brought in my lesbian audience. We had a good crowd, a great time, and everyone was happy. The second time I played there, they got the gay newspaper to sponsor me. Very smart—instead of saying, "Oh, my God, she's a lesbian; what are we going to do?"

I've done some educating in the folk community. I went to the Folk Alliance Conference and did the first queer support group there. A lot of work still needs to be done. Only gay people showed up, although that workshop was open to everyone.

As this interview concluded, two incidents shed light on Jamie's fluctuating location in the women's music hierarchy. We were talking in a hallway at the National Women's Music Festival, where Jamie had been invited to emcee but not to sing. Jamie called out a compliment to Lojo Russo, a new, younger performer who had just played her own featured set in the festival showcase. Lojo clearly had no idea who

Jamie was and simply did not recognize her as a popular festival artist and veteran performer. Ten minutes after this unsettling encounter, two women almost knocked me over in their eagerness to meet Jamie in person. They thanked her over and over for all she had done for women's music. The contrast between these two encounters brought tears to Jamie's eyes—and mine.

1. Alix requests that the L in Lesbian always be capitalized in references to her life and work; she maintains that Lesbians are a separate tribe and cultural people.

CHAPTER FIVE

Life Stages

And then there was the night that one couple made love in the cabin. They assumed that every-body was sleeping, that nobody could hear. They, uh, were trying to do it very quietly—until the end, when one of them said to the other, "Thank you. Thank you. Thank you!" And the next day everyone went up to them and went, "Thank you! Thank you!" And they never lived it down.
—Marcia, Campfest 1996

Lovemaking. Commitment ceremonies. Memorial services for a mourned loved one. Birthday parties; "cronings" for women reaching 50. Lesbian moms camping with toddler daughters; adult daughters introducing older moms to women's music. Romance blooming on the land—blushingly unexpected affairs, serious partnerships beginning, anniversaries celebrated. Festivals make visible lesbian life stages: self-discovery, celebration, passages. What must be kept discreet in the outside world becomes a major party on "the land."

There is heightened awareness of ritual in festival culture, not only because of the profound woman-centered spirituality and Goddess ceremonies regularly invoked onstage by artists such as Kay Gardner and Ruth Barrett. Most urgent is the need to repeat, or reclaim, critical life-stage celebrations—because "out there," in a homophobic society, our own partners may not be welcome home for holidays, at synagogue, at funerals, or at graduation parties. Those women who burst out of the closet only at festivals bring accumulated joys and milestones in their backpacks and recreate the past year's highlights in the good company of festiegoing allies. And where rituals from childhood haunt those emerging from dysfunctional families, festivals offer the chance to begin again, to design new rituals that can be anticipated annually without accompanying stress.

This chapter looks briefly at four different life-stage aspects of festival culture: adult romance and commitment, the young girls coming of age at festivals, perspectives on motherhood, and grief and loss expressed on the land.

Romance and Commitment ⋛⋚

Which part of the ad for a "women's music festival" attracts the lesbian festiegoer? Make no mistake, the music is terrific, but so are all the women, and they hail from such legendary locations as Brooklyn, Texas, Australia, Berlin, Montreal. Forget political processing and carpentry work shifts for now; festivals are all about women meeting women, platonically or seductively; building connections; celebrating lesbian sexuality. Here, as the popular joke goes, the majority are joyous "vagitarians" let loose at the Amazon buffet. And despite obvious challenges, such as the sheer lack of privacy and weather blowing hot and cold, lovemaking at festivals is an experience that few forget and many look forward to.

In no other environment is there such freedom for expressive affection between women, validated in song after song from the music stage (often explicitly, as in Gretchen Phillips's "The Queer Song," Heather Bishop's "I Wanna Be Seduced," Nedra Johnson's "Testify"). With the right performer, entire audiences become aroused: Our favorite romantics crooning onstage would certainly have to include Suede, Vicki Randle, Lucie Blue Tremblay, Linda Tillery, Kathryn Warner. And what about the wild sexual energy of very different bands like Two Funkin' Heavy and Sexpod or the environment created by Faith Nolan standing up and singing "Jelly Roll"? After a night-stage concert with these artists, who wouldn't want to return to one's tent with a new crush or longtime companion? And so the music (purchased and autographed at the performers' booth the next day) becomes a reminder, a souvenir, a keepsake of that loving.

There's no reason to pretend that "festival flings" don't exist—they do, and they are frequently the start of long-term committed partnerships. Festivals also stress the importance of having safe sex: Michigan's general store now sells dental dams alongside the insect repellent, rain gear, and Popsicles. (At one Michigan staff meeting, health care coordinators scolded frolicsome workers for helping themselves to the latex medical gloves reserved for actual emergencies). Whether the "moment" is ecstatic sex in a warm tent with a nearby drum circle matching one's own heartbeat, hushed seduction in a cabin packed with sleeping women, showering together under the stars, or rearranging the beds in that Indiana University festival dorm, there will be plenty of festiegoers walking or wheeling around with big smiles the next morning.[1]

Standard festival workshops address a range of sexuality topics, including presentations on what works for long-term couples. Role modeling along these lines is much appreciated at festivals, since the outside world hardly honors the sancti-

Kay Gardner performing at the opening of the National Women's Music Festival in 1989.

Toni Armstrong Jr.

ty (or tenacity) of committed lesbian relationships. Stage announcements at any festival invariably include tributes to couples who are celebrating seven, ten, 15, 20 years together—and powerful applause follows. One may catch a glimpse of a proud producer wiping away a tear as a beaming pair tell the story of how they met at that very festival on a windswept night X years ago: "I liked what she said in the workshop." "My car wouldn't start, and this beautiful, butch goddess appeared out of nowhere." "She came to my tent with a bouquet of flowers and a bar of chocolate."

It should be obvious that the performing artists also meet and mate during festival season, with even less privacy and with a more harried work schedule than those festiegoers on vacation. Despite the ever present dilemma of meeting the perfect woman only to discover she lives four states, three time zones, or two countries away, festivals provide the ultimate dating pool of kindred spirits. Here, there is no need to explain one's identity as an aficionado of women's music, festival culture, camping, lesbian political activism, woman-centered art, the Goddess, etc.—just being at the festival signals an openness to these basic interests and institutions. Festivals ingather a specific gene pool of talented lesbians: Certain women, born to do this work, reliably show up there.

Women who elect to hold their commitment ceremonies at a particular festival not only receive the most tender assistance and support but are also lauded for the service they provide to the assembled community: They enable festiegoers who may not have witnessed the union of two women to participate in the ritual of lesbian marriage. On such occasions everyone is invited. Most special of all are ceremonies where a popular festival artist offers to sing at the event. Over the years I have attended festival commitment ceremonies ranging from a full Jewish wedding led by a lesbian rabbi under a lavender *chuppah* at Michigan to a midnight wedding ritual held in a bayou at the Gulf Coast festival to a lakefront commitment celebration at the East Coast Lesbian Festival—and more. Festiegoers strolling through the crafts area are likely to observe many couples shopping for rings, and there's no sweeter sight, especially because at a festival, one need not lie or misrepresent oneself to the jeweler.

Do the festival couples last? How is courtship conducted in the midst of work shifts, sunburn, sound checks, and concert schedules? Campfest is a good laboratory for such research (and not only because two of its longtime attendees are noteworthy academic psychologists Joan Rabin and Barbara Slater, authors of a study on lesbian identity). Campfest, founded in 1984, has met almost continually at the same summer camp location in the Pennsylvania-Delaware-Maryland–New Jersey corridor. Camp Saginaw boasts not one but two elegant swimming pools and a dance hall, and producer Lee Glanton is most accommodating in arranging for groups or couples to retain "their" cabin year after year. These amenities and attentions enhance the comfort of relaxed courtship in a familiar environment.

Between 1995 and 1997 I interviewed dozens of couples, performers as well as campers, who had met at this festival during previous years and who were relationship legends on the land. A high number of returning festiegoers had met their partners at Campfest; these were women who chose to celebrate each subsequent anniversary in the company of seasonal friends. I discovered that two women had fallen in love during a workshop presentation I gave several years before; this happy couple invited me to read at their wedding. Two of Campfest's sound technicians met during a two-stepping dance workshop in 1992 and fell in love; six years later, they're still together and own a house. I became romantically involved for a time with a woman I met during one of Ubaka Hill's Campfest drumming workshops.

Two popular Campfest couples are Dianne and Doney and Leslie and Carol. Their stories certainly differ yet are fairly representative of festival romance. Longtime women's music artist Dianne Davidson fell in love with her sign-language interpreter, Doney Oatman, while performing at Campfest in 1995. Returning festiegoers Leslie and Carol, despite a family illness emergency, were determined to hold their commitment ceremony at Campfest in 1994 and ultimately videotaped it for their dying son. These interviews offer candid portraits of how partnerships develop in festival time.

Falling in Love:
DIANNE AND DONEY

DIANNE: It's really a great story. I didn't know any of the interpreters here at all. I had never done Campfest before; I'd always played at the Southern Women's Music festival on Memorial Day, and when that festival ended, I really missed it. So I decided to pursue the Campfest idea, but because I'd never performed much up here, there were a lot of women who were unfamiliar with my music. And one of those people was Doney. And though I know a lot of interpreters, I didn't know *her.*

DONEY: Alonna, who coordinated interpreters, asked if I wanted to do Dianne's set. You should know that before each festival the coordinator asks you your work preferences. I was fine working for Dianne, but what was her music like? I didn't know. And although Dianne sent me her material, I didn't have much chance to look at it before I arrived here—that's really rare for me. When I came to our sound check, Dianne was wearing these old ratty gray shorts and tacky tennis shoes and a baseball cap. Like she'd been out doing I don't know what and just rolled out of the rack. And for some reason, I was so attracted to how she looked.

Now, I don't come to festivals with "that" in mind—*ever*. I come to work. And at that point I had sworn off relationships. But I thought Dianne was really cute. We talked, and she kind of busted me on the fact that I hadn't really studied her music. When she ran through a song, I looked at Joy Duskin [another interpreter] and said, "Did you understand any of that stuff?" Not a word. She's got all this *language*.

Well, I introduced myself. And when we were done, I said, "Oh, by the way, what will you be wearing? So we can match." And in her smooth-talker Southern voice she said, "I thought I'd wear my purple silk shirt and my black pants with my black silver-tipped cowboy boots." I said, "I have a purple jacket! I'll wear that. I want to look decent if you'll be looking decent." Then she turned to me and said, "I don't think there's anything you *wouldn't* look good in." And I saw something in her eyes at that point. I know I did.

DIANNE: I thought she didn't like me. I thought, *What an incredibly beautiful woman, great energy. I'd better respect the boundary.* And we both assumed the other was in a long-term relationship, not single.

DONEY: I asked around a bit, found out that she was single but that she'd had her heart broken—*by an interpreter.* I needed to be careful. So I got some information. And unbeknownst to me, she was doing the same thing.

That night, we did the show. I was already infatuated. And it was just magic. We both felt it. There was sexual tension between us. But she still didn't know that I *liked* her. Then we happened to look at each other onstage. I looked at her, and I fell in love with her.

I spent the next two days at the festival keeping my left eye open for wherever she was and trying to concentrate on my work, to not be a goof about the whole thing. Then I saw a notice that she'd be signing her CDs at 11, so I just *happened* to pass by the Ladyslipper booth. And she jumped up and said, "Can I hug you?"

She wrapped her arms around me and didn't let go. I was shaking in my boots like a total idiot. Her warm breath was in my ear, and all I could think was that I hadn't bathed that morning. And I don't like to lose my cool, so even though by then it was the end of the festival, I just said, "It was good working with you too," and split. And I'm walking away down the hill thinking, *Idiot! There's no way for her to contact you. You didn't leave your name and address on her mailing list.* Dianne still didn't know I liked her.

DIANNE: I am so thick.

DONEY: She was always surrounded by clumps of performers. I could never get to her alone. My friends said, "What is it you want from her?" And I said, "I just want to find out if what I see behind her eyes is what I think it is."

DIANNE: The next part was right after dinner, that last night.

DONEY: My head was in my plate. Suddenly my friend Shirley whispered, "Dianne Davidson, 12 o'clock. Dianne Davidson, 3 o'clock. She's moving through the room. Will you please intercept her?"

DIANNE: I saw her walking up, and I thought, *God, what a beautiful woman.*

DONEY: I had decided to make the walk across that dining hall. To go get this woman. She's standing there doing her aw-shucks goofball act, toeing the sand. As I passed behind her, she reached out and grabbed my hand. I rolled around to her right side, and I whispered in her ear, "I don't know if you have the time or the inclination, but I would like to get together with you and just talk. Is that possible?"

DIANNE: And everybody's watching us. And I had no idea how to handle this situation. I couldn't think of anything to say. All my friends were looking at me. I knew they'd smash me later for how my face looked. All I could say was, "*Duh.*"

DONEY: I said, "How about later, after the show?"

DIANNE: *Finally,* we worked it out.

DONEY: She told me she was in a performer cabin, but she wasn't sure how to tell me which one. So I said, "Leave a light burning—I'll find you."

DIANNE: That was the night it rained. All the festie women were stuck outside of Radclyffe Hall while they moved sets inside, and I was down there for *the* longest time playing 'em camp songs, trying to get 'em in a better mood. I got soaked. When I got back to my cabin, I just changed into my sweats. I didn't think she'd come.

DONEY: Meanwhile, I had put on my best bib and tucker for meeting her after the show. And I couldn't get it wrinkled—it was this long, linen thing. So I'm sitting at a festival, in the dirt, with this long thing on, snarling to the women next to me, "Don't lean on this. Don't wrinkle it. Don't get it dirty!" I got everyone around me involved in keeping my clothes neat for my big date after the show.

Then the long walk up the hill, mentally preparing myself. So which cabin was Dianne's? One had a bright fluorescent light, the other, like, ten or 15 candles. First I knocked at the candles. But Dianne was the bright light.

DIANNE: In a lot of ways, we sat up and interviewed each other all night.

DONEY: Joy was very nervous because I never came home.

DIANNE: We spent all night talking about our stories, our expectations, and at 7 A.M. we went to breakfast.

DONEY: It was fun, it was relaxing, but it was very businesslike too in a lot of ways. Like, "I don't have time to mess around. What do you want? What are your values?"

DIANNE: Gentle but pointed. Should we let go before it got started? And it was about hopes and dreams.

DONEY: By the end of the evening, I knew this was the one.

DIANNE: We both knew. There was that fire, that spark.

DONEY: And still is. I'm the one she wants. I'm the one she brings it home to.

DIANNE: I approach everything I do with a different perspective now. It's a very delicate balance when we're still working together onstage, but I feel we nailed it the other night. We were able to share some of our playfulness, love, commitment, our wonder at the process of loving. I think couples aren't validated as often as I'd like to see, and the audience can relate to us. Just like we always look for role models, people who met later in life.

Married at the Festival:
LESLIE AND CAROL

CAROL: We're from New Hampshire, and we've been together eight years. We've come to Campfest every year since we got together, usually making it a two-week trip. So, in 1994 we decided to have our commitment ceremony here because this is where we feel the best.

LESLIE: The best and the safest.

CAROL: We wrote our own ceremony, planned it, picked songs—

LESLIE: Yeah, we thought we picked songs, but then when we got up here, we bumped into Justina and Joyce and asked them if they would sing. And they said, "Sure!"

CAROL: So they sang at our ceremony, and they opened with "Ancient Mother."

LESLIE: A lot of people at Campfest just chipped in. They set up the area for us, set up the reception; it was like the entire camp joined in, and so many came to watch.

CAROL: We had our ceremony over by the gazebo, and then everybody brought us gifts from the earth to lay on the altar. [Campfest producer] Lee Glanton gave us honeysuckle, and somebody else gave us two rose petals from the same rose. Re-

Satya Rhodes-Conway with her mother, Ann Rhodes, at the 1992 East Coast Lesbian Festival: two generations of festival workers.

Toni Armstrong Jr.

ally nice. We had our wedding cake made by the Mennonites down the road, and later, our friends Ann and Darlene had the top of our cake frozen in Ann's mother's freezer. So this year we brought it with us. We're going to eat the top of the cake this Saturday for our anniversary.

LESLIE: Now, at the same time that our ceremony was happening, Carol got a call that her son was in the hospital. He had leukemia. And he died shortly after we left Campfest, within two months. So in the midst of all of our planning, we knew he was very sick. But he said to us, "Please stay. Please have your ceremony."

CAROL: When I found out my son was sick, this couldn't have been a better place for me because everybody was so loving and supportive and caring. Lee Glanton even made arrangements to be sure that we could leave, that somebody could take us from camp and get us on a plane if we needed to. People here are just so caring.

My son was 25. I asked him, "Do you want me to come to the hospital?" And he said, "No. I want you to have your commitment ceremony." And so somebody from communications videotaped it so that when we got to the hospital, we could show it to him. So now we have this great video, with festival walkie-talkies going on in the background—

LESLIE: All during our ceremony you can hear the watermelon game in the pool, you can hear them building a wheelchair ramp—all the sounds of Campfest. I tell you, if we didn't have Campfest, we wouldn't make it through the rest of the year. It's our safe place. At one of my first Campfests, I cried and cried because I didn't want to leave. Parting was so hard.

CAROL: I've been coming since the very first festival in 1984, and Leslie and I got together in 1988. She didn't want to come that first time; she'd never been to a festival. But I said, "I *have* to go to Campfest." So she came, and we had a wonderful time, and when it was time to leave she didn't want to go. When we finally got into the car, she was so relaxed that she asked me, "How does anyone drive their *car* after this festival?"

LESLIE: And putting on a bra again was a traumatic experience.

CAROL: We do a lot of work shifts. One year there was rain, torrential rain the whole time, and a lot of women volunteered to put hay down so women wouldn't slip in the mud. But all we had for the job were broken tools. We had a broken hoe, a broken rake, a couple of rakes with no teeth. And we were marching up the hill singing, "Hi-ho, hi-ho!"

LESLIE: It was one of the best times we ever had, in the pouring rain.

CAROL: You know, our house is like a part of Campfest to keep us going year-round. We have our festival mugs, our wall-hangings—we sure bring home a lot of paraphernalia.

LESLIE: And now other people from New Hampshire are here and very excited. As I said, we're the work shift queens—that's what we're known for. We do work shifts in the kitchen, in greeting, and we drive for Cara, which is a lot of fun. We've also worked breaking down the stage, moving—everything.

CAROL: I liked being the toilet paper fairy, myself. I put new toilet paper in all the cabins one year. People *loved* me.

As these women spoke into my tape recorder, I was struck by the strong moral threads woven into both couples' stories. Dianne and Doney spoke about "interviewing" each other all night to see if they shared the same values. Dianne nearly missed the fateful date altogether by volunteering to perform in the rain for drenched festiegoers while a complicated set change was under way. Leslie and Carol coordinated their long-planned wedding around the needs of Carol's critically ill son, who ultimately lent his own vocal support for their ritual. These are family and community values that many homophobic critics fail to see (or respect) as normative in the lesbian community. For better or worse, many festivals become our extended families when our real families exclude us for living as lesbians.

As I write these words, at least ten of my closest friends are couples who met at festivals and moved in together. I myself fall into the category of meeting great women at festivals who live nowhere near me, but I accept the long-distance challenge if the relationship continues; my Visa card statement shows postfestival pilgrimages undertaken on Greyhound, Amtrak, United Airlines.

But what about the woman who has her ceremony or special romance at a festival, only to break up later on? How does this individual feel the next time she returns to the land? Are the memories too painful, and does such a woman choose to stay home? Or is the festival itself home and the poignant memories or personal ghosts accepted as part and parcel of the festiegoer experience? Poet Meredith Pond answered this question in her four-page piece "Home," originally read onstage during an open mike show at Michigan's August Night Café. Here is an excerpt:

Home. Where it is, where it was, where it will be. The place where our friend who hasn't been here for a while asks me, How can you be here without her? It feels so empty now. But I only shrug and answer, This is all I know. And besides, I still love her.

Tonight the Perseid meteor showers are scheduled for midnight and I wonder who makes the schedule for something like that. And maybe I fall asleep and maybe I don't, but all of a sudden I think of you and I feel more awake than I've ever been, the blood pulsing my heart in sync with drums that never seem to stop, a wild rhythm way back in the woods somewhere, women dancing around a bonfire. And right then a shooting star arcs across the horizon, blazing silver like the tail of Glinda's wand across the sky. Then off in different directions, the star splits in two and disappears, leaving me with sudden sorrow.

All alone now, I go back to the Goddess Circle and untie our rings from the chain of flowers and colored threads wrapped around Her carved oak body. Our anniversary is tonight—or would have been—right here where we first made love five years ago, where I'm kneeling now, under these stars, in front of the gentle face of this Ancient One, the protector of this sacred place. And I laugh, remembering that you had mosquito bites on your ass for a week after that. And how we rode around afterwards on the shuttle bus to the front gate and back all night long just to keep away from the bugs. I shake away the image of your body as I wrap these silver rings in doeskin and sage and strands of our hair. I make an easy bundle, tie a final knot, and tuck the bundle deep in the hollow of a linden tree at the edge of the meadow where I'll sleep tonight circled by stones, the medicine wheel, the wheel of time. What love we have left will always be here, safe in this tree, wrapped in silver and soft light and the memory of each other's arms.

Sleep forever, my love, in this mother tree, this secret place, soft with decomposing wood, and think of me the way you knew me once, before we began the list of what now and why not and you never do.

This land heals me, breathes life back into my heart, where 7,000 women call me home every year and we entwine forever in the hollow of this tree. No bodies this time, only dreams, quiet dreams of life without darkness, without each other, shooting star, shooting star.

Girls Coming of Age ⩔

As the oldest festivals reach the 20-year mark, they point with pride to an entire generation of girl children who grew up in festival culture with their moms or aunts, experiencing camping and artistic freedom from an entirely different perspective than that of the adult guardians. And present trends in the lesbian community show an increase in adoption and childbearing, not only because many couples are entering their 30s with goals of maternity, but also because child welfare laws (in a few states) increasingly permit lesbian adoption or foster care. Certainly festivals have always provided child care and children's activities, primarily welcoming girls (the controversy over boy children will be addressed in the following chapter). But the challenge of making festivals child-friendly is an ongoing process; for some, it is a politically loaded issue.

One woman commented to me that Michigan is a festival where any child with a scraped knee can wail "Mom!" and be assured of having 2,000 women turn around instantly. This is, however, the same Michigan where worker meetings explode over the question of children's exposure to drinking, smoking, and open sexuality.

On the one hand is the salient argument that parents bringing their children should be prepared for what any festival includes: adult language and romantic activity, performers (especially comedians) whose stage routines are "vulgar," the occasional whiff of someone breaking the rules by lighting up a joint, and perhaps sex toys or S/M literature in the crafts area. The parent or guardian must then decide how such encounters will be explained, avoided, or interpreted to the child. On the other hand, many workers contend that every adult in the festival community shares an obligation to ensure child safety and that a certain degree of self-censorship (or jumping up to assist a runaway toddler) doesn't have to be an undue burden. Effective compromises, hammered out after hours of dialogue, include restricting smoking and drinking to posted areas (adults appreciate this too) and advertising some performances as not "family-oriented." What hasn't changed is the understaffing and low status for child-care work, which is, ironically, perceived as "women's work" and domestic chore-ish by many lesbians. Despite our feminism, we often reproduce in festival culture the same attitudes present in patriarchal society. Certain girls have grown up attending Campfest, the East Coast Lesbian Festival, Michigan, Womongathering, and other events, accumulating a worldly nonchalance about adult lesbian culture that sets them apart from their peers in the schoolyard back home. The comments that follow from Maayan and Lesley (8 and 7 years old, respectively) naturally differ from those of teenagers Jenny and Connie (15 and 16). But both sets of girls make plain their awareness of adult behavior around them and can identify what makes them uncomfortable.

MAAYAN AND LESLEY

LESLEY: Our favorite things are going to Girl Space and Lucie Blue Tremblay. She is my adopted aunt. I adopted *her:* She asked if I would allow her to, and I said yes. She's really nice. To be with Lucie means a lot to me. Last year she let me up onstage with her, which was *so cool*.

MAAYAN: And today we performed the rainbow song. And we didn't need anybody to do the sign language because *we* did the sign language the whole time.

LESLEY: Onstage! I did it onstage!

MAAYAN: And today me and Lesley bought our parents presents.

LESLEY: And my mom was *so* thankful because I got her these earrings, and I got her this Goddess thing that she loved so much that she gave us each a dollar. So I bought this.

MAAYAN: Isn't it beautiful?

LESLEY: Rose will always let grown-ups pay the real prices. But if it's kids—especially us—she'll let us pay less. This was, like, $10, and she gave it to us for $1. She is *so nice* to little children.

MAAYAN: And today I bought a little stained glass rainbow flag. For my mom's friend. It was really pretty. And we went onstage with Ubaka last night—

LESLEY: Maayan, we were *not* on night stage with Ubaka. It was—
MAAYAN: Day stage. Everybody was playing drums. If you wanted to go in the circle and dance until the song was over, you could.

LESLEY: But to us, it would seem, like, half an hour to dance. And we went in the circle and danced for over ten minutes. We were tired because we stayed up over midnight!

MAAYAN: *Way* over. In the beginning she was pushing me. Then we were in the

circle, clapping with this one lady—

LESLEY: E-e-ew. And you said she smelled like *beer*.

MAAYAN: But we got to shake instruments. People brought their instruments, and they must have practiced really hard because they could do all the songs. Today me and Lesley played on the playground. And then we made T-shirts and painted them.

LESLEY: We will definitely be back next year. I *cannot* miss a year. Only once, when

Daughter and mother Adrian Hood and Alix Dobkin kicking back at the 1990 Michigan Womyn's Music Festival.

Toni Armstrong Jr.

it was Barbara dying. But I don't need to worry about that now. That was a long time ago—three years ago, when I was only 4.

JENNY AND CONNIE

CONNIE: The first year I was at Campfest, my mother brought both me and her girlfriend. I had finally gotten used to seeing all the naked women walking around, but then we had a spill at our lunch table, and my mom's girlfriend just took off her shirt and started wiping it up. And I, like, *flipped.* I turned bright red. I said, "You're my mom's girlfriend—I'm not supposed to see you naked!" I was only 10.

But I've been coming to Campfest for five years. Now I'm 15, and I love it here; it's, like, *so* awesome. I was running around naked yesterday. I love coming here because you can be so free and just frolic!

How do I explain the festival to friends back home? They are, like, *really* close-minded where I come from; there's a lot of prejudice and stuff. So, I basically just say that I'm going to camp. If they ask me what kind, I'll tell them it's an arts festival out in the woods.

JENNY: I was 15 last year. I just say I'm going to a women's festival, and that's it. They don't ask what a women's festival is. I've been to four Campfests now and to Womongathering.

CONNIE: Ooh, that's one place I haven't been, Womongathering, and I want to go *so bad.*

JENNY: *I've* been to Womongathering a *lot.*

CONNIE: Michigan is awesome too. It's *huge.*

JENNY: I went to Michigan for the 15th anniversary and the 20th anniversary festivals. On my way to my first Michigan, I got my period for the first time. And so, when I got there, AmyLee and some others did a ritual for me.

CONNIE: I couldn't believe how huge Michigan was. The person I drove with explained it was much bigger than Campfest. I worked at one end and camped all the way up at another. It took me half an hour to walk between them. When I wanted to stay out late, if the shuttle trains had stopped, I had to walk the whole way in the dark with only my little flashlight.

I have a lot of friends here at Campfest. We usually have our own little group of girls our own age, and we hang out. But I have a lot of friends who are older.

It's hilarious: The first couple of years we were here, everybody said, "Oh, so you're Connie's mother." And I spent all *my* time being "Leslie's daughter."

JENNY: My mom runs the Video Lodge. She comes here with all her friends from different places. And now I'm the "Dove Bar Goddess." I was selling ice cream, and they taped that sign on my *butt,* and somebody took a picture of it. I don't want *that* to end up in a book.

CONNIE: Actually, I was right here when I realized I was bisexual. I was seated all the way in the back when the Lounge Lizards came onstage. I fell in love with Zöe Lewis—right then and there. I could barely see her from the back, but I fell in love. *Weird.* Then I had my first real girlfriend at Michigan. We still write back and forth, but she lives in Oregon, which really sucks.

I love this place. I look forward to it every year. And I've changed so much. Two years ago I tried walking around without my shirt on, but I felt so embarrassed, I put it back on in 15 minutes. But then, yesterday, my friend and I got this urge to jump in the pool, and we didn't want to ruin the impulse by stopping to get towels. So we just threw off our clothes and came back up here naked.

JENNY: And then communications found out about it.

These four girls hardly exhaust the long roster of festival kids and adolescents, but they do bring up certain universal concerns. They voluntarily confirm what many adult workers believe: Kids dislike being around women who have been drinking, and adolescents are sensitive about nudity and sexual display. Jenny, usually a quiet member of Campfest's community, made it very clear that she wasn't ready to be a sex object, that her years spent as the hardworking ice-cream sales-girl should not be represented by a photo of the "Dove Bar Goddess" sign taped to her behind.

Can festivals be more child-friendly? For quite a few years, the Michigan festival featured a children's concert on Sunday morning; this has been replaced with comedy and acoustic stage performances, although the number of children attend-

139

ing has grown. Other festivals have tried to incorporate children onstage, and a few still offer a special children's show, but often this depends on performer initiative.

The question of "maternal instinct" remains volatile. No festiegoer denies that mothering and caregiving are important, undervalued contributions from the world's women, but not every festiegoer wants to moderate her own adult lesbian behavior during that rarest of all times, the lesbian vacation. And there's another problem: Approximately half of the babies born to women are male.

Motherhood ⇧⇧

On September 13, 1993, I became a mom. My son's name is Nia, and we are a family by adoption. I was present at his birth, and when he was delivered, the doctors handed him to his birth mother, who kissed him and hugged him and welcomed him into the world and then placed him in my arms.

And it's been an amazing ride! How many of you are single parents? My braids are off to *all* parents around the world. I am a single parent by choice; and I did not have a clue. That infant sleep-deprivation program! He wasn't a four-hour baby like the book says. He needed to eat every *three* hours. But he wouldn't sleep in between. He would, like, snack and snooze. And the days just got longer, and I never got to sleep. There were many, many mornings at 3 A.M. when I'd stare toothpick-eyed into the darkness going, "So, McCalla, was being an African-American lesbian-feminist singer-songwriter not *challenging* enough for you? You had to become a single parent too?"

He's 20 months old now but had to hit the friendly skies at two weeks old because Mom had gigs. His laughter is better than any melody I have ever written—or heard. I have never been this tired in my life, and I have never smiled this much. And I have never spent as much time periodically calling home to my own mother, apologizing for anything I might have done as a child. Because I had no idea how hard it is to be a parent.

The neat thing is feeling myself part of a process of a generation. When my parents met us at the airport, it was like I did not exist: I was merely the thing that delivered their grandchild to them. Here I was, a brand-new mom, watching, hoping I can give him enough so that he will be a kind, gentle, strong, compassionate person who walks on this earth, and my mom is watching me watching Nia and hoping *she* raised a strong compassionate person who's up for this task. I feel the generations going back and back and the ancestors gathered around us at a time when I know, at the very least, I had better be all grown up now.

This gracious speech was delivered by performer Deidre McCalla at Campfest in 1995 (see Chapter Six for her extended statement about bringing her son into women-only space.) It was a rare moment, hearing an artist acknowledge the many difficulties inherent in child rearing. Although many stage performers are mothers, only a few take advantage of time at the microphone to offer wisdom from their perspectives as parents. Tributes to mothers, however, are plentiful. Festival culture is, after all, the matriarchy, and *everyone* is some woman's daughter. Many, many festiegoers long to bring their own mothers to the annual women's music celebrations we call home. Yet how does one prepare a straight mom for what Maxine Feldman calls "Camp Dyke"?

My own mother has accompanied me to five different festivals (Sisterfire, Michigan, two Campfests, and Virginia) and will attend the 25th anniversary National Women's Music Festival with me in 1999. At a certain point in her gradual acceptance of festival culture, I felt the time was right for us to examine the mother-daughter dynamic as it fit within the supposedly matriarchal festival world. I also wanted to talk to performers who had brought their mothers along to certain festivals. The following excerpt is from an article I first published in the women's music and culture journal *HOT WIRE* in 1993.

I BROUGHT MOM TO THE FESTIVAL

By Bonnie J. Morris, daughter of Myra

The scene is a crowded dining hall at Campfest 1991. A torrential downpour has interrupted the Night Stage concert and forced everyone to relocate indoors. During the complicated transition of bodies and amplifiers, emcee Jamie Anderson entertains the rowdy audience with festival humor.

"How about a big round of applause for all the straight women here!" she shouts, adding, "How many straight women do we have?" From the sea of campers, one woman stands up—to enormous cheers. It is my mother, Myra. "Wow," breathes performer Zöe Lewis, to my left. "You brought your *mum* to the festival?"

But of course. My mother is now a festival veteran, having attended Sisterfire, Campfest, and the Michigan Womyn's Music Festival as well. She is a high-spirited, open-hearted dance teacher who took me to peace marches and political demonstrations while I was still in kindergarten; it seems only natural to bring her now to my community of allies in women's music and culture.

Myra's reactions have been mixed as she bravely sallies forth through man-hating lyrics and tofu surprise. And I know I'm privileged to have her friendship, the basis for shared adventure.

Festival culture is, by design, overwhelmingly matriarchal. It is one of the few actively matriarchal movements in the contemporary United States, supported by thousands of diverse and multicultural women yet rarely publicized in the "mainstream" media. The music, workshops, theatrical performances, and woman-made crafts available at festivals intentionally draw attention to our foremothers, our female bloodlines, our mother-daughter rites of passage (no matter how stormy), our visions and heritage as kinswomen from ethnic traditions. And yet within this very harvest of mother-naming, many women are in pain because their actual mothers do not condone or understand feminist politics or a lesbian lifestyle. Thus, when my own mother agrees to enter my world as an occasional festiegoer, we are greeted with wistful awe: "I could *never* bring *my* mother to a festival." "I wish my mother could accept me and learn more about my music, my interests." "My mother would *die* if she came here and saw some of the titles of these workshops!" "Yeah, and my mother would *flip out* over the nudity, the sexual slang, the soy milk. I could hardly flirt with anyone if she was along."

Inevitably, I am told, "Your mother must be, like, *way cool.*"

Grief and Loss ⇌

As we get older, lose our parents or partners or other loved ones, cope with illness, festivals take on new meaning as healing spaces and resting places. I once expressed a desire to have my ashes scattered around the land of the Michigan festival. When I confided this wish to Alix Dobkin, convinced that my plan was original and daring, she gave a knowing snort: "You think women haven't been doing that privately for their friends and partners for *years* in those woods?"

For health and insurance reasons, plus obvious other considerations—such as the extreme paucity of festivals held on permanently owned private land—there are no festival burial grounds just yet. Nonetheless, grieving is part of any festival's emotive fabric, all the more so when our own artists and workers succumb to female-specific cancers. Women and political issues are not the sole focus for festival grieving, as in 1995, when festiegoers grieved noisily over Jerry Garcia's death and completely ignored the loss of important lesbian poet and novelist May Sarton (not to mention the 50th anniversary of the Hiroshima bombing). In other years the battle against cancer is a victory, as when festiegoers around the country contributed emergency funds for Kay Gardner's successful treatment and recovery. Flyers soliciting health care donations are common in a community where many artists (and campers) still lack insurance.

One of the most powerful manifestations of mass grief occurred in 1994, when Michigan artists and crew struggled to maintain composure following the death of worker Sara Woolery (known to most of us as Deerheart). Sara's loss to breast cancer resulted in extraordinary demonstrations on the land. One physician stood upon the night stage and, in the open field, led 5,000 women through careful instruction in breast self-examination. Later, the same audience attended a concert by the lesbian-affirming rock band Girls in the Nose, whose signature song, "Breast Exam," is an open and urgent invitation to make breast exams part of sex play.

A similar need for ritual after the presumed suicide of African-American lesbian writer Terri Jewell led to a spontaneous memorial at the 1996 National Women's Music Festival. And the Friday night Shabbat service at Michigan, which attracts more Jewish women (and onlookers) than any other event in Jewish women's programming at festivals, of course includes the mourners' Kaddish, where those attending are specifically invited to name loved ones lost in the previous year. Interestingly, because the Michigan Shabbat is so profoundly a Jewish "family" space, the loss of gay Jewish men to AIDS is mourned quite openly, compared with other festivals and rituals where the focus stays on women. One Jewish Michigan festiegoer annually offers a prayer to Oscar Schindler in honor of his efforts to save Jewish lives.

But if death is acknowledged, elderhood is certainly respected with great joy, and here the personification of survival and spirit is Ruth Ellis, who is in her 90s. Ruth's memories, captured in part in the anthology *Lesbians of Color,* make her a valued participant at the Michigan and National festivals, where she often sets up visiting hours and par-

The late Laura Nyro at the 1989 Michigan Womyn's Music Festival. Seldom has the mainstream media acknowledged this singer's lesbian identity.

Toni Armstrong Jr.

ticipates in the Sunday morning foot or wheelchair races. Campfest's beloved elder B.J. Owens once offered a workshop about her own life, advertised in the festival program as "Come Meet a Butch Lesbian Who's Older Than Dirt." Michigan's "Raffle Rose," Pat Dodson (mother of worker Karen Dodson), achieved fame by blithely stage diving into the mosh pit during a Tribe 8 concert. Ageism certainly troubles festivals in other ways, but the very oldest usually are celebrities and seem to enjoy that role.

For each life stage, festivals offer a wealth of workshops, ceremonies, comfort zones, or helping hands. The luckiest are those whose birthdays fall during festival season and hear a crowd of 2,000—or even a favorite artist—sing to them. Most of us seldom receive such tribute to the simple fact of our being alive. Once again, we see that the artist or techie at the microphone has the power to create family feeling in various ways. In my own capacity as Campfest emcee in 1993, I used Lynn Thomas's cellular phone onstage to call my mother in Maryland and then had every woman in the Campfest audience shout "Happy birthday!" to her.

If festivals, however, are in large part about growing older together, fresh problems of disagreement and consensus will continue to emerge every year—as they do in any big family. The next chapter takes a look at controversy.

1. "And please return the beds to their original position in the dorm room" is a standard last day stage announcement at the National Women's Music Festival, where festiegoers stay in the residence halls of Indiana University.

CHAPTER SIX

The Politics of Discomfort: Controversies and Compromise

Well, if anyone is here from the black American tradition of call and response singing in the church, I could probably count you on two hands. It is awful lonely at this festival sometimes....
Oh, no! Did we say something political?
—The Washington Sisters, emcees, unnamed festival, 1989

What, conflict in paradise?

But of course.

Whether the crisis is a medical emergency, a controversial performer, certain groups' challenges to festival policy, blatant incidents of racism, or a weather disaster causing concert interruptus, there will be at least one "issue" each festival season—more often, two or three. These, regrettably, often serve as the main gossip headlines available to nonfestiegoers, exacerbating the stereotype of festivals as politically eruptive space. Whether due to prolonged debate after the fact (in the pages of periodicals like *Lesbian Connection*) or because some festiegoers relish passing on unflattering chat about producers and celebrity performers, festival conflicts quickly gain prominence in lesbian community discourse. Trouble in paradise means that the festivals are *not* paradise for everyone, after all.

This chapter begins with the radical premise that festival discomfort can be a positive learning experience. And it must be understood that the discomfort comes in two packages: environmental and political.

At outdoor festivals such as Michigan, minor discomfort is simply one by-product of the environmental structure. Camping out in the elements means lacing up a sneaker redolent of male raccoon, sharing a cramped audience hay bale with an inebriated loudmouth, standing in line for a cold shower (and then watching powdery dust coat brand-new festiewear). At any given time, we're all less than comfy; indeed, we are chilly, sunburned, allergic, muddy, or bug-bitten. And, alas, just at the moment when many of us hope to make sexy impressions on new pals! This is the apolitical face of festival discomfort: plain old bodily weariness, the yearning for a Laundromat and a pizza, loud cabinmates, or, in the case of the determined nudist, setting one's porous beach chair atop a colony of fire ants at Rhythmfest. Most first-timers at larger festivals spend much of their weekend wandering about with a map, trying to memorize mealtimes or coordinate activities so that schlepping back and forth to the tent can be reduced to a minimum. Battling the elements is not as much of a challenge at indoor festivals like National, but even there the accumulated lack of sleep from days of delirious music-industry networking can affect behaviors and health.

Having attended the Michigan Women's Music Festival since 1981, I can readily attest that veteran familiarity with a festival's layout greatly reduces personal stress. Lillian Gilbreth, the motion-study pioneer and mother of 12 made famous in *Cheaper By the Dozen,* applied her economy-of-motion insights to household management. In festival culture the same principle applies: One may vastly reduce unnecessary treks around the land by knowing ahead of time where to camp, when to eat, when to plant one's chair for a concert, and when lines are thinnest at the snack stand. However, even the most experienced festiegoer can have her modus operandi wrecked by unplanned illness, injury, or—as we all grow older—greater need for rest and a toilet. I gained a new appreciation for festiegoers with unique medical needs the year I attended the National Women's Music Festival while recovering from an allergic reaction to penicillin.

To the best of their abilities, festival organizers do strive toward reducing personal discomforts. Health care, child care, massage, a blanket bank, support groups for newcomers, 12-step meetings, camping tips in the program, and workshops on infinite topics welcome the festiegoer concerned about surviving the weekend. But minimal comforts (showers, snacks and tampons on sale, a medical area) cannot satisfy unusual needs. Accommodating women with disabilities is a more complex festival

ABLEISM, ACCESS, MICHIGAN, AND YOU

Maybe you've seen me year after year here, zipping along the paved paths, or rolling slowly down to night stage. Maybe you've wondered why there aren't more powered wheelies here. My guess is you've been more likely to think how lovely it is that there is a space for "people like me." Have you waited in porta jane lines with me? Carried on a conversation at the Cuntree Store with me? Come across me in General Camping or Bread and Roses or at the Twilight Zone? How about at workers camp, or trying to make a phone call? No, you haven't seen me in any of these places because they are not accessible to women on wheels. This year you almost didn't see me at all.

The powers that be from WWTMC attempted to initiate a policy that would exclude all vehicles from Downtown Dart. With much organizing, six of us were allowed in. Last year there were twenty two. We need to sleep in our vehicles and be close to downtown for numerous and varied access reasons. Some of us found it too difficult to fight for inclusion, or acquiesced to camping situations that would make us more dependent and less mobile. Some of us found it impossible to challenge our institutional behavior or internalized ableism that says we should be grateful for and accept what is offered us. Some of us still believe that if we move beyond segregated space and into integration of people with and people without disabilities that we will lose what little privilege we have managed to obtain. Some of us want our own separate space to be away from the oppressive behavior of non-disabled people and choose not to struggle for an environment that is more than separate but equal.

And then there are those of us who believe that we have the right to piss and shit where you do, to take showers with you, eat with you, sit with you, camp with you, and work alongside of you to build a women's community that is truly inclusive of women with disabilities and not just providing "services" that we don't even get to define, organize or implement. Those of us that feel that way are women with disabilities and our allies who believe in equal access for all.

We are women who want to see anti-ableism education and access consultation become integrated into all the goings on at Michigan. We are women who do not want to settle for a DART, segregated service provider, model of access but rather desire the option of integrated as well as separate space. We are women who have the expertise, knowledge, and ideas to begin to implement integration at Michigan without harm to the land or ecosystems, and without unreasonable expense. We are women who recognize that for a time the Michigan Women's Music Festival model of access was the only model in the women's community, the group committed to "allowing us in" when most feminist groups were still not even addressing basic access issues. We are women who recognize that it's time for producers, workers, and festi-goers to listen to those of us doing the ground-moving work of creating accessible integrated community and providing anti-ableism education.

We are women who want WWTMC to implement systems designed by people with disabilities to begin addressing the ableism and non-compliance with the Americans With Disabilities Act that exist at the Michigan Women's Music Festival. Please join us in encouraging Lisa and Boo to stop discriminating against women with disabilities by hiring and consulting with those of us who know how to envision and implement a community that invites and welcomes integration of women with and without disabilities.

Stop by the yellow van with the "Ableism Keeps Us Apart" banner in Downtown Dart and chat with us. Attend an anti-ableism workshop held daily at 12:30 at the same van or look up our workshops in the program. Please come and experience for yourself how it can be if ableism is interrupted, integration initiated, and separate space honored. Please let the producers know through your evaluations, phone calls, and letters the time to change is now and that you support WOMEN CREATING ACCESSIBLE COMMUNITY'S attempts to provide anti-ableism education and access consultation to the Michigan Women's Music Festival.

© 1993 Women Creating Accessible Community

Flyer distributed at the Michigan Womyn's Music Festival.

issue, which came to a head at the first East Coast Lesbian Festival in 1989. Where entire groups of women feel marginalized, invisible, or unplanned for, we find a second category of festival discomfort: political.

It must be said that a primary form of political discomfort at festivals is the isolation or even hostility heterosexual women experience. This flourishing bias is rarely discussed. While most festivals advertise a welcome for all women, there is an obvi-

Lin Daniels and K.C. Cohen at the 1989 Michigan Womyn's Music Festival.

Toni Armstrong Jr.

ous lesbian majority attending and performing, and women who identify as heterosexual are often put on the defensive. T-shirts, bumper stickers, stage performances, crafts, and workshops celebrate a woman-loving sensibility, and residual "straight bashing" does indeed occur. It occurs in remarks from the stage and from the audience, in lyrics or comic routines by some performers and in the disappointed audience groans that greet a performer's announcement that she's heterosexual.

Because many of us would like to bring our (often straight) mothers or daughters or coworkers to festivals as our guests and because the number of girl children and teenagers attending continues to grow, this mocking attitude toward women who like men can cause tension and resentment.[1] ("This is supposed to be a *women's* festival, but it's really a *lesbian* festival." "I didn't pay $200 on the sliding scale to be insulted." "I'm married to a great guy who supports my feminist politics; from what I see, your woman lover belittles your beliefs in front of your friends.") However, there are two interesting responses to this problem. One is the emergence of a support group for straight women at the Michigan festival and elsewhere. The other is the viewpoint that it may be appropriate, even healthy for straight women to experience being in the minority and having their preferences questioned—if only for a few days in their lives.

Within any festival season, more attention is given to controversial incidents than to the attitudes that create them. A number of incidents have already become legendary in festival culture.

Some Famous Controversial Incidents ⪮

North East Women's Music Retreat, 1985: Program guidelines forbidding S/M displays or activities lead some "vanilla" campers to wear pro-S/M buttons out of solidarity.

Sisterfire, 1987: Held on public grounds, one of the few festivals to admit men cracks under a storm of conflict after two men enter and refuse to leave the women-only art booth staffed by Lin Daniels and Myriam Fougere.

Michigan Womyn's Music Festival, 1988: An outbreak of shigella leaves workers as well as festiegoers violently ill; conspiracy theories fly, though county health inspectors praise the festival for quick response to the crisis.[2]

East Coast Lesbian Festival, 1989: At the first gathering for this festival, disabled activists block the gate in protest of the land's inaccessiblity; later, anonymous campers harass the cabin of two women who have brought a male infant to the festival despite the policy of women- and girls-only space.[3]

Michigan Womyn's Music Festival, 1989: Workers draft a statement of protest after white performer Dianne Davidson sings a song of tribute to the African-American caregiver from her childhood years; the statement of protest is read on the night stage the following night, after Dianne has left the land; Dianne is ostracized for years.[4]

Michigan Womyn's Music Festival, 1990: S/M activists rent a plane and fly over the land, dropping a hail of flyers protesting the festival's policy toward S/M visibility. An antiracism parade through the crafts area leads to individual merchants being charged with cultural appropriation and harassed for using Native images in artwork sold.[5]

Campfest, 1991: A bisexual activist seizes the microphone from emcee Jamie Anderson and accuses the festival of perpetuating "biphobia."

Michigan Womyn's Music Festival, 1991: A white musician's performance on an Australian musical instrument called the didgeridoo, or yidaki, is stopped after an aboriginal woman on the land points out that only aboriginal Australians are meant to play the sacred instrument of aboriginal culture.[6]

East Coast Lesbian Festival, 1992: Performance artist Shelly Mars ignites a storm of controversy with her show featuring a strap-on dildo and scenes of sexual aggression.

Michigan Womyn's Music Festival, 1993: During the tenth anniversary celebration of the Women of Color tent, a white woman enters the tent designated as a sanctuary for women of color to ask if the women present can sell her drugs. Antiableism activists distribute a flyer protesting the "segregation" of women with disabilities in a campground area specific to their needs.[7]

Campfest, 1994: Producer Lee Glanton makes a rare speech onstage in defense of her decision to ask several campers to leave the festival (the expelled party included individuals thought to be transgendered men).

Michigan Womyn's Music Festival, 1994: Transgender activist Leslie Feinberg sets up "Camp Trans" outside the Michigan gate to protest and debate the festival's woman-born–only policy. Women protest the scheduled performance by radical thrash band Tribe 8, standing at the entrance to the night-stage bowl with signs accusing the band of promoting eroticized violence against women. (More on Tribe 8 in Chapter Nine.)[8]

Campfest, 1995: Due to miscommunication about the festival's women-only policy, artist Deidre McCalla arrives with her adopted toddler son and refuses to perform unless he is allowed into the festival; later, both Deidre and producer Lee Glanton update the festival audience about the situation.

Michigan Womyn's Music Festival, 1997: Officially, stage diving is banned because of safety concerns, but many women ignore these guidelines, and in the resultant mosh-pit mayhem, two security workers suffer dislocated shoulders; the more disillusioned of the two injured women demonstrates her dismay by wearing a protest sign on her sling: INSECURITY WORKER.

This is by no means a complete list, but the purpose of this book is not to air all our dirty laundry. And even the aforementioned controversies are but public incidents. Private grievances go on behind the scenes ad infinitum *et* ad nauseum. Ironically, at larger festivals many women remain blissfully ignorant of a controversial moment until after they've left the land. Plenty of women tune out of the body politic by choice: They're honeymooning in a cozy tent, wandering with glazed eyes and extended credit cards through the crafts area, catching up with an old friend, and talking with her for hours when everyone else is at the night stage concert. Hence they miss the controversial moment onstage or the hot workshop that leads to a statement of protest that leads to a "girlcott." In short, not all women see the issues that flare and fade; only a core of activists or personalities concerned are likely to be affected. This is not necessarily a good thing.

The Issue of Racism ⋙

Perhaps the greatest sorrow for all who believe in festival culture as a model of cooperation is that every year, racism shows its sharp claws. Most festivals are predominantly white in attendance, despite planned racial and ethnic diversity in terms of staff, performers, and workshop topics. Although white festiegoers may experience festival culture as a radical shift for them, marveling at women-only, lesbian-tolerant space and its accompanying freedoms, women of color arrive to find they have their same old minority status in a sea of now-topless white liberals. Accompanying stereotypes are revealed through one painful incident after another, yet efforts to create safe gathering spaces within festival weekends for women of color to meet and talk are misunderstood, even resented, by some white festiegoers. "A workshop by and for women of color only? Isn't that, like, reverse discrimination?" asks

Teresa Trull, Deidre McCalla, and Linda Tillery performing at the 1986 Michigan Womyn's Music Festival.

Toni Armstrong Jr.

the white woman who has always assumed the privilege of inclusion.

Sadly, a virulent form of racism is that expressed between white women, neither heard nor seen by women of color but reflecting attitudes brought into festival culture. As recently as 1998, I was dismayed to have several different festiegoers (strangers to me) express racist opinions they assumed I would agree with because I am white. One new festiegoer, fresh from the military, questioned performer Faith Nolan's songs about racism in Canadian society and complained to me, knowing only that I am a historian. She wanted me, the white professor with the Ph.D., to confirm or deny Faith's interpretation of historical events—even though Faith was available just a few feet away to interact with her own audience and take such questions herself.

Nor is racism always a black-white construction. One issue hovering over nearly every festival is the degree to which white and black festiegoers appropriate Native American rituals, music, and dress. Women leaving patriarchy (to use Carolyn Gage's phrase) may seek a new spiritual path influenced by indigenous traditions but without fully understanding how white ethnic consumerism exploits first peoples on the earth. Z. Budapest, a popular festival speaker and expert on European-heritage Goddess spirituality, challenged her audience at the 1989 West Coast festival: "You look ridiculous, you white women wearing the Indian feathers. *Get them out of your hair.* You think you're Native American? You're not. Be proud! Look to your own white European heritage, there is plenty of earth-based spirituality there. And bakery! Women's herbs, women's baking—that's your heritage."

Native American women do attend and perform at festivals, encountering both white and African-American women who talk about "unlearning racism" while dressed in Washington Redskins and Cleveland Indians sweatshirts. Festivals regularly feature music by Native American and native Hawaiian performance groups, such as Ulali, Two-Spirit Thunder People, Zelie Duvauchelle. In 1989, Michigan hosted Maori artist Mahinaarongi Tocker from Aotearoa, New Zealand. The diverse representation of aboriginal music, however, cannot always prevent casual appropriation of images and beliefs in festiegoers' language, dress, and consumerism.

Festivals can be loving, happy, creative ingatherings and still feel alienating to the women of color searching for faces like their own. And for black lesbian artists with limited resources, the frustrating choice is whether to spend a vacation at a primarily white festival or at a possibly homophobic conference for activists of color. Writer Julie Blackwomon illustrated this concept in her 1981 short story "Kippy"; the story's narrator is the young daughter of a black lesbian:

> Before we moved to Pierce Street, my mom and I lived in a woman's collective in West Philly. A collective is a house where five or six women shop for food, cook, do laundry, and pay bills together, just like a family, even though some are black and some are white and some have college degrees and make a lot of money and some don't make much money at all. The first year we lived in the

collective, four of our housemates took me camping at a women's music festival in Michigan while Mom and Terri went to a black women's conference in New York. I liked living in the collective. It was like one big happy family. Only most of the family was white.[9]

In calling this chapter "The Politics of Discomfort," I know that I have lumped racism and natural disasters together as festival "discomforts." I realize that I and many white festiegoers have the luxury of seeing racism as a series of single incidents. Racist incidents on the land are remembered singularly, just like the natural disasters—the five-day thunderstorm at Michigan in 1987 or Hurricane Bob's unwelcome redistribution of yellow jacket nests at NEWMR in 1991. These are temporary eruptions for white women. But racism is the ongoing story for women of color, on and off the land. And the disinterested white festiegoer has the luxury of believing that racism, like hurricanes and thunderstorms, is just some unexplainable phenomenon that "hits" festivals now and then.

Furthermore, as black lesbian comic Karen Williams often points out, the seemingly benign camping discomforts described earlier do take on a political meaning for some low-income women of color. Many dislike the tacky outhouses that come with the festival ticket price. "Where I come from, we don't call it camping, we call it homeless," is a standard line in Williams's stage routine. Toni Morrison makes a similar point in her novel *The Bluest Eye:* The worst fate for a troubled family comes when "everyone is outdoors," with no place to sleep but under the stars. Racism in the United States has an economic base; hence, while many affluent feminists enjoy camping out and doing without as a contrast to regular life, some women of color whose families have been forced into substandard housing for generations see festivals' leaky cabins and Porta-Janes as troubling to daily dignity. Speaking in Marlon Riggs's film documentary *Black Is/Black Ain't,* Angela Davis commented that many African-Americans seek to distance themselves from rural, agrarian ways or conditions because of their association with slavery. And some festivals, with work shifts, crew overseers, and big-shot producers to whom homage is paid, may seem vaguely reminiscent of plantation-style living. Cabin sleeping and community outhouses can be avoided if one brings personal camping gear, but rainproof dome tents, down sleeping bags, and collapsible folding toilets all cost money.

Karen Williams's jokes about tofu (see Chapter Seven) also reflect the tension between those who grew up viewing meat as a luxury in the family stew pot and those who put down meat eaters as politically incorrect. "I'm trying to get to the point where I eat steak all the time," says Karen, and my friend Jules, a mixed-heritage woman who grew up on welfare in rural, white Pennsylvania, nods in understand-

The Washington Sisters accompanied by Mimi Fox at the 1990 Michigan Womyn's Music Festival.

Toni Armstrong Jr.

ing. Some white women who come to festivals as vegetarian activists get pious when festiegoers complain about meatless meals, not recognizing the symbolism of meat as reward, as plenitude. The vegetarian with attitude is such a lesbian stereotype that in 1989, Michigan kitchen workers and artists Kay Turner and Gretchen Phillips of the rock band Girls in the Nose recorded and performed a song, "Meat," a humorous look at festival politics: "We'll heal ourselves with crystals and drink ginseng tea / We'll eat with chopsticks and talk about monogamy."

In the early 1990s the East Coast group Feminists for Animal Rights bought large ads in festival programs at Campfest and at the East Coast Lesbian Festival. While well-intentioned, these ads began, "If you are a woman who eats animals, did you know that you are participating in the starvation of 40,000 children each day?" It probably did not occur to FAIR that some festiegoers reading these ads might, themselves, hail from cultures or communities threatened by hunger, where meat represents survival.

Lesbian filmmaker Heather Lynn McDonald investigated this issue in her documentary *Kitchen Talk USSR*. Traveling through the former Soviet Union, McDonald filmed a woman who observed that Americans have everything desirable on their grocery shelves yet freely choose not to consume entire levels on the food pyramid, whereas Russian women would gladly eat anything but have almost no goods to choose from. "I would never live with anyone who ate meat," proclaimed one friend of mine, unaware that her statement sounded very much like a de facto romantic rejection of chicken-soup–slurping Jews like me—and meat-eating Native peoples, most Arabs and East Asians, many African-Americans, and so on. The point here is that food and housing *are* racial and ethnic issues. When white festiegoers complain, "Why don't more women of color attend?" they don't always stop to examine the politics of diet and shelter or what sorts of diet and shelter have appeal.[10]

Increasingly, music issues have attached to this question of racism; we are, after all, discussing women's music festivals. Concerns raised in the past decade include: What does it mean when white women play sacred aboriginal instruments onstage when few aboriginal women have the money to travel to international music events themselves? What does it mean when traditional African drumming circles are interrupted by white women who assume the gathering is a jam session for all percussionist passersby? Can a festival acknowledge the homophobic politics of fundamentalist Christianity while simultaneously featuring sacred music or the African-American church tradition of gospel singing? To this last question, the Washington Sisters, Sandra and Sharon, have responded, "We would never ask anyone to leave behind their cultural traditions, and we ask that *you* not ask us." Likewise, Mexican antiracism activist Papusa Molina suggests, "Alliances must be between equals. And asking anyone to leave part of themselves behind is not equality."

Open communication about the ethnic heritage of musical traditions helps to prevent most misunderstandings. Yet discussion of such issues doesn't feel "fun" to festiegoers who prefer entertainment without politics. When scholar and artist Linda Tillery or vocalist Tiana Marquez or choral directors Melanie DeMore and Allowyn Price explain the herstory behind songs of slave resistance, some restless white festiegoers feel the moment isn't "lesbian" enough to hold their interest and head toward the snack bar. At one festival I watched white women wiggle and grumble during the Washington Sisters' performance of "Lift Every Voice and Sing," the African-American national anthem, during which it is customary to remain standing. These reminders of separate American histories, black and white, insert a note of political discomfort—for those who insist on seeing it that way. For many years, white Jewish folksinger Alix Dobkin made a point of performing "Lift Every Voice and Sing" herself, to educate her audiences.

"Unlearning Racism" is a standard festival workshop. Festivals offer ample opportunities to engage in dialogues across race and ethnic lines and typically bring in workshop facilitators who have years of expertise: AmyLee, Margaret Sloan-Hunter, Papusa Molina, Jana Olsson, Amoja Three Rivers and Blanche Jackson, Mel Bramyn. Participating in such intensive workshops is never an easy experience, but it may be a life-changing one. Many white Christian women, reared in families where raised voices or conflicting viewpoints at the dinner table meant trouble and slaps rather than an exchange of lively opinions, find the verbal styles of African-American or Jewish, Arab, and Latina women "confrontational" or aggressive. Some white women want to be handed answers about racism rather than doing the difficult homework themselves.

In Papusa Molina's workshop for Michigan festival staff, Jewish workers agreed that, as Jews, we seem pushy merely by being visible, since Jewishness is not "normative." Our Jewishness is pushy because it makes folks deal with a non-Christian heritage and calendar year, forces them to add "Um, or Happy Hanukkah?" to their sincerely intended "Merry Christmas" greeting. Anti-Semitism continues to plague festivals in ways small and large: At Lin Daniels's East Coast Lesbian Festival in 1991, an anonymous note dropped in the suggestion box accused the festival of "cultural nepotism" for having "so many" Jewish workers.

How to approach these issues? For the white woman who's had little ongoing social contact with women of color (and that's most white women), the cringing liberal need for approval makes honest dialogue all but impossible and turns every salient point raised by a woman of color into a perceived "attack" that has to be Band-Aided. This point has been explored by many black and white theorists, ranging from bell hooks and Bernice Johnson Reagon to Minnie Bruce

Pratt, Jane Rule, and Naomi Wolf; all conclude that white feminists are hooked on "safety." But complete comfort may be a clue that no progress is being made during, say, an antiracism workshop.

In her classic 1984 text *Feminist Theory: From Margin to Center,* bell hooks writes:

> The fierce negative disagreements that have taken place in feminist circles have led many feminist activists to shun group or individual interaction where there is likely to be disagreement which leads to confrontation. Safety and support have been redefined to mean hanging out in groups where the participants are alike and share similar values.... Solidarity is not the same as support.[11]

Yet festivals are one uniquely American institution where there is dialogue across ethnic lines and where maintaining that dialogue is a clearly stated goal. The Women of Color tent at Michigan, founded in 1983, is not only a clearinghouse and sanctuary for women of color, but also sponsors discussion workshops for all women.[12] WOC tent cofounders Blanche Jackson and Amoja Three Rivers prepared a guidebook in 1990 entitled *Cultural Etiquette* to help women move beyond "well-intentioned" stereotypes, and white activists are part of the extended staff leading antiracism workshops at Michigan. All workers at Michigan are encouraged to join the "Unlearning Racism" workshops. In 1991 the Michigan festival added a permanent space for Jewish women's concerns in the community center, and exploring anti-Semitism became the theme for a hugely successful workers' workshop in 1997. It is a measure of the extreme dedication of Michigan's antiracism staff that Mel Bramyn helped put together the August 1997 anti-Semitism workshop during a period of chemotherapy treatments for breast cancer the previous winter.

Most festivals have a tent, room, or workshop program for women of color. The East Coast Lesbian Festival was the first to offer a Jewish lesbians tent; the West Coast festival also offered Jewish women's space. A Passover Seder, instructive to the overwhelmingly non-Jewish festiegoers, has always been part of Wanda and Brenda Henson's Gulf Coast festival. NEWMR hired an antioppression staff in 1990 to coordinate antiracism workshops. The Michigan festival offered a Town Meeting

Day of antiracism workshops in the summer of 1989. These examples—and the participation of many festiegoers in such activities—demonstrate the possibility of festivals serving as nuclei for social change.

Drumming: One Success Story of Compromise ⩘

An example of a workshop and jam-session trend that initially sparked some mis-understanding is drumming. Drumming has enjoyed a profound artistic and social renaissance at festivals. For many festiegoers, falling asleep in a warm tent to the sound of distant drum rhythms evokes an immediate sense of caring, of a tribal community wherein music is always a part of the landscape of creation and expression. Others liken the sound and feel of the drumbeat to a heartbeat and, specifically, to the sound of the mother's heart surrounding a fetus in utero, a comforting, life-giving background pulse. And certainly there are also weary festiegoers who view late-night drumming as recreational noise disrupting their sleep.

Drumming rhythms and compositions tell or accompany ritual stories and rites of indigenous peoples all over the planet. In many instances of African, Indian, and Native American religious traditions, drumming circles are sacred and specific to a tribal ceremony. Particular types of drums and drumming styles once used by men only have been revived and popularized by women in ethnic diaspora communities as a means of continuing traditions and beliefs threatened by encroaching Westernization or racism. Drumming is thus a significant aspect of women's music because of its oral storyline, its configuration as a medium of ritual for women of color.

Most festivals bring ritual drum performances to the stage, such as ecstatic soloist Edwina Lee Tyler or the Japanese-heritage ensemble group Sawagi Taiko from Vancouver, Canada. Such performances draw acclaim not only for their artistic merit but also because feminist audiences thrill at seeing the athletic strength exhibited by strong women drummers. Drummers for women's bands are often hidden behind their own equipment or behind their band vocalists; Barbara Borden and Carolyn Brandy both played drums for the group Alive! for years before getting their own sets at Michigan. But African or Taiko drummers take over the entire stage, sometimes leave the stage to play amidst the audience, and are able to feature the drum itself as the main event.

However, the complex herstory of spiritual drumming is not always known to white festiegoers, who sometimes notice private drumming circles at festivals and jump right in with their own bongos. By the 1990s, the problem of untutored drop-ins in more ritualized drumming circles had prompted the introduction of intensive drumming workshops open to women of color only. For many white women, this felt like a slap in the face, particularly when noted performers such as the Taiko ensemble offered intensive Japanese drumming workshops for non-Asian women of color but not for white festiegoers. Some white women just discovering both festivals and drumming felt unwelcome at late-night drumming circles on the land and complained of reverse discrimination.

What emerged from this problem was a careful campaign to educate white festiegoers about the specific heritage of drumming and the symbolism of its instruction in closed workshops for women of this heritage. What's fascinating is that the same women who complained about being shut out of a closed drumming circle were perfectly free to start a circle of their own but retained a sense that the *real* action was behind the trees where *authentic* (African) jamming was under way. The recognition of that authenticity should trigger an accompanying awareness of history, of how that authentic Africanness came to be in America, but often it does not.

The festiegoer who thinks, *They're so cool. Why can't I play?* may be lamenting that only in festival time will she have an opportunity to party freestyle, shirt off, with other skilled drummers. But this is different from the black festiegoer's desire to study African drumming traditions in order to preserve and celebrate black women's spirituality or ancestors. Because most festivals draw a white majority, open drumming workshops or circles can quickly surround the women of color present with hundreds of white festiegoers, replicating the minority status they endure outside the festival and shifting attention from shared ritual to appropriated ritual. Some African-American women are fed up with entertaining white onlookers.

This is a significant issue because there are some sacred objects, some spiritual moments that are *not* open to all—or to the camera and tape recorder of all—yet as Americans, we are raised with a tourist mentality toward the spectrum of world cultures. Traveling through Asia as faculty for the Semester at Sea program in 1993, I cringed at seeing my white colleagues plunge into temples or other holy sites with video cameras whirring intrusively while the "natives" attempted to worship. In other contexts—a prearranged guided tour or an invitation from hosts—such visits to a different culture can certainly be educational. But a difficult lesson for white Westerners seems to be that simple idea that we cannot always be in the center of whatever is going on. And where some festiegoers understand this principle as it applies to men respecting women-only space, not all support women of color who seek to network apart from the white majority during some festival workshops.

Fortunately, this potentially explosive area has been vastly soothed by the emergence of the charismatic drum artist Ubaka Hill. Her presence at festivals through-

Linda Uyehara Hoffman (front) and Lisa Mah of Sawagi Taiko, an Asian-Canadian drumming troupe, at the 1997 Michigan Womyn's Music Festival.

Toni Armstrong Jr.

out the 1990s has revitalized drumming as a community act. Ubaka's drum poetry and compositions are stunning in and of themselves, but it is her work as a drum orchestra conductor that has built a bridge for the *entire* drumming population at festivals. From her first festival appearances, Ubaka initiated a format of inviting festival drummers to rehearse with her and come onstage for a finale. She was also the first drum artist in any festival context to offer intensive drum workshops for Deaf women. This "open-drum" policy, coupled with her loving but disciplined drum orchestra rehearsals, attracted scores of women, most of whom did not even own drums yet. A heart-stopping vision for those few festival craftswomen who specialize in making delicate and valuable djembe drums is the sight of 50 clumsy beginning drummers running into the crafts booth to announce breathlessly, "We're going to be in Ubaka's workshop, and she said we could borrow some drums from your booth to practice with, and we need them—*right now.*"

Summer 1995 was Ubaka Hill's turning point. First there was that rainy night at Campfest, when nearly every woman on the land filled the old video lodge up to its rafters and drummed hypnotically for hours, drumming and dancing and then drumming again, standing, seated, embracing, using any available percussive tool when all drums and shekeres were occupied—tin plates, spoons, open palms on a girlfriend's thigh. This spectacular gathering was followed by Ubaka's first night-stage appearance at the National Women's Music Festival one week later (after which one rapt festiegoer declared, "Ubaka could be some kind of *messianic leader.*") and the release of her first CD, *Shape Shifters,* on Ladyslipper's label. Finally, there was the first Drumsong Orchestra on the acoustic stage at Michigan's 20th anniversary festival later that same season. The newly enlarged acoustic stage was filled with 156 women drumming in concert as Ubaka invited up her own great role model, longtime Michigan performer and drum mentor Edwina Lee Tyler.

With the public linking of these two solo artists—whose works insist upon both the sacred and the playful as paired drumming elements—the Michigan audience saw drumming's religious significance and the power of traditional sounds; now a new generation of drum students are willing and able to respect the times and places of discrete drumming circles. That is one step forward in the group process of using festival season to explore the fight against racism.

Gender and Sexuality ⩩

Apart from racism, the most common festival controversies involve male children on the land, S/M displays, and, more recently, festival admission sought by male-to-female transsexuals. These three issues are unique in that they involve explicit testing of festival rules outlined in programs, brochures, and policies. They also invoke the cry of "minority rights" (e.g., the unique needs of nursing mothers or of sexual or gender minorities) and thus have burgeoned into civil liberties questions well beyond the scope of this chapter.

Without question, festiegoers and workers identifying as S/M enthusiasts have long been treated as delinquents on probation at festivals, even while stage artists get laughs and knowing cheers for making jokes about tying up or "topping" women. Rhythmfest producer Michelle Crone noted in Chapter Two that she deliberately sought to build a festival where S/M leatherwomen would be welcomed as regular workers. While S/M lesbians have always attended festivals, they have often encountered land policies prohibiting public displays of S/M activity altogether—usually with the justification that festivals offer safe spaces for women in recovery from violence and that whips and chains or dog collars in public space don't suit this goal.

The 1980s saw an explosion of debates on the subject, notably in the rival books *Against Sadomasochism* and *Coming to Power,* but the issue became blurred in the 1990s by the growing popularity of sex toys, which received enthusiastic approval from lesbian "sexperts" Susie Bright, Pat Califia, and Joann Loulan. The notorious small aircraft flight over the Michigan festival in summer 1990, when S/M activists dropped flyers onto the land protesting their second-class status, has been the most dramatic expression of protest to date, although the controversy over the band Tribe 8 (addressed in Chapter Nine) reopened S/M debates in 1994.

Today, sex toys are routinely sold at the Eve's Garden crafts booth at several festivals, and purchasing a lavender dildo at a festival is no longer a statement of S/M practice. The progression toward greater tolerance may be seen through a series of minor incidents: Amy Ziff of the trio BETTY used a whip onstage during her 1989 Michigan performance; the 1996 Michigan workers' talent show included a satirical song about fisting; and during the 1997 National Women's Music Festival, the older trio of artists Saffire, The Uppity Blues Women joked from the stage about "packing a lightning rod" purchased in the crafts area. At Michigan, performer Mimi Bazcewska critiqued one of her own stage performances: "A friend told me I should have been topping rather than bottoming my audience." Another popular artist, who has often performed at Campfest, could not have been more forthright in voicing her excitement over the purchase of a thigh harness at the National Women's Music Festival.

Forsaking, for now, a time-consuming philosophical-political discussion of S/M sexuality as practiced privately between women, we can conclude that festivals have been torn between permitting all women to express their sexuality freely and drawing a line at exhibitions deemed offensive (or inappropriate for children to see). The impossibility of drawing that line clearly or fairly has kept S/M festiegoers at a distance but exotically discernable, somewhat like whale sightings. By 1991, the North East Women's Music Retreat had changed its policy to include an S/M camping area. The Michigan festival, struggling not to sanction S/M by setting aside a specified campground, instead offers any number of workshops (pro and con) on S/M theory and practice, including a hilarious "S/M Barbie" gathering in 1992. Veteran festiegoers at Michigan know that the Twilight Zone camping area is where S/M play parties take place at night, and there are specific guest passwords for those invited, but longtime Swiss worker Pyramid ("Let's break the ice with some flogging!") continues to campaign for a staff sex tent and bordello.

The presence of male children is another clear challenge to women-only space. Most festivals offer child care and permit mothers of young sons to bring along male children up to the age of 3 or 4 (age 8 at the Gulf Coast festival.) For festiegoers with male children over age 5, this request to uphold women-only space elicits heated complaints. At worst, festival organizers have been likened to Nazis, even when, as at Michigan, they do provide a separate summer camp program for boys over 3 (Brother Sun Boys Camp) near the main festival area. Consider the following excerpt from Susan J. Wolfe's essay in the 1982 volume *Nice Jewish Girls: A Lesbian Anthology*:

> The Michigan Womyn's Music Festival announced that male children would not be allowed on festival grounds. Male children over the age of 6 were to be placed in a camp about ten miles away.... It has not been easy to be a Jewish Lesbian feminist mother with a son. Forced to choose between my summer time with Jeffrey and attending the Michigan Womyn's Music Festival, I pre-

served my sisters' space by staying home. I refused to place my Jewish child in a camp because of his undesirability to lesbian separatists. The festival organizers' ignorance of the Jewish experience
with institutionalized camps was disappointingly apparent.[13]

Claiming that Michigan producers Boo Price and Lisa Vogel are Holocaust
ignorant is a fairly extreme way to make a point. But extreme rhetoric is the name
of the game in discussions on male children in women-only space. One anonymous separatist covered a woman's cabin at the first East Coast Lesbian Festival
(1989) with signs reading TAKE YOUR BABY PRICK OUT OF HERE because a festiegoer had brought her ten-month-old male infant to ECLF. In presenting calmer
arguments for the preservation of women-only space, lesbian theorist Julia Penelope, artist Alix Dobkin, and others stress the point that creating a festival by and
for *women only* means honoring that goal, even if mothers of sons must find temporary child care for a few days. ECLF coproducer Myriam Fougere made a film,
Sacred Space, in which eight well-known lesbians address the point that it's important for young boys to learn that they cannot enter or dominate all spaces
with their needs, that some spaces are indeed women-only. While criticizing
those women who choose to behave cruelly toward small boys, Alix Dobkin has
noted that little girls who attend festivals deserve girl-only space in their living
and playing areas—they shouldn't be compelled to compete with boys during the
special few days of a women's festival. Examining the problem in her book *Call
Me Lesbian,* veteran festiegoer Julia Penelope wrote:

> There is no space on this planet that men do not claim as theirs
> "by right." However much space they dominate, it never seems to
> be "enough" for them. Wimmin- and Lesbian-only spaces chal-
> lenge the male "right" to occupy and control territory. In this cul-
> ture, "it's a man's world." Whatever is "public" space is theirs. Men
> assume they have the right to occupy any "public" space" because
> it's *their* world. Women's lives have been confined to the "private"
> sphere. But men control the private as well as the public sphere....

> If Lesbians want to raise males, they should be teaching them
> that wimmin have the right to establish our own spaces, that
> no man has any right to be where we don't want him, that "No"
> doesn't mean "Yes."[14]

The issue remains unresolved, in part because festivals have very differing policies on the cutoff age (not to be confused with castration, please!) for male toddlers. Festivals' militant monitoring of boys on the land has been ridiculed by gay male author Armistead Maupin in his festival satire "Wimminwoods," a chapter in the *Tales of the City* installation *Significant Others*. But here too compromise is possible.

Another Case Study in Compromise: Campfest, 1995 ⩫⩫

At Campfest 1995, longtime Olivia artist and performer Deidre McCalla, unaware that Campfest bars male children of any age, brought her 18-month-old son Nia to the festival. She had sent a series of communications to the staff ahead of time about her intentions, but somehow these never reached producer Lee Glanton, and at the last minute a crisis developed over whether or not Deidre would be permitted to bring a male child into the festival. After a day of arbitration between Deidre, Lee Glanton, and *Lesbian Ethics* author Sarah Hoagland, Nia became an official guest of Campfest, and Deidre went onstage with the following speech:

> The situation was, I did not know this was a women-only festival. None of the material that was sent to me or to other performers mentions this. I had my agent send a message to Lee at the beginning of May [saying] that I was planning on bringing my 18-month-old son and that if there was a problem, to please get back to my agent. No one called me. We also talked around May 13 with the production coordinator, again mentioning that I was bringing my son; again, no problem was indicated.
>
> There was a gap of information. That information never got

to Lee. And as soon as it did, which to my understanding was Wednesday of this week, I was already en route. There was really very little that could be done. I would not have brought him if I had known, but he was here. It's an issue that will continue to be discussed among us.

My son is here. I really need to be here. A festival cannot be all things to all people. I do see a need for women-only space, although at this particular time in my life, during my son's age, and the relationship between parent and child at this age, I probably would not choose to participate in that type of space—at this time in my life. I sincerely hope that we continue to make options, to be gentle with each other; and I want to thank Lee Glanton in particular, for the way in which this was handled.

Lee Glanton, in turn, gave her own speech from the stage:

It's been an odd day at the festival. Everything is going along marvelously well, and under the surface there have been other, more emotional kinds of issues going on. Some of them are very individual, between women who for one reason or another had grievances or had felt hurt by each other, and others have been opportunities to be divisive in the present. It has shown me once more, so clearly, that when women keep their hearts open and focus on searching for ways to be cooperative, to seek solutions that will allow everyone dignity, then we can accomplish just about anything.

What Lee Glanton tactfully alluded to in this nod toward "processing" was not only Deidre's controversial test case: Campfest 1995 also saw the first interaction onstage between performers Alix Dobkin and Dianne Davidson since Alix was made to read a workers' statement charging Dianne with racism at Michigan in 1989. Alix and Dianne also used time at Campfest for successful rapprochement; only those festiegoers and workers familiar with the notorious 1989 incident at Michigan could really feel the power of reestablished trust when Alix brought Dianne onto the Campfest stage with the introduction, "My good friend, a good old soul." And perhaps most remarkable was a late-night conversation I overheard between the two potential pariahs, Dianne and Deidre, at Campfest 1995. Longtime friends (as recording artists for Olivia Records), they sat on a bench at midnight talking about Deidre's decision not to be separated from her toddler for even a weekend. "If we value motherhood, talk about abandonment issues, stress parental bonding, then there has to be some respect for women with babes in arms," said Deidre. Dianne replied, "And that's all I ever meant when I tried to sing about my childhood care-giver. My parents did not parent me; a black woman did. But there's no way to talk about my love for that primary caregiver without getting everybody hopping mad." I wished that everyone interested in festival racism and the issue of male children had been present to overhear this very complicated, intimate conversation between two artists, one black, one white.

It's fascinating that for years Campfest was perceived as the least political of the ongoing festivals, a point producer Lee Glanton actually resented. (Producers can't win: Their festivals are either too PC or not controversial enough.) While Campfest is indeed billed as "the comfortable women's festival," in 1991 Lee gave a poolside speech clarifying her outlook:

> I wish to share once again what my philosophy of this festival is. This is simply the work that I have chosen to do. It annoys me to be told that this festival is apolitical. I don't know of another festival where 700 to 900 lesbians manage to coexist without telling each other how to compost their broccoli. Diplomacy and cooperative behavior and accepting one another's differences and coexistence in our particular community, where we have an enormous number of different, strongly held beliefs, which we are only too eager to share and rarely interested in listening to, is an enormous political accomplishment.

Transgender on the Land ⩗⩗

Finally, there is today's hot issue: transgendered festiegoers. During the 1990s, two key activists pushed for change in Michigan's women-born-women–only policy: Nancy Burkholder, a male-to-female transsexual, and Leslie Feinberg, author of the powerful novel *Stone Butch Blues* and the history text *Transgender Warriors*. Their desire for a greater understanding of transgender politics led to the unofficial establishment of a "Camp Trans" outside the Michigan festival gate in summer 1994. This peaceful demonstration encampment, offering daily workshops, surprised some festiegoers by its low-key presence (although much of the controversy limelight at Michigan 1994 was admittedly stolen by the band Tribe 8).

The murder of young female-to-male transsexual Brandon Teena, which thankfully resulted in the conviction of the homophobic murderer, has been an emphatic point in Feinberg's articulate lecture series. Feinberg burst upon the lesbian political scene in 1993 with her autobiographical novel about passing for male in the pre-Stonewall era, and from her first festival appearance at the National Festival in 1994, she emphasized at-risk transgendered youth and the responsibility of the festival community to avoid shaming women like herself who appeared to be and had lived as male. What is compelling in Feinberg's rhetoric is her point that lesbian culture (and by extension, festival culture) has often worshiped the butch as a heroic icon. The "real" lesbian, the dues-paying tomboy, has been portrayed in literature and culture as she who dared to assume masculine dress or masculine privileges. Butch iconography is also a subject too complex to explore here in entirety, but suffice it to say that women's bookstores are overflowing with novels and social research on butch role phenomena and sexuality. The problem for festival staff is that if indeed festival policy mandates exclusion of anyone born male, whose unhappy job is it to "catch" the apparent transsexual? And what if the very women harassed for suspicious masculinity are in fact the heroic stone butches of Feinberg's cadre?

The potential for harassment of masculine women is one angle, but the real debate is over festival policy against transgendered men living as women. On one side

PANTY CHECK!

In 1991 the Michigan Womyn's Music Festival began enforcing a hitherto unpublished "womyn-born womyn only" or PANTY CHECK policy. The Festival GENDER POLICE are empowered to interrogate any Festiegoer regarding her sexual origins. If you refuse to answer their questions, or if in their opinion you appear to be transsexual, then you can be expelled from the festival, regardless of the anatomy between your legs or any legal identification you may possess.

I was expelled from the 16th Michigan Womyn's Music Festival by festival security women on Tuesday morning at approximately 12:45. While waiting at the main gate for a friend arriving on the chartered bus, I was approached by the security women who questioned me about whether I was a man. I answered that I was a woman and I showed them my picture ID driver's li-cense. Then one of the women asked if I was transsexual. I asked her what was the point of her questioning. She replied that transsexuals were not permitted at the festival because the festival was for "natural, women-born women" only. I replied that nowhere in any festival literature was that policy stated and I asked her to verify that policy. She contacted the festival producers, Lisa Vogel and Barbara Price, and verified that transsexuals are not permitted to attend by festival policy. When I asked to speak to the producers directly, she said that they would not speak to me, that she was their designated contact person. Then she asked me if I had had a sex change operation. I replied that my medical history was none of her business but that I was willing to submit to genital examination to satisfy her concerns regarding my sex. She declined, saying she would not feel comfortable doing that....

Nancy Burkholder
Weare, N.H.

Excerpt from a flyer rallying for support against the Michigan Womyn's Music Festival's "womyn–born womyn only" policy.

are those who argue that any man desperate enough to undergo a sex-change operation should be permitted to attend as a woman, since an intended and deeply felt
female identity is his/her obvious location. Many other women, however, are acute-
ly uncomfortable with the idea that in presumably women-only space, campers who
lived most of their lives as men—raised as men, with male privilege—are now welcome to sit in on intensely personal workshops or, say, discussions about rape. The
celebration of female life and energy that is festival culture seems mocked by the inclusion of men who have *selected* female identity; they are not, to use Alix Dobkin's
phrase, *survivors of girlhood.* The real limbo is for those few potential festiegoers who
since birth have manifested androgynous sexual characteristics: so-called hermaph-
rodites or intersexuals. How female does one have to appear at birth to count as female? In such cases, future admission to Michigan is probably not foremost on the
individual's mind during childhood socialization, but scientists, such as Brown University's Anne Fausto-Sterling, and transgender humorists, such as Kate Bornstein,
continue to press the issue of sex variance in our community.

The question of allowing transgendered men into Michigan, the most famous
women-only event in the United States, is complicated by the freedom-of-
speech issue: At Michigan, transsexual rights *activists* are discouraged from distributing literature critical of festival policy.[15] There are, no doubt, transgendered
men quietly attending women-only festivals every year; their presence becomes
controversial only when they "come out." (Several young women I met in the
Michigan worker community also knew of two gay men who had attended a past
Michigan festival, passing as lesbians.) Because of the lesbian community's historic sensitivity to the experience of living a secret, closeted life, some lesbian festival workers have grown quite sympathetic to transgender causes, while others
insist that this is just another example of men getting all the attention and trying to own the only spaces where men aren't allowed. For her strong stance on
women-only space, Alix Dobkin was *un*invited to lead the June 1998 Dyke
March in Philadelphia after first receiving and accepting an invitation from the
organizers. Now a number of activists in the Lesbian Avengers have taken up the
agenda of pushing Michigan to welcome "trans-festiegoers." Is it not possible for
there to be *one* event, *one* annual festival, intended for women born female? One

does not see any "transracial" persons demanding entry to Michigan's Womyn of Color Sanctuary. But this analogy angers some activists.

Whether festivals retain their agrarian flavor or move to resortlike facilities, accommodate the needs of all groups or uphold policies some find exclusionary, discomfort and political tension remain a primary part of the turf—and can be constructive learning experiences. The causes of specific festival conflicts can be attributed to multiple variables—with a theorist for each. "We get stirred up when

1992 Michigan Womyn's Music Festival emcees Linda Tillery and Karen Williams.

Toni Armstrong Jr.

there are too many bees in the hive," jokes Kay Turner of the rock band Girls in the Nose. Ubaka Hill says, more seriously, "There's a thin line between personal freedom and community cooperation." Affirming the Michigan festival's rule of no male music vocals on the land (unless absolutely necessary for a multicultural performance), Toni Armstrong Jr. said, "We're not talking about the rules in a lesbian nation. We're talking about going without men's music for *one weekend*. You can't go without Nine Inch Nails for one weekend? Can you say *Walkman*?" These three different comments (all overheard at the 20th anniversary Michigan festival in 1995) acknowledge community tensions. There are a lot of movers and thinkers congregating at any one festival, there is a yearning for every conceivable freedom in that short time "away" from society, and there have to be some temporary compromises as we grapple toward a week of cooperative living and collective utopia.

In the popular film *Groundhog Day,* actor Bill Murray finds himself trapped in snowy Punxsatawney, Pa., living the same bad day over and over, seemingly without cause. Recalling a vacation day he spent making love on an island beach, he complains, "*That* was a pretty good day—why couldn't I relive that day over and over?" Festivals incite controversy because everyone wants to return annually to their own magic Groundhog Day, a reliable and unchanged Brigadoon, or what sound engineer Karen Kane calls "the bubble." We expect the perfect spiritual buzz, the perfect women-only version of our imagined ideal, served up and lived over and over each festival season. Since personal visions of utopia differ, we do indeed wind up with both lesbian gospel choirs and lesbian Shabbat rituals on the land, with women burning sage and women demanding smoke-free space. It is not always possible to prevent one person's spiritual high from spilling over into another's view.

Am I an affront, seemingly disrespectful or antisocial as I sit writing in my journal during Ubaka's workshop? For me, she is muse, and it's a *Groundhog Day* joy to use her drumming as my ultimate writing music. Is Christianity an affront when the Michigan gospel choir sings about the infallibility of Christ? Yet with lesbian vocalists in the house, that is the ultimate triumphant Sunday morning for so many African-American lesbians unwelcome in their home churches.[16] Is S/M an affront? Drumming for women of color only—an affront? The political weather vane turns in the wind. One must chiefly beware getting stuck in the festival toddler stage, as a giant white 2-year-old howling, "Mine! Me!" seeing oneself as the center of the universe; workshops, politically pious though they may seem, are the useful schooling so many festiegoers need, learning, again, the reality of sharing.

1. At the Michigan Womyn's Music Festival in 1982, a posted notice for a workshop led by the John Brown Anti-Klan organization read SNEAKY STRAIGHT INFILTRATORS PRETENDING TO BE INTERESTED IN LESBIANS PLEASE KEEP OUT. But an anonymous festiegoer added her own graffiti: NEED THIS BE SO HOSTILE?

2. See Laura Post, "The Michigan Bug," in *HOT WIRE,* v.5, n. 1, January 1989, pp. 34-5.

3. See Julia Penelope, "Wimmin- and Lesbian-Only Spaces: Thought Into Action," in *Call Me Lesbian* (Crossing Press, 1992).

4. For an interesting discussion on the public shaming of performers (from an artist's viewpoint), see Laura Post, "Monica Grant: The Politics of Hissing," in *HOT WIRE*, v.8, n.3, September 1992, pp. 44-5.

5. See Lisa Vogel and Boo Price, "Michigan Festival Responds," in *Off Our Backs*, December 1990, p. 14; and Kay Gardner, "Are White Spiritual Feminists Exploiting Native American Spirituality?" in *HOT WIRE*, vol. 7, n.1. January 1991, pp. 52-3.

6. See Joanne Stato, "Cultural Appropriation," in *Off Our Backs*, October 1991, pp. 20-21.

7. See "Ableism, Access, Michigan and You," copyright 1993, *Women Creating Accessible Community*.

8. See "Michigan Commentary: Solution to Violence? Or the Normalization of Violence?" in *Off Our Backs*, November 1994, pp. 16-20; Caitlin and Gunilla, "Seps' Letter on Michigan," in *Off Our Backs*, January 1995, pp. 18-9; Trish Thomas, "Five Years of Tribe 8," in *Girlfriends*, July-August 1995.

9. Julie Blackwomon, "Kippy," in *Lesbian Fiction*, ed. Elly Bulkin (Watertown, MA: Persephone Press, 1981), p. 79.

10. It's important to note, though, that the Michigan Womyn's Music Festival now offers its worker-performer community (often 600 to 700 women living in the backstage grounds) an "ethnic" midnight meal.

11. bell hooks, *Feminist Theory: From Margin to Center* (Boston: South End Press, 1984), pp. 63-4. In her career as a theorist, hooks has chosen to use lower case letters when her name appears in print.

12. See Tatiana de la Tierra, "In Living Color at Michigan," in *Deneuve* magazine (now *Curve*), July/August 1994.

13. Susan J. Wolfe, in *Nice Jewish Girls: A Lesbian Anthology*, ed. Evelyn Torton Beck (Watertown, MA: Persephone Press, 1982), pp. 172-3.

14. Julia Penelope, *Call Me Lesbian* (Crossing Press, 1992), pp. 53-4.

15. See Davina Ann Gabriel, "Mission to Michigan," in *Transisters*, issue 10, Autumn 1995.

16. See Sylvia Rue and Dee Mosbacher's film *All God's Children*, about homophobia and black church communities.

CHAPTER SEVEN

There Is a Sense of Humor Here: Trends in Festival Parody

What is tofu? I throw my old sponges away.
—Karen Williams

Summer is the sound of 6,000 women laughing together in a field. And often we're laughing at ourselves.

We know that in the eyes of our more skeptical friends and loved ones, this decision to spend every summer festival hopping seems mad, especially as we all grow older. Who wants to vacation in a mine field of political disagreement? Whose idea of utopia is a rain-swamped pup tent downwind of an overflowing outhouse? Why *pay* to leave air conditioning and summer barbecues for a mosquito-flecked tofu line? Why would any woman go to more than two festivals per year—isn't that just dyke Deadheadism at its most pathetic? These are the withering remarks we endure annually. Yet festivals created a significant, original, and memorable way for an entire generation of lesbian feminists to have *fun* together.

Perfectly sensible, otherwise sensitive friends of mine become Scrooge incarnate when I pay homage to festival culture. One pal regularly requests, "When you get back, just let me know what this year's big controversy was about," as I depart, starry-eyed, for Michigan each August. The belief is that festivals are mirthless endurance tests: lesbian United Nations meetings with sunburn added.

The uninitiated—and women who have themselves endured personally unpleasant festivals—will always offer such doubts. One bad festival experience can turn committed lesbian feminists into acrimonious critics; this was the case for journalist Lindsy Van Gelder, who had a lousy time at NEWMR and then slammed festival culture in her 1992 *Los Angeles Times* piece "Lipstick Liberation." (She later visited Michigan with her partner and coauthor Pam Brandt, and they gave a more balanced report in their 1996 book *The Girls Next Door.*)[1] Yet others have turned gentle festival mockery into an entire category of humor and art. Musicians joke about festivals in song lyrics. Comedians write their best material on the challenges of camping or eating during festivals. And lesbian cartoonists have contributed a wry new genre of festival strips, succinctly capturing trends and politics for posterity.

One can learn a great deal from these humorists. This chapter will look at a cross section of festival satire in fiction, cartoon art, and performance since 1981.

Stage Humor ⩤⩥

Festivals *are* humorous events. They offer real situation comedy because most of us *don't* live like this year-round. We do indeed poke fun at our recognizable archetypes: the otherwise dignified feminist philosophy professor trapped inside a collapsed tent, the inevitable fortissimo snorer in a jam-packed cabin,[2] the uniquely fashionable young woman who comes to breakfast wearing only a buck knife and a yarmulke, or even Skip Drum, the beloved games coordinator at Campfest, who waltzes into the dining hall each year stark naked but for the pastel ribbon tied to her pubic hair. Stage announcements almost always provide a belly laugh: "Thursday's sexuality workshop has been moved from Cabin A because of plumbing problems." Festival culture *is* funny.

As an emcee, I've often used festival-humor stories to amuse the audience during set changes. There was the time I was mistakenly kissed and groped from behind by some woman who thought I was her girlfriend; when I turned around and smiled, she gasped in dismay, "Oh, my God, *you're* not Lorraine!" There was the time my mother warmed up rain-drenched performer Leah Zicari by roaring a blowdryer through Leah's pants. And there was the time I laid awake at Michigan trying not to listen to new arrivals in the next tent make wild love ("Oh, honey, you taste so spicy tonight!"). When I met these lusty neighbors over breakfast the next morning, I tried not to remark, "And you must be the spicy-tasting one," as we all shook hands in our best butch manner.

Professional humorists gladly take advantage of festival in-jokes and camping fiascos to hone new material, writing entire sets about the anthropology of festival culture. Every comedy artist worth her salt who performs at a festival will usually open with jokes about incidents that have happened on the land since she arrived, even if this is a departure from her regular material. It can hardly escape the performer's notice that much of her audience is topless or, conversely, bravely huddled under rain gear and umbrellas. And festival audiences delight in hearing their own experiences confirmed by lesbian celebrities. We don't all make albums, tour, sign autographs, appear on the cover of *Hot Wire* or *Curve* or *Girlfriends,* but we do share the challenges of festival weather, housing, and cuisine as the great equalizers. Audiences feel closer to a performer who tries out festival language and satire. As a result of this dynamic, most festivals offer a dose of self-parody and increasingly showcase lesbian comedians as part of the regular stage lineup—in response to the audience's demand for good humor.

Producer and comedian Robin Tyler, whose own entertainment career as a stand-up comic burgeoned into two popular women's music and comedy festivals and a women's safari and cruise business, is the prime example of the cultural marriage between women's music and lesbian comedy. Beginning with Robin's performances, recordings, and festivals, the '70s and '80s gradually saw the addition of feminist and lesbian comedy acts to the "music" stage, and half a dozen women were established as festival headliners: Kate Clinton, Sara Cytron, Lea DeLaria, Marga Gomez, Suzanne Westenhoefer, and Karen Williams. True to the American comedy tradition, most of these entertainers draw on their experiences with an ethnic identity or family upbringing within the larger framework of their lesbian experience. By the mid 1990s the market for skilled comedy with a gay edge permitted both Kate Clinton and Lea DeLaria in particular to establish full-time careers as entertainers well beyond the festival circuit—including television, film, and theater appearances. Marga Gomez appeared in the Hollywood movie *Sphere.* Georgia Ragsdale, a veteran of several festivals, has appeared on *Ellen* and costarred with Margot Kidder in the feature film *Never Met Picasso*. One might even argue that festivals helped pave the way for someone like Ellen DeGeneres to be accepted as a national lesbian heroine; certainly festivals have created new consumer audiences for lesbian humor as a genre of American comedy.

In some instances, therefore, festival humorists have a better shot at mainstream bookings (and income) than festival musicians because comedy clubs continue to thrive on controversial "adult" material. On the other hand, some funny women present lesbian humor on the festival stage but nonetheless symbolize "family values" on television. Here the example is comedian Diane Amos, who wowed the 1993 Michigan day-stage audience with anecdotes about her lesbian moms—and then promptly became a household face to millions of Americans by appearing in a series of TV commercials for Pine-Sol cleanser.[3]

Festival humor is hardly restricted to the hired comedians. Emcees, pressed to fill time during prolonged set changes and sound checks, are notorious jesters: Sue Fink, Maxine Feldman, and the New Zealand Topp Twins are as well-known for their hilarious emcee work as for their music. Comedy songwriter-musicians who tour festivals include the Seattle-based duo Dos Fallopia (Lisa Koch and Peggy Platt); their show includes an unforgettable parody of festival culture: two characters named Compost Morningdew and Dolphin-Free Tuna Woman, whose song "My Vulva Is Singing" includes erotic flash cards for the audience. Other festival performers who interweave lesbian satire and original music are Anne Seale and Sasha Hedley, the Lesbian Lounge Lizards (Zöe Lewis and Julie Wheeler), Jamie Anderson, and the Derivative Duo (Susan Nivert and Barb Glenn). There are also Deaf lesbian comedians (Susan Jackson and Patty Wilson), humorous lecture presenters like Joann Loulan, and the uniquely outrageous Judith Sloan, who combines comedy with hard-hitting political critique and characterizations. Performer Monica Grant takes an additional risk with her hilarious spoof of Ferron's "Shadows on a Dime."

I noted at the onset of this chapter that the best memories of any festival include the sound of thousands of women laughing together—deep bass guffaws, helpless gasping, hysterical giggling, knowing chuckles of life experience and recognition. Sue Fink once remarked, "You know it's a small community when you recognize your friends' laughter in the audience." Most of us go to festivals to share in that laughter. The following excerpts, transcribed from several different festival comedians' live performances and emcee announcements, demonstrate the varied approaches to festival humor.

Maxine Feldman, emcee, and October Browne, announcements
East Coast Lesbian Festival, 1990

MAXINE: We need one more worker for the kitchen. Listen—you know how things work here—the more hands that get out there, the quicker it's done. And that applies for a *lot* of things. So, speaking of trash, also reported by the trash queens are sightings of extra rolls of toilet paper throughout the camp. I don't know—are they running away? What do they do? Ah—in the empty cabins. They are free! Don't let those little rolls of toilet paper feel alone: They are lesbians too. They want to be near you. Now, recycling is going well. Apparently Earth Day had an effect on dykes this year. But for a persistent minority who put cans in the trash bins and paper in the compost—shame, shame, shame. Hissy boo. This just in from the trash queens: You may flush your poo paper, but please throw your pee paper away. I'm not making this up; I just read what they tell me. Now it says, "Is your plumbing not working? Go to the political tent."

OCTOBER: I was over at the Eve's Garden booth looking at the dildos. Oh, of course I was only browsing to do an article on how politically incorrect they are. I did discover that if I rubbed one on my trousers it would glow in the dark. All right then, announcements: 1) Today's tea dance was cancelled due to technical difficulties. 2) Soft bull dykes—let's play—meet tomorrow and play games. Huh? *Oh,* I'm sorry; it's *softball* dykes.

Sharon and Sändra Washington, emcees
North East Women's Music Retreat, 1988

SHARON: Now you all need to know that Lyme disease is caused by the bite of a small tick. You may not see the tick; it might bite and drop off before you even know you've been bitten—

SÄNDRA: Like some relationships.

SHARON: So you want to watch for a red, hard spot that is hot to the touch. [*Appreciative whoops and shrieks from the audience.*] You are not making it easy up here. I don't even want to say this next part. I'll try my best. Ah, you want to watch for a red, hard spot that is hot to the touch and gets bigger as time goes by. [*More screaming and laughter from the audience.*]

SÄNDRA: Well, I think we all know what *that* is.

SHARON: This is a very serious medical announcement, now. Look, it says the spot can be very itchy but isn't a problem if recognized and treated within a reasonable time frame. [*Still more hilarity offstage.*] I'm the shy one of the two of us, and I sure wish I'd given this announcement to Sändra.

Karen Williams, performer
West Coast Women's Music and Comedy Festival, 1989

Bill Pappas

I don't know about you but I got the tofu blues. What is tofu? I throw my old sponges away. And no whole grains? What is holding your ass together? I don't know if it's a *class* thing or not, but I'm trying to get to the point where I eat steak as often as possible. And what gets me are the women who say, "No preservatives." We live in the threat of a nuclear holocaust. I am not going up in a tofu poof. I want as much steak and preservatives saving my thin ass as possible....

OK, I don't do camping. Maybe it's because I'm from New York—we don't call it camping, we call it homeless. I do hotel *real well*. True story: I went on my first camping trip with high heels and stopped on the way to pick up my clothes from the cleaners. I'm no good at putting up tents. I like to watch about eight butches struggle for hours to put up a dome tent. I'm the campsite hostess, bringin' 'em little drinks and snacks. But when it's up, I make the inside of the tent look *like a* Maui condo!

Karen Williams, performer
Rhythmfest, 1992

I'm in culture shock here, you know. Every time I pack my freshly pressed blouses to come for one of these campfests, I fucking freak out. And to have to go in the porta-toilet, or whatever these outhouses are called. I leave my penthouse apartment to come here so I can drink rusty water and shit in a hole. And we call this lesbian culture—but it's gonna change soon. You know why? 'Cause there's so many of us over 40. [*Wild applause.*]

Any minute now all of the over-40s are gonna say a collective, "Fuck it!" All the rest of the festivals are gonna be in hotels, trust me, with real sheets. I am gonna stay up until I leave this festival—I have not been in the bottom bunk of a bed since I was 4. This is my last festival of the season, and I've done it all, even eaten rabbit food. I've been indoctrinated. I understand how this works. But why we think we deserve mud and holes, I don't know. It's obvious we're all getting older. My little friends who picked me up in the airport-shuttle van and drove me here, they're 22. And they talk incessantly—about the same shit we talked about 20 years ago.

Sara Cytron, performer
East Coast Lesbian Festival, 1993

Nick Granito

It's a great feeling to be here with all you wonderful women. And I think this is a terrific place for a romance, don't you? I have a friend, Marcia, who had a very unexpected romance recently at a women's festival. She's 38, and at a Welcome the Goddess ceremony, she met somebody who's only 23. Imagine—somebody who's still filled with youthful energy and enthusiasm. The first night they were together, the woman turns to her and says, "I want to be the most amazing lover that you have ever had." Marcia says, "Sure, go ahead. Try. I'm rooting for you."

Sara Cytron, performer
Campfest, 1995

So here we are at a women's festival. It's fantastic, and I know there have to be a few festie virgins out there—yes? [*Wild cheers.*] Oh, my God, that first time you go—it's unbelievable. You can't believe you're with all these women. You start to bask in the sunshine, you start to sway to the music, and pretty soon you start to feel oh-so *natural*. And then you gotta take off those unnatural, confining clothes, and then your breasts are hanging free and loose. And you look to your left, and you see these naked women and a mountain. And you look to your right, and you see—Ms. Weber from the personnel department! Oh, my God—Ms. Weber's here! Uh, nice to see you again, Ms. Weber....

Well, we've certainly developed our own alternative culture at these women's festivals. Where else can you go and hear over the loudspeaker, booming through the trees, "Will Running River Schwartz please meet her girlfriend Oat Bran at the light bondage tent immediately." Then there are always a few women who have their heads completely shaved except for a women's symbol going around the crown of their heads like a trimmed hedge and down the back. And whenever I see these women, I think, *Where do these women work?*...

You know, many lesbian gatherings—like many lesbians—tend to be very environmentally conscious. You can usually get vegetarian food, you have to smoke outside, and there are usually bins available to recycle bottles, plastics, and aluminum cans.

And because we're such ecologically responsible lesbians, we go even further: We recycle our lovers. You know, a lot of lesbians are addicted to very short, very intense relationships. They're like the bulimics of relationships. They have the binge-purge syndrome. But the great thing about lesbian relationships is that when they're over, you don't just dump someone, which would be very wasteful. Instead, you pass her on to someone else.

So, if you get tired of your lover while you're here this evening, please be considerate and drop her in one of the Lesbian Lover Recycling Bins located conveniently throughout the area, and I'm sure someone will pick her up who can use her.[4]

Lea DeLaria, emcee
Rhythmfest, 1992

LEA: I need a bath! I am a city girl, OK? When are they going to hold one of these goddamned festivals in the Holiday Inn? I can't take it. Oh, don't *boo* me just 'cause I'm scared of bugs. It's a great way to meet girls, OK? Next time you're in your tent or your cabin and you see some babe you like, you run screaming out of that tent: "There's a spider in my tent! Get it out! Get it out! You—the big butch babe—the big, butch, good-looking babe—get the spider!"

Now, when they asked me to emcee, I just knew they were going to make me do a *million* stupid announcements. There's nothing that makes me happier than knowing I'm standing onstage in front of a couple thousand women boring the fuck out of them. But now listen, a lot of people worked to get this festival together. It doesn't just magically happen, although we all like to think that. We like to think that we just wave our crystals in the air, and this festival magically happens. But that's not the way it works at all—even though [Rhythmfest producer] Michelle Crone takes care of all *her* aspects of the festival that way. She doesn't really do anything, just stands there with a big honking crystal, holds it up to the sky, and says, "Goddess, do this for me." [*Backstage, Michelle responds by lifting her shirt.*]

Michelle just showed me her tit! The prude of the century! Come on out here, Michelle. We all want to see it. Everybody wants to see it!

MICHELLE: So far, we raised $2,875 for the next March on Washington. If someone will make that $3,000, I will come up onstage there and show my breasts.

LEA: Three thousand! You got it! [*Michelle comes onstage and flashes the audience.*] Ah, my whole life I have waited for that moment.

Ugh—a fucking moth in my eye. Oh, great! Now somebody's saying, "Don't kill it! That's my grandmother in a different life." We l-o-ove pointing our fingers at each other. We have a real problem with that, don't we, women? A real semantics problem. Why say something in one word when you can use 20? I will never forget getting a brochure that said, "Do not wear any perfume or deodorant, as it is offensive to women who are environmentally impaired." What the fuck is "environmentally impaired"? You don't know that you're standing outside? What is wrong with the word *allergic*? The word m-a-n does not appear in the word *allergic* anywhere—why can't we say it?

Linda Moakes, performer
North East Women's Music Retreat, 1988

Now we're being intimate. Are people getting comfortable here at all? *I'm* kind of a happy camper. Why don't we all try saying that together: I am a happy camper. That's an affirmation, right? You know what affirmations are? That's when you lie to yourself until it's true. Now let's all chant together: I understand quantum physics.

Marga Gomez, performer
Campfest, 1991

Are you in tents? I'll say you're intense. I'm from San Francisco, and this is my first time in Pennsylvania. When I go to festivals with my girlfriend, I always feel so butch, even though I don't put up the tent. I feel butch just being there. "I'll carry the canteen, babe. Here, let me rip open that Wash'n Dri for you."

Marga Gomez, performer
Rhythmfest, 1992

I asked my Aunt Sonia, "Why? Why am I homosexual?" She said "Why? Why, the Gomezes have always been homosexual. There was your great-great aunt, Sappho Gomez. We called her Sapphita. She used to wear a lot of Corinthian leather—and she organized the first women's music and bullfighting festival."

I'm just glad to be here because it meant we could stop driving. It's great when you get to a festival on Wednesday because that's when the Porta-Janes are brand new. You open it up, and you just look for a while because it's so blue. It's like a glacier—pure, pure, pure, blue, blue, blue!

Georgia Ragsdale, performer
Northampton Lesbian Festival, 1993

Let's take a moment to separate the butches from the femmes, shall we? I'll just come into the audience—I can already see the women in front freezing up and going, "I am a chair." Here's the test: Do you more frequently wear lipstick or Chap Stick? [*To an audience member*] Your name is? Ann. And you are a teacher? What an unusual profession for a lesbian. Do you prefer power tools or power earrings? Do you prefer a strapless or a strap-on? You don't have to answer that. Is that your girlfriend? It's a long story? That's OK, you don't have to explain. You're from Dallas? Well, goddamn, what a coincidence that we never met *there*—but we probably have ex-lovers in common.

Suzanne Westenhoefer, performer
National Women's Music Festival, 1993

Toni Armstrong Jr.

So this is the Midwest! Hi, I'm Suzanne Westenhoefer, lesbian comedian. I do lesbian comedy in straight clubs across this great nation of ours. Yes, I get up in front of straight people and tell them how fun it is to be gay. It's my version of S/M. I do stand-up in New York at the Improv, Catch a Rising Star. But there's this one club—they didn't want me. I had a really great audition, and this little guy comes up afterwards and goes, "Oh, you were really great but I don't think that we can use you. Because we groom our people for television, and I don't think there'll ever be lesbians on TV." Like, *no* lesbians? What about Wimbledon? And I guess you didn't know about Miss Jane Hathaway on *The Beverly Hillbillies*. And that is because heterosexuals are afraid of us. And I like straight people—I just don't want them teaching our kids….

I was at Michigan, and they made me camp. It was heinous. In a tent! On the ground! I whined for 48 straight hours. I would rather peel back my own scalp and suck out my brain with a straw than camp. Camping is an evil, horrible thing. So, I get there, and I have this little pup tent. And Alix Dobkin comes over to me and says, "Hi, Suzanne, how you doing?" And I'm, like, sobbing. She says, "Come over to my tent, and I'll give you a jacket." I didn't even have a jacket. So we walk over to her tent, and she's got the exact same size tent that I have—and she's got, like, a bed, shelves, central heating. I said, "How long have you *been* here?" I had, like, a sleeping bag, a piece of foam, and a pile of leaves. Alix gets into it; I do not. So there I am at Michigan, and this woman walks up to me and says, "I guess you've heard that we now have female condoms." Where the hell does that go? On *our* little version of what the men got? Eighty-two to a package?

Kate Clinton, performer
National Women's Music Festival, 1994

Toni Armstrong Jr.

Hello, hello. Happy anniversary! The 20th anniversary! Which I looked up in my etiquette book. It's a very small book. I found that for a 20th anniversary you give china. But after the Tianamen Square thing, I just can't, do you know what I mean? But I am retaining my own Most Flavored Lesbian status, thank you....

The 20th anniversary! June 1974—I was not even *out*. I was teaching high school English in Massachusetts. But by November 1974, I was out. I don't know if it was the trickle-down effect of this festival, but I would like to thank you so much....

Ten years ago was the first time I came to this festival. I'd wasted so much time that I thought, *Well, I'll just tell* everyone *that I'm a lesbian.* And in 1984, I came here and did a show, my "unplugged" show—not wearing a tampon. For the longest time, that's what I thought it meant....

In 1984, Jasmine was on the night stage. Oh, I wanted to come back as a saxophone. "Better check my reed—I don't know if it's moist enough yet." Being here now, in the Midwest, I feel like I'm on the set of *Bad Girls.* Did you see that? Cowgirl Barbies! During that movie I wanted to come back as a saddle.

Nancy Norton, announcements
Campfest, 1996

The largest announcement card tonight, which I'm supposed to read to you with dignity, is about the Campfest toilets. As a Virgo, I actually enjoy this. And it's written so beautifully: "Campfest toilet etiquette, colon." Isn't that cute, to have a colon for this particular announcement? "Due to the very sensitive nature of our facilities"—we even have neurotic toilets, codependent. Not taking this shit no more! And this must be really fun for Joy, our sign-language artist, to interpret. OK, so, the announcement continues: "Small size paper bags have been issued"—and they probably *have* issues—"Please deposit—quote, unquote—damp paper in these bags." I cannot wait until I have my own sitcom and can reflect on this moment in my career. "And please fold over these paper bags, for aesthetic as well as hygienic value. The trusty trash womyn will come by twice a day. Remember, if it's yellow, let it mellow; if it's brown, flush it down." And since I am a nurse, I'll add that if it's white, please get a hepatitis test.

Dorothy Hirsch, performer
Gulf Coast Womyn's Festival, 1997

Fran and I are very glad to be back here again. Last year was a big adventure for us. I had never been to this part of Mississippi; I had read about Camp Sister Spirit, was excited about coming. We flew into New Orleans and rented a car. As the sun set and we got onto smaller roads, Fran decided that asking directions was a good idea, pulls up next to a clump of good old boys with belt buckles—on *my* side of the car. I had purple hair with Etch-A-Sketch designs in it and a sheaf of papers that said *lesbian* all over....

Finally, we pull up to the biggest lavender gate we'd ever seen. What do we do now? There was a tiny hole, and some printed directions said, "Press the button and state your business." I looked for a speaker mike, but apparently your statement just goes directly to God. I felt like an idiot, putting my finger in a hole in a fence, like vagina dentata or something. So I shouted, "Hi, I'm Dorothy Hirsch! I'm supposed to be performing here!" And a voice from the heavens drawled, "All right, I'll open the gate."

Fran's nerves snapped: "Nothin's happening! We supposed to do something here or what?" But that gate suddenly rose. Three tons of lavender steel. Fran hit the gas. And then we came to a little clump of women. A white girl with dreads and a New Zealand accent sent us further down to park. All these women were as sweet as they could be, but this one big girl—she was impressive. A monument to womanhood. Long dark hair parted in the middle, Indian bead thing, a jog bra that protected some of the most gorgeous—and a bowie knife about 12 feet long. And this apparition, this goddess on the land, stuck out her hand and said, "Wolf."

Fran and I looked at each other and thought, *Oh—respond in animal nouns.* Fran said, "Tiger!" and I said, "Chia pet?" And as we all stood there staring at each other, this woman bounded by wearing a clown outfit, and someone said, "That's Brenda Henson."

❖❖❖❖❖❖❖❖❖❖❖❖❖❖❖❖

These examples, culled from many summers of festival comedy and emcee announcements, demonstrate several trends in festival humor. The obvious first is an assumption of the audience's lesbian orientation, which allows the performer to flirt with and tease the audience (and other stage performers). Lea DeLaria is the best example of in-your-face sexual humor; the excerpt in which Lea incorporates a spontaneous flirtation with festival producer Michelle Crone into her act also shows the good-natured participation of festival staff in stage pranks and playfulness.

A second trend is the general mockery of festival cuisine, housing, and bathrooms, where festivals are campground-based. Note that Suzanne Westenhoefer's diatribe on camping at Michigan was tactfully delivered not at Michigan but at the National Women's Music Festival, which meets on a university campus with private dormitory beds and dining services. It is true that as festival culture itself approaches its 25th year, the original festiegoers have steadily aged and are less comfortable with tents, outhouses, lining up for mass chow. Sara Cytron, Karen Williams, and other performers fondly poke fun at the newer generation of young, enthusiastic festiegoers, who lack the perspectives of the over-40s. Karen Williams also makes the more specific point that for many black Americans threatened with homelessness and continually struggling to escape substandard urban housing or the legacy of Southern rural poverty, sleeping on the ground and using a filthy portable toilet hardly seems like liberating recreation (as discussed in the previous chapter). Karen did indeed fulfill her dream of "Hotelfest" by organizing the first Women's Comedy Festival at the Embassy Suites Hotel in Cleveland, Ohio, in November 1993.[5]

One important part of festival humor not visible in these excerpts is how comedians' routines are interpreted for the Deaf. Almost all festivals use sign language interpreters for every stage artist so that Deaf and hard-of-hearing festiegoers can enjoy the performance. Stand-up comedians—usually solo performers with large egos—were once upon a time unaccustomed to sharing the stage this way but have gleefully adjusted, inventing an entire new subcategory of festival humor. When Kate Clinton pauses during her act to take a sip of water, she makes interpreter Sherry Hicks dip her own fingers in a water glass. Karen Williams and Lea DeLaria both delight in making their interpreters sign the word *pussy* over and over. Jamie Anderson waltzes with her interpreter during one song. Dos Fallopia (Lisa Koch and Peggy Platt) do a parody of a mother-daughter country-and-western band, "The Spudds"; during this act Peggy customarily insults their sign-language interpreter and then snarls, "So what? She can't hear me," leaving both Deaf and hearing women in the audience howling with laughter. Lisa Koch also performs the raunchy comedy song "You Make My Pants Pound," in which the interpreter must creatively sign the song title over and over. As interpreters change from festival to festival, this particular song has endeared a wide variety of sign-language artists to new audiences. (It really must be seen, not described.)

There are also Deaf comedians and actresses, including Susan Jackson and Patty Wilson, who perform at festivals. Patty Wilson introduced Deaf festival humor at the 1988 North East Women's Music Retreat; Susan Jackson appeared several times at Campfest and at Michigan. When Deaf artists perform, the American Sign Language interpreters voice for them: non-Deaf fans of ASL interpreter Sherry Hicks are often surprised to hear her Arkansas accent for the first time.

Festival performance is bawdy. Our natural functions are out in the open; we're all getting older.—humor must be a constant companion. But politics or conflicts can change the good mood. Thus, humor also targets the overly serious among us.

Political Correctness: Festivals in Fiction ⪢

I attended my first festival in 1981. In that same year, author Lisa Alther's Southern coming-of-age novel *Original Sins* was published by Knopf. Alther's semiautobiographical heroine, Emily, who moves from Tennessee to New York City and eventually comes out as a lesbian, experiences her first festival with all the mixed emotions of an authentic festie virgin:

> That weekend Emily went with Maria and Kate to a women's music festival. The college amphitheater, with its elaborate polished oak woodwork, was packed with women of every size and shape and color, dressed mostly in jeans or overalls, flannel shirts or sweat shirts, boots or tennis shoes. A woman in jeans and suspenders and a flannel shirt, with close-cropped hair, played a guitar and sang love songs to a woman in her backup band. From the corner of her eye Emily saw Maria and Kate were touching fingertips, trying to be unobtrusive so that Emily wouldn't feel left out. But she did anyway. All around her, women had their arms across each other's shoulders, were holding hands and pressing thighs. Emily felt titillated. Women making love to women. It was unheard of in Newland, and Emily had always been drawn to anything Newland forbade. If Newland forbade it, it couldn't be all bad. She decided she adored these tough defiant women lounging all over each other.[6]

However, Emily, now separated from her activist husband after years of putting up with his constant political proselytizing, is leery of festival morals. She craves a vacation from political angst:

> On one side of the stage was a woman interpreting the song in sign language for the Deaf. On the other side, a woman did a

karate demonstration. Women were passing cardboard buckets through the audience for donations to a lesbian mothers' defense fund. Emily sighed. Civil rights, Appalachia, Vietnam, American Indians, migrant workers, Chile, Puerto Rico. Emily, under Justin's tutelage, had done them all. Now it was Women. And next week the sisters would be stacked in someone's attic like cast-off hula hoops. Political consumerism. Fuck it, she'd been taken in too many times by this Cause of the Month mentality.[7]

Lisa Alther allows Emily to express a standard impatience with so-called political correctness; Emily's sarcasm is the sarcasm of the festie virgin whose erotic homecoming is constantly interrupted by political guilt trips from stage authorities. Can't festivals simply be recreational or romantic good times? No topic raises hackles on all sides like the topic of political correctness. However, most festiegoers can laugh at Rhonda Dicksion's cartoon of a woman condemned to burn in hell because she ate hot dogs at a festival or Susan Baylies's "Michigan 2000" cartoon featured in Chapter Three.[8]

Surprisingly few authors of lesbian fiction depicted festival culture during the 1980s. But along with Lisa Alther, there was Noretta Koertge, whose 1984 *Valley of the Amazons* lampooned a very thinly disguised Michigan Womyn's Music Festival—again, as seen through the eyes of a festie virgin:

> Somehow she had unconsciously thought the festival would sort of be like summer camp—lots of songs about rotten peanuts and pruney faces, everyone keen on fire building and proper bedrolls. But it wasn't like that at all. Whatever was going on here was much more intense—and much more anarchistic....
>
> But then it suddenly occurred to her—the crucial difference between this gathering of Amazons and a Girl Scout Roundup was sexual freedom.[9]

Valley of the Amazons is very funny, and it includes a considerate dedication ex-

plaining that the novel was "written with great affection." However, Noretta Koertge later went on to attack political correctness professionally. During the mid
1990s she coauthored (with women's studies critic Daphne Patai) *Professing Feminism: Cautionary Tales From the Strange World of Women's Studies,* a volume charging
academic feminism with doctrinaire brainwashing and pro-lesbian, antimale bias.

Satire by insiders—by women who, like Lisa Alther or Rhonda Dicksion, are
obviously committed to lesbian culture and art—is "our" humor—in the same
way that members of a specific ethnic group may mock their own customs in
nicknames or jokes that become racist when used by outsiders. But what happens when men poke fun at festival culture? Some lesbians were uncomfortable
with the parody of festival culture presented in Armistead Maupin's novel *Significant Others.* Veteran festiegoers were aware that Maupin, a gay man, could
not possibly have any firsthand knowledge of a women-only festival. However,
Kate Clinton recently revealed in her 1998 book *Don't Get Me Started* that it was
she who served as Maupin's friendly informant.

In *Significant Others,* the fictive festival "Wimminwoods" introduces a hostile lesbian separatist archetype named Rose Dvorak, who stops a lesbian mother from
bringing her son into the festival grounds. This satire takes on a serious issue in festival culture—the concept of women-only space—and uses it to demonstrate the
apparent intolerance of festival organizers. Maupin ascribes a butch stridency to lesbian festival authorities like Rose, then questions why such seemingly strong women
would feel threatened by the presence of small boys. Maupin's work is very much
loved by gay, lesbian, and straight readers alike, but because his lampoon did not exactly represent festival culture in a favorable light, some lesbians charged that this
was a (male) disservice to female readers contemplating their first festival.

However, it should be noted that plenty of women enjoy creating opinions about
festivals they have not attended. And gay men also have a prolific festival culture all
their own: the Radical Faerie gatherings dating back to the 1960s, as discussed in
Stuart Timmons's 1990 biography *The Trouble With Harry Hay.*

There are also festival humorists who have voluntarily built bridges of understanding about women-only space. Lesbian cartoonist Alison Bechdel explained
festival separatism in a little-known strip that intentionally depicted gay and lesbian

activists in caring, good-natured dialogue. Alison is best known for her hugely popular comic series "Dykes to Watch Out For." In summer 1993 she had her own special issue in the long-running *Gay Comics* series, and reprinted her "Servants to the Cause" feature about a gay newspaper collective. Here, we see the collective's members discussing why women's music festivals are not coed.

Explaining festival culture to men has also served as a storyline for N. Leigh Dunlap's lesbian cartoon series "Morgan Calabrese" in which she also points out festiegoers' love-hate relationship with camping discomforts and political processing. Along these same lines, writer Jorjet Harper, whose humorous columns on lesbian life were collectively published in the 1994 book *Lesbomania*, contributed a column entitled "Michiguilt" to the fall 1993 issue of *HOT WIRE:*

> "So what's a little discomfort when it comes to experiencing lesbian culture?" says my Right Brain. "Isn't lesbian culture worth a few bug bites?"
>
> Michiguilt. OK. I'll go. I'll go.
>
> "Sure," says my Left Brain. "And she can be a part of all that marvelous political *processing.*"
>
> That's it. I'm not going.
>
> Right Brain:" But it's Lesbian nation! Beautiful Michigoddesses…"
>
> Left Brain: "…Mishugennahs! Dust, heat, thunderstorms…"
>
> Right Brain: "…and so many women stark na…"
>
> I'm going.
>
> In the midst of this Michigaas, I ran into a very well-known Chicago lesbian activist, who asked me if I was going to the festival. "I don't know," I groaned.
>
> "I'm going," she said, "finally." She leaned toward me, lowered her voice, and said, "I've never been before. *Shhh*, don't tell anyone."
>
> How many lesbians are walking around hiding this secret shame?[10]

Varieties of Festival Comic Art ⪼

After politics, fashion and relationships are the most popular topics for festival cartoons. An early Alison Bechdel panel features "do and don't" grooming tips for four popular lesbian summer vacation destinations of 1986: festivals; Provincetown, Mass.; martial arts camp; and the women's peace camps (then flourishing at Puget

©1986 by Alison Bechdel, from Dykes to Watch Out For (Firebrand Books, Ithaca, N.Y., 1986).

Sound; Seneca Falls, N.Y.; and Greenham Common in England). Alison also contributed "Festival Hell," acknowledging that festiegoers often dream about festivals—even while attending them. In contrast, cartoonist Kris Kovick's panel gently mocks the affluent festiegoer who samples wildness and abandon by going shirtless.

HOT WIRE had the foresight to record a conversation between Alison Bechdel and Kris Kovick, who share a September 10 birthday, as a "Confabulation" article in 1990. Here, they discuss festival influences on their cartoon art:

> ALISON: God, my first women's music festival—there were all these women there who looked like me!

> KRIS: Isn't that fabulous. The first time I saw you, I thought, "Oh, wow, we look alike!" That's a great feeling. Now tell me about your

first women's festival, because I'm trying to do a card to give to a woman who's going to her first music festival.

ALISON: It's probably a very dated response; I mean this was 1980. I was just coming out.

KRIS: Did you go by yourself?

ALISON: No, I went with my girlfriend. First of all, it was seeing all of these women who looked like me. I thought I had invented my own personal aesthetic—the way I like to wear my jeans baggy, the way I had my hair cut short, and the way I moved and talked. Then all of a sudden there were thousands of women who were like that—what is now sneeringly referred to as the '70s androgynous lesbian style.

KRIS: "Sneeringly?" I still have those clothes. I'm not sneering. I'm just out of fashion.

ALISON: What I also realized at this first festival is that you can buy this culture. There were all these merchants. You could buy the labrys, the music, the T-shirts.

KRIS: Yeah, the feminist mall.[11]

YOU'RE A RICH WHITE NORTH AMERICAN FEMALE AT A WOMEN'S FESTIVAL AND FEMINIST MALL IN THE WOODS. YOU HAVEN'T USED A HAIR DRYER IN DAYS. WEARING NOTHING BUT A WATER BOTTLE & A PAIR OF SHORTS, YOU ARE EXPERIENCING EPIPHANY. IT MAKES YOU FORGET THAT YOU HAVE DIMPLES INSTEAD OF KNEES.

Festival cartoon by Kris Kovick.

©1986 by Alison Bechdel, from Dykes to Watch Out For *(Firebrand Books, Ithaca, N.Y., 1986).*

Despite the tendency for satirists to choose either political correctness or camping challenges and fashions as subject matter, there are also festival cartoons that raise important questions about safe-sex behavior. Alison Bechdel, who has sold her work at her own Michigan festival crafts booth for many years, used the rain-deluged 1987 festival experience as a springboard for this storyline on lesbians and AIDS. (Alison was not the only festival "insider" to suggest caution in sexual behavior that year. Aware that the driving rains were sending most festiegoers into their tents to pass the time in erotic recreation, performers Holly Near and Tret Fure both spoke from the 1987 Michigan stage about the importance of "loving safely.")

Alison Bechdel's character Lois is well-established as a seductress and Don Juanita–about-town in the "Dykes to Watch Out For" series. Elsewhere in festival satire, humor about wild girl behavior remains a strong counterpoint to the presumed prudery of political correctness. Festival culture lets lesbian social and

©1988 by Alison Bechdel, from More Dykes to Watch Out For (*Firebrand Books, Ithaca, N.Y., 1988*).

©1988 by Alison Bechdel, from More Dykes to Watch Out For (Firebrand Books, Ithaca, N.Y., 1988).

Kris Kovick pokes fun at the lesbian generation gap.

sexual styles dominate "public" life for a few blessed days of each year. This includes the incorporation of S/M activists and leatherwomen into the festival body, and as noted in the previous chapter, the presence of dog-collared women has sparked debate ever since festivals began. Again, our "insider" humorists remind us gently that *all* women attending a festival are there to have fun—some in leather and spikes, some in Birkenstocks and tie-dye. Kris Kovick is superb in depicting these clashes of generation, sexual style, and fashion. Her cartoons remind us that changes in the 1990s are not the end of lesbian festival culture but the beginning of greater tolerance, diversity, and playfulness across two and three generations.

Performer Back Talk ⋙

No one is better equipped to poke fun at festival culture than the weary festival performer, whose stature and livelihood depend in part on summer festival gigs. A partial list of touring musicians who have written or recorded songs with tongue-in-cheek references to festivals includes Lucie Blue Tremblay, Pam Hall, Rhiannon, Karen Escovitz ("Otter"), Monica Grant, Zöe Lewis, Gretchen Phillips, Kay Turner, Sue Fink, Leah Zicari, and Tribe 8. These artists' lyrics range from joyful to cynical to taunting.

Lynn Breedlove, Tribe 8

From the song "Neanderthal Dyke":

Neanderthal dyke
Neanderthal dyke
I never read Kate Millet
I ride a big bike
Feminist theory gets me uptight
Get in some heels and lipstick babe
and I'll spend the night
Hey pseudo-intellectual sluts
You went to school
Did you learn how to fuck?
"Will it play in Michigan? Is it correct?"

ZÖE LEWIS

Toni Armstrong Jr.

I'll be ten years old next Tuesday
And my Mama said to me that we're gonna go away
To a place where we can feel free…
To a women's festival in the country!

I had one mother and now I got two
And we live together and our love is true
And I'm really happy that they brought me
To the women's festival in the country.

You can ride on tractors, listen to bands
And there's a woman with a drum, she's got talking hands!
We never wear clothes and we feel comfy
At the women's festival in the country.

A clown painted my face and we played silly games
And I made lots of friends with mystical names
(Oh, hi Moonbeam!)
We eat vegetables for breakfast, lunch and tea
At the women's festival in the country.

I've seen bottoms and bosoms all sizes and shapes
But when I look down at mine they're just little grapes
But next year they'll be bigger, you'll see
At the next women's festival in the country.

We sleep in a tent and we hide from the rain
And the toilets aren't johns, they're Porta-Janes!
And my mama says that I'm much luckier than she
'Cos when she was my age there was no women's festival
In the country
La la la la la la la

And the boys that are here are very very young
And they never let in men
But I did see one
In a truck, collecting poo and pee
At the women's festival in the country

I'll be ten years old next Tuesday
And I want my birthday *here*, I don't *want* to go away
Back to the rules of society
I want to live here at the women's festival
In the country!

MONICA GRANT

Somewhere over Walhalla, capital M capital I,
There's women's land that I've heard of once in a *Gaia's Guide*.
Somewhere out in Walhalla, lesbians fly
They fly out to Walhalla; why then, O why can't I?
Someday I'll wish upon a star, another girl with a guitar—
They'll hire me!
Where troubles are processed through and through,
Hangin' with the techie crew—
That's where you'll find me!
Somewhere out in Walhalla, skies are gray
And the dreams that girls dare to dream come true every day,

SUE FINK

"Camp Nowannaweenie"

We go to Camp Nowannaweenie,
Not an itsy-bitsy teeny weenie,
We go to Camp Nowannaweenie,
Where the girls don't need no boys.
We don't need Harry, Dick or Jim-bo
When we get down and do the lezzie limbo
We go to Camp Nowannaweenie
Where the girls see eye to thigh.

This last example has an interesting herstory. Between 1990 and 1994, Sue taught "Camp Nowannaweenie" to festival audiences throughout all regions of the U.S.— at the North East Women's Music Retreat, Gulf Coast, the East Coast Lesbian Festival, Campfest, the National Women's Music Festival. It's one of the only in-joke festival songs known by so many separate festival audiences. And since festivals often use summer camp facilities, Sue's song also amuses those festiegoers who are still Girl Scout counselors themselves or who first realized they were lesbians while at teen summer camp. (Like me, Sue Fink was a Los Angeles Camp Fire girl.)

However, one committee at NEWMR condemned Sue's satire as racist in 1990. Sue maintained that she was intentionally commenting on the historic appropriation of Native American names by white summer camps in America. But because Sue sold Camp Nowannaweenie T-shirts with a Native American woman on the shirt logo, she took a good deal of criticism. To clarify her stance, she chose to donate her T-shirt profits to the Native women's struggle at Big Mountain.

"Camp Nowannaweenie" is but one example of a comedy risk in a climate of political concerns. Washington, D.C., artist Dorothy Hirsch, whose comedy routine includes a lesbian charismatic preacher called Mother Daughter Sister Woman, had to convince Gulf Coast festival producer Wanda Henson that such satire would not offend the many "recovering Holiness" festiegoers in Mississippi. Magician comedian Ann Lincoln, who incorporated the traditional dove-in-a-hat and rabbit-out-of-thin-air gimmicks into her magic shows at Campfest and the National Women's Music Festival, anticipated complaints from animal rights activists in her audience and declared, "No lesbians or animals were hurt in the production of my show." Her gentle reminder that lesbians too are often under attack in a homophobic world is a good example of humor used intelligently from the stage by a new festival performer.

Sub-sub-subcultural humor may be found when a specific group at a specific festival gets up onstage to delight the audience with insider jokes. Michigan's infamous "No-Talent Talent Show" is traditionally performed by and for the 600-plus worker community on the night before the festiegoers come through the gates. On this occasion, work crew revues offer original lyrics—usually of an "artistic" nature guaranteed to raise Jesse Helms's blood pressure. In 1996, techies and land-crew staff sang Broadway musical parodies about decision processing, mail deliveries to the land, registration, producer Lisa Vogel—even a kitchen satire to the tune of "My Favorite Things":

Black beans and barley and barbecued tofu
Bagels and cream cheese and rice by the bowlful

Coffee and herbs that will make your hair curl
These are a few of the foods in our world

When the truck breaks (shit!)
When the bee stings (ouch!)
When I'm PMS (fuck you!)
I simply remember my favorite things....

But some artists grow weary of festival culture and turn their talents toward exposing its apparent political inconsistencies. One such example is the one-woman play *White Girl With Guitar*, written by former festival performer Leah Zicari. Leah, a classically trained musician, enjoyed numerous festival gigs before quitting the festival scene in 1993 and refocusing on theater. The following scene from Leah's biting satire shows the familiar frustration of a new festival performer trying to decipher festival etiquette:

LEAH ZICARI

White Girl with Guitar

(*Leah enters and approaches the registration table. She has a sleeping bag, two guitars, a box of tapes and press material, and a large suitcase. She dumps her stuff on the table. "Annie Orientation" is there. She is not wearing a shirt.*)

ANNIE: [*Exuberantly*] Hi!
LEAH: Hi. I'm here to register.
ANNIE: Another festie who's brought her guitar! We're gonna have some great music around the campfires this year.
LEAH: Well, actually, I'm performing at the festival.
ANNIE: OH! Who'd you say you were?
LEAH: Leah Zicari.
ANNIE: [*Flipping through her files*] How d'ya spell that?

LEAH: Z as in zebra, I, C as in Charles, A-R-I.

ANNIE: Let's see. Z...Z...Z...Zicari! Here we go. [*Surprised*] Hmm. It says you're playing Night Stage.

LEAH: I sure am.

ANNIE: [*Somewhat disappointed*] Oh. I thought it was Lea DeLaria who was performing.

LEAH: No. Leah Zicari.

ANNIE: Well, I look forward to hearing you. You must be pretty good if you made it to night stage. Sign in here. [*She does.*] Left arm, please. [*Leah extends her arm, and Annie puts a purple hospital band on her wrist*] Your packet contains a program, a map, a complete list of merchants, workshops, and the rules. [*She hands her the packet, and Leah opens it immediately and looks through the contents*] Now please sign here.

LEAH: What's this?

ANNIE: An insurance liability waiver. [*Leah signs once*] In triplicate. [*Annie flips the next two pages for her*] OK, now let's go over the rules.

LEAH: We have to go over the rules?

ANNIE: You can't enter the grounds unless you sign a form stating you've read the rules and regulations.

LEAH: You have to watch me read them?

ANNIE: Don't be ridiculous! I have to read them to you. [*Leah sighs and gets out her copy of the rules from the packet.*]

LEAH: This festival's philosophy is to ensure that this festival is a physically and psychically safe experience for womyn. It is our commitment to be an IN-CLUSIVE retreat appealing to many DIVERSE groupings of women. To this end, we actively struggle against the ways we are DIVIDED. Specifically, we will not tolerate racism, looksism, anti-Semitism, classism, ageism, sizeism, mental or physical ableism, or homophobia.

LEAH: It seems that the only thing you do tolerate is intolerance.

ANNIE: [*Glares at Leah while reading last line*] This is not meant to be the final list of ways in which we are divided against each other.

LEAH: [*Becoming impatient*] OK, so what you're saying is that you don't want to see practices which exclude women from other women. That the idea of this festival is for women to come together in a spirit of complete unity?

ANNIE: [*Smiles*] Exactly!

LEAH: How do you manage that?

ANNIE: [*Drawing her attention to the map and pointing as she goes*] We have a lot of specialized tents. There's the twelve-steps tent, the lesbian moms tent, the disability tent, the political tent, the singles tent, the Latinas tent, the Womyn of Color tent, the goddess worship tent...

LEAH: [*Interrupting*] But these tents are all separate. How does that promote unity?

ANNIE: By allowing us to explore our differences.

LEAH: [*thinks about it for a minute*] Oh! So I can go to the Latinas or Womyn of Color tents to learn about other women's cultures.

ANNIE: [*Shocked disbelief*] You can't go into those tents!

LEAH: Why not?

ANNIE: Because you're not a womyn of color. It's a place for them to go and be with their own sisters.

LEAH: Isn't that segregation?

ANNIE: Not at a womyn's music festival.

LEAH: [*Completely puzzled*] Oh. [*Pause*] Well, I see you have a singles tent. Do you have a couples tent?

ANNIE: We don't promote couple-ism. Coupled women have a tendency to stick to their own kind.

LEAH: [*Pointing to map*] Here's the tent for goddess worshippers, where's the tent for Christians? I like to pray before I perform.

ANNIE: We don't allow the religions of the patriarchy on land.

LEAH: Isn't that against the first amendment?

ANNIE: Not at a womyn's music festival.

LEAH: But you have a Jewish lesbians tent. Judaism is the patriarchal precursor to Christianity.

ANNIE: That's different. It's the Jewish, left-handed lesbian daughters of Russian socialists tent. They are against all religion.

LEAH: Then why do they bother to mention their Jewishness?

ANNIE: To get "oppressed group" status at the festival.

LEAH: What is "oppressed group" status?

ANNIE: That's so women who come from minority or other oppressed cultures can attend the festival at a lower price.

LEAH: You mean to tell me that if I wasn't a white woman, I would be paying a lower registration fee?

ANNIE: Yup.

LEAH: Isn't that racism *and* classism?

ANNIE: Not at…

LEAH: [*Says it with Annie*]…a woman's music festival. I think I get the picture.

ANNIE: Then sign here. [*Leah does.*]

LEAH: [*Extending her hand to shake*] Thank you.

ANNIE: [*Shying away from her hand*] We don't shake hands like men around here. We have a salute. [*She demonstrates the universal sign for "vagina".*]

LEAH: What does that mean?

ANNIE: It's sign language for "vagina." [*Leah picks up her stuff*] Here, let me help you! [*Annie helps*] Have a great weekend…what'd you say your name was?

LEAH: Leah. Leah *Zicari.*

ANNIE: [*Saluting*] Have fun!

Other performers use humor to expose the difficulties inherent in touring. Jamie Anderson is a performer who travels through enormous regions of the United States in her truck while on tour each year. A popular festival artist, she remains aware that mainstream commercial success brings far greater comfort and affluence than the festival circuit. Jamie is also a cartoonist, and in one sketch she poked fun at the commercial entertainment hierarchy—which keeps most lesbian artists struggling economically.

Finally, no overview of festival humor would be complete without a look at the work of Leanne Franson. This Canadian artist produces cartoons which resonate with the younger, international community of festival workers at Michigan; her comic book and postcards on the Michigan working experience are the most au-

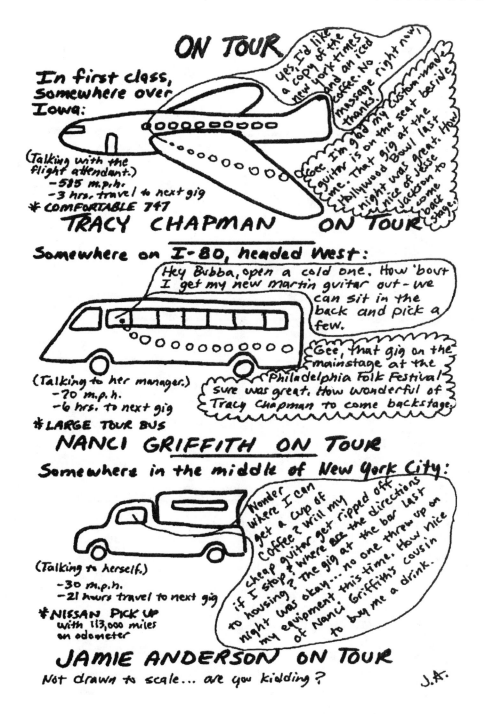

ON TOUR

In first class, somewhere over Iowa:

(Talking with the flight attendant.)
- 585 m.p.h.
- 3 hrs. travel to next gig

*COMFORTABLE 747

TRACY CHAPMAN ON TOUR

Yes, I'd like a copy of the new york times and an iced coffee. No massage right now, thanks.

Gee, I'm glad my custom-made guitar is on the seat beside me. That gig at the Hollywood Bowl last night was great. How nice of Jesse Jackson to come back stage.

Somewhere on **I-80, headed West:**

Hey Bubba, open a cold one. How 'bout I get my new martin guitar out - we can sit in the back and pick a few.

Gee, that gig on the mainstage at the Philadelphia Folk Festival sure was great. How wonderful of Tracy Chapman to come backstage.

(Talking to her manager.)
- 70 m.p.h.
- 6 hrs. to next gig

*LARGE TOUR BUS

NANCI GRIFFITH ON TOUR

Somewhere in the middle of New York City:

(Talking to herself.)
- 30 m.p.h.
- 21 hours travel to next gig

*NISSAN PICK UP with 113,000 miles on odometer

Wonder where I can get a cup of coffee & will my cheap guitar get ripped off if I stop? Where are the directions to housing? The gig at the bar last night was okay... no one threw up on my equipment this time. How nice of Nanci Griffith's cousin to buy me a drink.

JAMIE ANDERSON ON TOUR

Not drawn to scale... are you kidding?

J.A.

This original cartoon by Jamie Anderson first appeared in HOT WIRE.

thentic representation of crew humor in festival culture. When not drawing festival satire, Leanne works in the Michigan staff massage tent, bringing relief to tired backs and shoulders.

by Leanne Franson

These many examples of festival satire by "insiders" should put to rest the stereotype that lesbians have no sense of humor about our culture. What is lost in translation is the camaraderie we experience as a festival audience, in recognizing and

howling at our own foibles. Still, despite the wide spectrum of festival humor available through cartoon and performance art, many nonfestiegoers remain convinced that "issues" rather than fun dominate festival culture. And that is because festivals continue to be raked over the coals in the lesbian press and gossip mill by disgruntled festiegoers with specific complaints.

1. See Lindsy Van Gelder, "Lipstick Liberation," in *The Los Angeles Times Magazine,* March 15, 1992, p. 30, and (with Pam Brandt) "The Way We Were: The Michigan Womyn's Music Festival," in *The Girls Next Door* (New York: Simon and Schuster, 1996.)

2. The Gulf Coast Womyn's Festival at Camp Sister Spirit in Mississippi, however, includes in its guidelines a plea for more tolerant attitudes toward snorers.

3. However, it should be noted that the festival artist with the most successful television career to date is percussionist Vicki Randle, beloved to women's music audiences for almost two decades before winning a gig as conga player in Jay Leno's *Tonight Show* band.

4. C. Harriet Malinowitz and Sara Cytron, February 1996.

5. See Judith Sloan, "First National Women's Comedy Conference Diary," in *HOT WIRE,* May 1994.

6. Lisa Alther, *Original Sins* (New York: Knopf, 1981), p. 397.

7. Ibid., p. 398

8. Rhonda Dicksion's cartoon originally appeared in the Naiad Press volume *The Lesbian Survival Manual* (Naid Press, 1990), and is reprinted here with permission.

9. Noretta Koertge, *Valley of the Amazons* (New York: St. Martin's Press, 1984), p. 66.

10. Jorjet Harper, "Michiguilt and Other Musings," in *HOT WIRE,* September 1993, p.

11. Alison Bechdel and Kris Kovick, "Confabulation," in *HOT WIRE,* September 1990, p. 13.

CHAPTER EIGHT

Festivals on the Front Lines:
From Sisterfire to Camp Sister Spirit

W hat occurs when a festival spills over into the surrounding community, creating a year-round lesbian presence? Is it possible for locals to get wind of
the festival institution and organize a homophobic backlash? What about when festivals meet in public space and invite men in? How has such interaction changed
and challenged communities where festivals put down roots?

For the most part, annual festivals are self-contained. In the case of Michigan, the
United States' largest women's music festival, the secluded land is privately owned
by the festival. The 4,000 to 8,000 festiegoers and crew who appear each August are
"parked in" while there and rarely leave the land during the festival except in the case
of medical emergencies, supply runs, or shuttle buses to and from the Grand Rapids
airport. The one tiny grocery/convenience store nearest the land site turnoff enjoys
such a burgeoning profit during festival week each year that it traditionally sets out
a WELCOME sign for arriving festiegoers. Rumor has it that struggling locals roam
the land with metal detectors during the winter months, gleaning the countless
pieces of lost jewelry and pocket change sowed by dancing festiegoers each summer.

In contrast, the National Women's Music Festival first met at the University of
Illinois's Champaign-Urbana campus from 1974–1980, moved to the campus of Indiana University in Bloomington for the 1982–1997 era, and in 1998 moved over
to Ball State University in Muncie, Ind. The festival environment included at least
a few men and, in Bloomington, depended upon the assistance of male and female
IU dormitory and dining-hall staff. For Bloomington residents the business gener-

SISTER SPIRIT INCORPORATED   PROJECT: CAMP SISTER SPIRIT
LIABILITY RELEASE FORM

Sister Spirit Incorporated, or any Sister Spirit Incorporated representative or volunteer, shall not be held liable for any injury, accident or loss while I am on Camp Sister Spirit grounds, located at 203 East Side Drive in Ovett, Mississippi. I am responsible for myself, any person under the age of 21 in my care, and my personal property. I am also financially responsible for any damage done to the property of Sister Spirit Incorporated by me or anyone for whom I am responsible for their actions. The responsibility for any child's person, actions and property shall be the person signing this agreement. It is the responsibility of the child's/children's caretaker to supervise your child/children's activities.

I am aware of the homophobic and womyn-hating public attacks made against Camp Sister Spirit by a regional group, Mississippi For Family Values, the media, churches, known persons and unknown persons. I understand violence could possible erupt from the above named sources. Should this occur, I am committed to taking/making a non-violent stance and supporting this philosophy of Sister Spirit Incorporated. I will not take any action of rebuttal.

I am aware that human rights and civil rights of persons living at Camp Sister Spirit have been violated. The Federal Civil Rights Laws do not protect Lesbians and Gay Men.

I agree to follow the leadership of the land's full-time caretakers, Wanda and Brenda Henson or anyone designated by Brenda Henson, in an emergency or in their absence from the land. This agreement is governed by the laws of the State of Mississippi.

PLEASE PRINT

Name_____

Child/Children's Name(s)_____

Address_____

City_____ State_____ Zip_____

Phone Day_____ Phone Evening _____

Date_____

Signature_____

Witness_____ Witness_____

Release form presented to all artists and festiegoers attending the Gulf Coast Womyn's Festival.

ated by several thousand temporary guests—and the extraordinary artistic talent of the musicians, writers, and actresses visiting town, whose performances were accessible to locals during the university's academic off-season—stifled any latent controversy. "Cool! Are you from the festival?" was the average response from working IU students who mixed festiegoers' milk shakes in town. Elsewhere, festivals have been held at rented summer camps or remote land spaces where there is little likelihood of an impact on the local populace.

In three cases, however, regional festivals have had a specific setting that identified them, for better or worse, as community institutions. There could not be greater contrast between the three: Sisterfire, in Washington, D.C.; the Northampton Lesbian Festival, in Western Massachusetts; and the Gulf Coast Womyn's Festival, at Camp Sister Spirit in Ovett, Miss.

Sisterfire began in 1982 as one of the few U.S. festivals open to men. Produced by Roadwork, the company founded by Amy Horowitz in 1978, Sisterfire expanded from a one-day to a two-day event in 1984 and, for several years, met at a public junior high in liberal Takoma Park, Md. Far from alienating the local community, Sisterfire's multicultural and multiracial philosophy succeeded in attracting the approval of both Takoma Park mayor Sam Abbott and Washington, D.C., mayor Marion Barry. Their letters of support were proudly displayed in the 1984 program all festiegoers received. Mayor Barry, a controversial figure who was nonetheless very supportive of gay and lesbian events in the D.C. region, actually declared June 23 and 24 of 1984 to be Women's Cultural Days, with specific appreciation for Roadwork. That 1984 festival was recorded live, resulting in the first festival album marketed for sale (the Michigan festival followed suit in 1985, recording its tenth anniversary stage performances as a double album).

Recalling the initial collaboration between Roadwork and acclaimed D.C.-based vocal group Sweet Honey in the Rock, producer Amy Horowitz explained: "The idea was born out of bold hopes and a special mix of naïveté and chutzpah. We knew we were taking a risk in producing a festival consisting solely of women performers to which the public [all genders and orientations] would be welcomed. We were conscious of a lack of role models and a fundamental lack of skills in building multiracial institutions.... We were propelled by a sense of purpose."[1]

Sweet Honey in the Rock members also took risks in being identified (whether locally, nationally, or internationally) with a women's music cultural movement dominated by white lesbians. Bernice Johnson Reagon commented that "having been nurtured and reborn through the rich sands of Black Nationalism, I understood this as a radical movement, and Sweet Honey decided we could do this collaboration.... There was clearly a Movement energy that I understood and respected."[2] But the excellent relationship Sisterfire enjoyed with its urban-suburban setting underwent a devastating test in 1987, when the festival relocated to a large racetrack and tempers flared in the summer heat. An incident involving two African-American men who

Sue Fink directing the 1992 Gulf Coast Womyn's Festival performer chorus. Author Bonnie Morris is at far right.

Toni Armstrong Jr.

demanded entry to a women-only crafts booth staffed by lesbian separatists received such ugly publicity—with differing versions and explanations circulating for months in feminist periodicals—that Sisterfire never recovered.

The women's community that was Sisterfire's mainstay divided over the question of whether racism or woman hating defined the notorious incident; some alleged that allowing men into a woman-centered event inevitably produced such misunderstandings and proved male inability to respect female space. Separatism, not lesbianism per se, challenged Sisterfire's relationship with the surrounding community. But Washington, D.C., is a town already weary and defensive about the daily separatism of black from white in terms of power, educational opportunity, and economic resources. Hearts sank at the symbolism of Sisterfire's predicament. Eventually, Roadwork disbanded, and though festivals burgeoned elsewhere, throughout the 1990s, D.C. lacked a regular festival venue and a lesbian production company.

Other regional producers picked up the gauntlet. In 1990, Northampton was named "Lesbianville, U.S.A." on the front page of the *National Enquirer*. Home to historic Smith College, near sister female institution Mount Holyoke College and boasting the additional academic resources of Amherst and Hampshire Colleges and the University of Massachusetts, Northampton has one of the most affluent and educated lesbian populations in the United States. The Northampton Lesbian Festival, originally a one-day event that later expanded to two days, had its share of frustrating land searches, but producers Zizi Ansell and Diane Morgan variously held their event on town property, at a rural inn, and, one year, on the Hampshire College campus. This nomadism resulted in the festival being visible to local men and women.[3] The economic power of the Noho lesbian community, however, secures certain privileges: When ABC's *20/20* produced a special on "Lesbianville U.S.A.," broadcast on national television in fall 1992, the program featured not only excerpts from festival performances but also interviews with primarily white and affluent professional women in the town. University professors, real estate agents, business owners, writers, and artists typify Northampton's lesbian community, and while infighting and insularity have somewhat tarnished its reputation as a lesbian heaven, "The Valley" retains mystical appeal for many young dykes on pilgrimage from smaller New England hometowns.

In great contrast, the town of Ovett, Miss., where the Gulf Coast Womyn's Festival found its permanent land, more or less declared war on lesbians. The story of Wanda and Brenda Henson's fight for a feminist retreat in their home state eloquently demonstrates the inconsistency in equal protection for lesbians around these United States.

The Mississippi Spirit ≋

By now most festiegoers and, indeed, many Americans in general are familiar with the saga of Camp Sister Spirit. Wanda and Brenda Henson's battle with the citizens of Ovett, Miss., has been enhanced by media coverage from *The Oprah Winfrey Show, 20/20, The Jerry Springer Show, Larry King Live,* and newspapers across the country. The Hensons, whose original goal was simply to provide quality community outreach and educational resources to women in rural Mississippi, have become controversial folk heroines in the Southern land they insist they will not leave.

Mississippi is the poorest state in the nation. It graduates the fewest students and pays the lowest wages. It is a right-to-work state where women, black and white, struggle to find promising job opportunities. Haunted by the bloody civil rights years of voter registration drives and lynchings, Mississippi's black and white residents remain divided though united in a profound Christianity that has also made controversial headlines of late (certain public schools include daily Christian prayer and Bible reading despite the presumed separation of church and state). [4]

In spite of these challenges, Mississippi draws on a rich oral tradition of women's words and stories. The language of women speaking and singing is woven into the lush coastal geography and deltas. This too is a culture and a place where women look to one another with love and commitment. Here, song traditions draw from Native American languages, Cajun cadences, slave lullabies, blues, gospel hymns, fishing, and riverboat legends. In response to those who mock the idea of a lesbian festival taking root in Mississippi, Wanda Henson's quick reply is that these are her people and this is her environment—why should a woman-loving identity make refugees of individuals, require all activists to relocate to urban gay communities like San Francisco?

The arrogant assumption that progressive Mississippi women have the resources to move out of state is another point. Uprooting every lesbian feminist is not just a slap in the face to folk with kinship ties and emotional history in their own land: It is impossible for those women who lack the discretionary budget to leave town. Women without the cash flow to attend the more distant festivals might well benefit from an affordable, local festival at home, tailored to their own concerns. With this in mind, Wanda and Brenda Henson founded the Gulf Coast Womyn's Festival in 1989. What no one could foresee was that this small statement of grassroots feminism, based in the belief that every region deserves its own festival, would become a national symbol of the fight against intolerance.

Wanda and Brenda first met in January of 1985 at an abortion clinic defense during the anniversary of *Roe* v. *Wade*. Brenda hailed from a Unitarian family in Ohio, while Wanda grew up in Mississippi's strict Holiness subculture and preached as a young woman; nonetheless, the two women had much in common. Both had married at 16. Both had two children from their young marriages. And both had left behind husbands who battered them, electing to start life over in service to women in need.

As a committed lesbian couple, legally sharing the surname of Brenda's mother, the Hensons found a model for community change in the first festival they attended—Robin Tyler's Southern Women's Music and Comedy Festival in Georgia. Reminiscing about that life-changing first festival, Wanda later told *HOT WIRE* readers, "I went into Robin's festival a desperate, tired woman, full of pure hopelessness…and for the first time began seeing people that were expressing things like what I thought." She added: "When I hear sisters say to me that the feminist movement is dying, I feel like, *You can't die—we haven't had our chance yet.* I get real desperate over that because I know where I was, and I see it in my sisters every day. There's so much hopelessness, lack of education, and poverty here among women."[5]

Zöe Lewis at the 1992 Gulf Coast Womyn's Festival.

Rather like the radical feminist writer Sonia Johnson, who transferred the visionary fervor of her Mormon upbringing to festival activism and rhetoric, Wanda caught inspiration from Robin Tyler's festival and began working and fund-raising to open a women's bookstore in Mississippi. Southern Wild Sisters Unlimited opened in November 1987, and a host of other Henson projects followed. Brenda would eventually joke, "Instead of a community starting a bookstore, our bookstore started a community." The Hensons' goals were twofold: to host cultural events that were clean and sober alternatives to the bar scene and to work politically on child custody, incest, and other issues (Wanda lost custody of her children for being a lesbian, although she later regained that custody).

With the support of festival veterans Therese Edell and Sue Fink, who trained the Hensons in everything from sound production to emcee work, the first Gulf Coast festival met in 1989 at a Girl Scout camp and attracted over 250 festiegoers. Brenda boasted proudly, "Wanda put the whole thing together in 90 days with 33 volunteers—her spirit is catching." With almost no precedent for its Gulf Coast cultural focus, the festival quickly gained a reputation for emphasizing regional delicacies such as red beans and rice, boiled shrimp, and a Mardi Gras night with a parade of women throwing Moon Pies and beads into the audience.

In support of Southern women who, like Wanda, felt overwhelmed by the contrasting messages of Pentecostal and feminist spirituality, the Hensons also began hosting a separate event, Spiritfest, in 1991. By the festival's third year, Wanda and Brenda were still renting from Scout or church camps and anxious about land privacy, yet their commitment and friendly outreach continued to attract top-quality performers. And because the festival met on Easter weekend, the only spring holiday for the state's workers, the Hensons instituted a Passover Seder as well, educating Mississippi women about Jewish culture and inviting all festiegoers to partake in this appropriate ritual of liberation.

The festival came up against its first real ideological backlash when the Methodist camp used in 1991 refused to rent space for 1992, citing concerns about the Jewish Seder ritual. A verbal contract notwithstanding, the camp board denied use of its facility well after the Hensons had begun advertising the 1992 festival. As a result, in 1992 the Gulf Coast Womyn's Festival had to switch to a Boy Scout camp where male caretakers were very much present and male violence at the outside gate created a series of confrontations. Angry, weary, and desperate to continue her search for safe land, Wanda Henson greeted the 1992 festival audience with a moving lesson on anti-Semitism and organizing.

WANDA HENSON

opening night speech at the Gulf Coast Womyn's Festival, 1992

Good evening, and welcome to the fourth annual Gulf Coast Womyn's Festival. This is the second time that we've had to change camp plans. And I come here tonight as an *angry* Southern woman! I am sick and tired of the oppression we live under, and what I've been through this year *nobody* should have to have endured. It was bad enough when the Girl Scouts—the people who taught me integrity, the place where I got my first hickey when I was 9 years old—it was bad enough when they told me that I couldn't have their land back. I'm here tonight to tell you they lied to me. And I'm angry.

I'm angry at the Methodist Church camp that we were at last year because they are liars too. Two days after festival last year, our money was embezzled by the camp director. They asked us to keep it all a secret. A grand jury was held—I was not invited to the proceedings. But the judge ordered a reimbursement of money to this festival because they had severely overcharged us. I'm having to sue them, and I want my money back! I wouldn't set foot on that land if the judge gave it to me. I want land that is sacred woman land, and I want land that comes from our hearts, and I want land soon. Real soon. If we don't get this land back, this Boy Scout camp, next year we'll be at a university, and what that means is that every year we have lost more and more and more.

To backtrack, in January, I went pleading to the Methodist camp board. I wanted their land again. We gave a long, long ordeal—about an hour and a half with them—and all they could do was sit and ask me a multitude of questions about the Passover Seder. They didn't understand why there would be a Seder at our festival, and wanted to know all about it. And sisters, I didn't see anti-Semitism when it was staring me in the face. But we are all *here* today because of it. So if you never thought your lives would be affected by it, as non-Jewish sisters, then you're wrong because here we are. And each year it will be because of oppression, because they will find a hook to land us with, and I'm sick of it.

I hate to have to start the festival off like this again. But I'm telling you, I'm angry, and I'm tired of it. I wrote some little thoughts down about organizing, so

I'd like to share with you what goes on in my head all year long.

Sisters, we must organize ourselves with a new mind-set; then we can build a new meaning for ourselves and transform, bring life to the existence we now live. One thing that has kept us apart as Southern women, forever, is our individualism, and it is not serving us well at all. We must learn collective action with responsibility. Then our society and our reality will change. The power for meaningful change is within our hearts, and we can do by our own hands; no one can do our work for us. We must begin by building trust with each other. And that is what the Gulf Coast Womyn's Festival is all about.

Consciousness-raising groups in the Deep South are a must; we must get them. And we must take the responsibility, each one of us here tonight. It is necessary. We need to face the reality of our issues together; we can no longer sit back and wait for change to happen. Our denial has rendered us powerless and without voice. Our anger is consuming us.

Who will build these spaces? What sisters am I talking to tonight? And who is gonna risk being in that space? I know hundreds of sisters here on the coast who are afraid to be in this space because they don't know what this festival is about. Think about it: The greater risk for us is to choose not to be here. We must come together to understand what our strengths are, then we must share our differences so we can accept each other and each others' truths. My sisters' truths will then become a part of my truths.

That's what the Gulf Coast Womyn's Festival is all about: It's about bringing all of our groups together. And feminism is what this festival is about, for we must become feminists. Feminism is the politics of this space, and I sometimes like to think it's the politics of my morality. Already we have evidence to show what can happen when women embrace feminism in the Deep South. Look at this festival—this is our fourth year! We are here because women embraced feminism. Because we wanted to live in freedom, like our sisters do outside of our existence here.

We are here because we love women, because our lives are valuable, because we can no longer leave our lives to chance. We are here because we know it is up to us to create safe space—a space that is free of oppression, for the empowerment of ourselves.

Sisters, the winds of change are blowing across the Gulf Coast, and tonight I hope you feel the winds of change....

〰〰〰〰〰〰〰〰〰〰〰〰〰〰〰〰〰

By the following year, the festival was forced to meet in one corner of a Louisiana state park, where an early evening noise ordinance and patrolling park rangers placed obvious limitations on festival freedom. Yet even under circumstances that would have seemed intolerable to, say, veterans of the Michigan festival, Gulf Coast festiegoers made clear their appreciation for *any* organized lesbian event. For example, the state park location made it easy for festiegoers to drive into town for snacks and supplies at any time—a convenience most festivals lack—but few Southern women attending left the land, preferring to invent a parked-in feeling like that of the Michigan festival.

I overheard the following conversation: a woman inviting her lover to drive into town for munchies. The invited partner rooted herself more firmly into a splintered picnic bench, gestured to the many lesbians conversing around her, and replied with almost transcendental serenity, "Now, honey, why would I leave heaven to go to the grocery store?" Only Wanda could have expressed more searingly the important role a local festival plays. In a word, *heaven*.

At that same 1993 festival, the producers indeed took their moments at the microphone. Wanda and Brenda Henson, who had closed their women's bookstore and gone back to school for graduate training in education, were now far more experienced speakers and had successfully raised the seed money for a land purchase, winning a $14,000 grant from the Minneapolis-based Lesbian Natural Resources foundation. After 1993, the Gulf Coast Womyn's Festival would no longer be "homeless," and a cheerful Wanda Henson, drawing on her background as a preacher, wowed the festival audience with a revival-style update on Gulf Coast organizing.

WANDA HENSON

Saturday night speech at the Gulf Coast Womyn's Festival, 1993

This past year, all of my friends have begun to say, "Wanda Henson, just hush; we ain't in the mood for no more projects. You just about to kill us!" Well, Gulf Coast women have been busy, busy for five years now—busy doing all the stuff you might not know about: We have a food bank that we make available to old women, primarily, up to the tune of 40,000 pounds last year and 60,000 pounds this year. We also have a second-hand shop that sisters run themselves, making the money to get the food, and we got a Federal Emergency Management Assistance grant for this, and the Catholic Church funded us $1,000 this year.

So, you see, I tell you my work is in Mississippi, but it's just about the same here in Louisiana: Working in this part of the country, we're working with very poor people. For instance, one third of all Mississippi women cannot really read or write. And it means that you work in jobs that are horrible—if you can get work. And so the poor have very few choices in my state. We started our work at the basic level; it's been really tough, but it's growing, and we're happy. We are now ready for the challenge of the land.

We keep talking about this land, this land, this land, and many sisters keep saying, "Well, when are you getting this land?" When are *you* getting the land? You? It's not a *you.* It is o-u-r. It has to be a community effort. Right now, the community has raised around $10,000. There is also $13,950 that has been raised as a grant from Lesbian Natural Resources, sisters up in Minneapolis. We've done fund-raisers in all the different communities: Tallahassee, Memphis, Jackson, Mobile, New Orleans, a couple [three of them] in New Orleans. And there's been individuals who have stood up in meetings and said, "This is important. Take out your checkbooks and write your checks."

It dawned on us that we don't know exactly what women can do for community money. This is because of classism, and I'm eat up with it. I'm eat up with internalized classism. We have not had the chance for what feminism could be, in the Deep South.

Now, sisters that have had privilege, able to get out of this area and go other places, have a lot of wonderful feminist spirit. But for sisters that can't leave, there's just literally hundreds of suicides happening all around. You know what happens when you don't have hope? This work is saving lives, sisters, and we are desperate for this land space.

This year the patriarchy has pushed us out of Mississippi, and it's gonna push us out of Louisiana. What I have learned from my history is that the civil rights movement wouldn't have got off the ground like it did if Ella Baker had not gotten with the folks and organized, and she said that the black farmers owned their land and couldn't be moved off it. They could stand in defiance and defend their land. And I'm screaming now because that's what poor women do when they're upset and they need something. Thanks for being here. It does me a world of good to do this because when I'm at home doing this, everybody's worried about me. They don't like it when I cry, and they say, "Don't get upset." But if we don't get upset, what happens to feminists? What happens to you when you have the passion of love in your heart for your sisters? What happens is internalized stress, and there's a lot of cancer in our communities. So it is with passion that I work.

Actress, comedienne, writer, and oral historian Judith Sloan performing "Sophie," one of her many character portrayals, Gulf Coast 1992.

Toni Armstrong Jr.

What's gonna happen when we get our civil rights but sisters are sitting in a closet? I know what happens when the laws change and the people don't. That's why it's hard for sisters of color to trust coming to this space, to come to Mississippi in the first place! Because of the racism that's in this community. And if you can say that you're working on this shit, then sisters *can* organize across the lines that are separating us.

But you're gonna come home to apathy. You're gonna come home to sisters who look at you like you're a strange woman because you dare to come to a festival, because you went to a Seder and learned, as a Christian, about liberation and freedom.

They're gonna look at you, and they're not gonna understand. And then you're gonna be oppressed by your own people; your own people is gonna look atcha and make fun of everything you say. That is my experience, But what I know is, I can't wait 30 or 40 years until there comes a trickle down in the patriarchy here.

And one by one we will change. And if we don't change, I challenge you to get the black women's anthologies and read what Pat Parker had to say. She said, "Where will you be when they come? And they will come!" I can't remember poetry—I made an F on it in the 11th grade, dropped out of school over poetry. Actually, I was pregnant. Thought I was heterosexual! But I use that poem to piss people off. I was at the March on Washington in 1987 when her booming voice came over the microphone. There were 650,000 people there, but everyone stood still, and we heard what Pat Parker had to say. Pat's not with us any more, but her words live on. Read that poem! Use it to piss off everybody you know! And then, once they get angry and start talking, then maybe you can move them off their apathy and into a space that is for freedom.

If you look around this room, there are some empowered sisters here. We have our first group of lesbian-feminist–identified sisters from the state of Louisiana on the national women's music scene, Sisterbeat; from Mississippi, our first lesbian-identified women's musician on the national scene, Pam Hall; and sisters from Florida beginning in the women's music scene now. This is the *first* wave of feminism coming through here. We can't ride on the third one that some folks tell me about.

But if you think there ain't no way that you can do something, I want to tell you I felt that way too, eight years ago, before I went to *my* first festival, the Southern Women's Music and Comedy Festival, Robin Tyler's festival. After I left there I went up to her and told her, "Sister, you have changed my life forever. Forever!" And I just cried and cried in her arms. I didn't know how to organize, but we did a craft show, made a little money, started from there.

I was in the Pentecostal Church with 30 sisters; you can laugh, but that's the culture I come from, in case you hadn't noticed. I used to preach in children's church. A sister at a festival told me I'd never be effective with my speaking style, and it silenced me—up until last year. I've longed to get up on stage and say the things that are on my heart, but it is my speaking style that I was afraid of, that sisters would not understand. But it's the language that I have! When I was in the Holiness Church, we met every Saturday morning, and we made peanut brittle until we had blisters on our hands. This was serious business because we wanted a church. And I dare say, the South would not be where it is today if we didn't have those damn churches. I got five churches within two blocks of my house, and there are 200 within an eight-mile stretch on the lower coast of Mississippi, and not one of them gave $1 when I sent out a plea for money for people living with AIDS. Not one. Buncha hypocrites! And if I'm stepping on your toes because you claim Christianity, well, I'm just telling you about the people that I've had to deal with.

Anyhow, we made peanut brittle, we had blisters on our hands, every Saturday. And come Monday, when the women at the sawmill got out and the women at the paper mill got out, we stood there. We stood out there in our long dresses and our hair poked up like this and looking the way Holiness sisters look, and we asked, "Can you buy some peanut brittle?" And every time they'd buy it, we'd say, "Bless you, sister." "Thank you, sister." "You're doing the Lord's work." And we raised $65,000 in two years, selling peanut brittle.

So when we needed food for our food bank, I decided to make little bracelets and send them to feminist bookstores. I made $1,500 in a year! I don't have a jewelry pattern; I just got me some leather and string and a couple little beads, put it all together, and said, "This is a bracelet. Help support us. We're working for change in Mississippi." And the sisters heard me. And so now we've been making food available where there was none, where sisters had to choose between medicine and food the last week of the month. That's the level of poverty I'm talking about, see?

Toni Armstrong Jr. from *HOT WIRE* magazine said to me, "Hang on, Wanda; one day the sisters will not remember *not* having the land." That day will come. It will!

So, I want to leave you with a challenge: What will you do? What can you do? I don't know you. I don't know what your circumstances are. Every one of you gonna leave out of here with a different interpretation of what I mean.

Being foremothers—of the groundwater of the deep South feminist movement—we have a challenge. I want to invite you, I want your input—just come on, and we'll process. Or maybe we'll just visit with each other, figure out what to do. I invite lesbians, bisexual women, straight women, celibate women—any woman who is here, who has found it important to be here. Just come on, even if you think you might not know how. Just come on.

❖❖❖❖❖❖❖❖❖❖❖❖❖❖❖❖❖

Wanda skillfully reminded her audiences that for a Southerner, one's place—having a place—is everything. Yet her mission appealed to supporters from all regions. The stage was set for a land purchase, and in summer 1993, Sisterspirit Inc. paid $60,000 for a 120-acre former pig farm in Ovett, Miss. The goals for the land went beyond having secure festival space: The Hensons were dedicated to creating indigenous lesbian culture, building a feminist educational retreat, and maintaining their community work running a food bank and a literacy program. They also sought an economically self-sufficient "landyke" community, using this term to reach interested women through the country lesbian magazine *Maize*. The new land, quickly named Camp Sister Spirit, was situated in a dry county and effectively continued the Gulf Coast festival's policy of clean and sober space. The land site was the most affordable option for the Hensons. Yet it quickly placed the women under scrutiny—not only from their overwhelmingly born-again neighbors but also from Northern festival activists critical of the site. Writing about the ensuing months of controversy, feminist author Phyllis Chesler noted:

> Questions abound. Why should the feminist government-in-exile choose Jones County, the historical heart of the Klan, as its first outpost on earth? Why build a future where you're not wanted? (Tell that to the Israelis and the Palestinians.) "Why not in Mississippi, the poorest state in the nation, and the most oppressed?" Wanda asks. "It's where I was born, where I'm from." Anyway where exactly are radical lesbian feminists wanted? And where is land as cheap (120 acres for $60,000) as in Ovett, Mississippi?[6]

Trouble first began in November, 1993, after a copy of the Camp Sister Spirit newsletter, *The Grapevine*, was removed from the Henson's mailbox and made available to local Christian activists. On November 8, a dog resembling the camp's three-month-old puppy was found shot through the stomach and draped over the mailbox, with a sanitary napkin attached to the side of the mailbox, reading "Die Bitch"—a clearly symbolic statement of hostility to women's interests and an incident that has consistently been denied and misreported by local law officials. Bomb threats, obscene letters and phone calls, roofing tacks placed on the driveway (as well as spikes commonly used during war to disable tires), and incidents where camp volunteers were shot at or driven off the road followed. Despite keeping meticulous records of these threats, the Hensons—and caretakers Cheri Michael and Pam Firth—were up against the biases of local law-enforcement officials, who clearly opposed their presence. On January 3, 1994, Jones County sheriff Maurice Hooks himself passed the collection plate for the "Ovett Community Defense Fund" at one of the many anti-Camp meetings.

As the "outside" press quickly zoomed in on what looked like new civil rights egg on the face of Mississippi, state and local leaders quickly rallied to protest the "gay agenda" in their midst. The Mississippians for Family Values group formed, led by James Hendry, for the sole purpose of driving the Hensons from their land, enlisting the support of Beverly LaHaye's Concerned Women for America organization. U.S. representative Mike Parker (D-Ovett) expressed his opposition. Paul Walley, attorney for the Perry County board of supervisors, quickly began investigating state sodomy and building code laws that might force the Hensons out. Eventually, the local threat grew so intimidating that by February of 1994, Attorney General Janet Reno asked for mediation from the Justice Department and sent a letter of support to the National Gay and Lesbian Task Force.

In spite of Reno's few gestures, however, the spotlight of the U.S. Justice Department did not create change in the situation, and a war of words—in both print and television media—escalated. Ironically, although in many respects the Gulf Coast festival was one of the newer women's festival gatherings in the United States, its producers were the first to become household names across the country—names with faces, as the Hensons described their plight on the *The Oprah Winfrey Show* in

December 1993, on *20/20* in January 1994, and on the *The Jerry Springer Show* and *Larry King Live* (as well as in *Time* and *Newsweek* articles) in February and early spring. Astonished festiegoers turned on their televisions to see, for the first time, festival founders as media spokeswomen. If the Hensons offered a grassroots rather than glamorous media image, they also brought home—in a new era of "lesbian chic"—the message that tolerance and visibility were privileges enjoyed by only a few gay and lesbian communities nationwide. Transformed into educators whose testimony moved millions of viewers, the Hensons were forced to take to the road and support their cause through speaking engagements and fund-raisers.

Throughout calendar year 1994, while festivals and gay and lesbian pride events flourished in other American states, the Hensons traveled through a blizzard of college campuses and conferences while Pam and Cheri (and Wanda's adult son, Arthur) kept the camp secure and built its first structures. A glance through news clippings from the eight-month period between November 1993 and July 1994 shows the degree of hatred:

November 21, 1993:

We're raising kids in this part of the country. I would not want my kids exposed to that type of lifestyle.... The only solution I can think of is to come together as a community, pool our resources and buy back our land. I don't know how many would be willing. It's just a suggestion, in case we run out of legal options.

—James Hendry, *Hattiesburg* [Miss.] *American*

December 5, 1993:

I expect that the value of my property is about half of what it was before. I can't let church groups camp on my land no more because with young'uns and all, I can't be responsible.

—Ray Tucker, *Hattiesburg American*

I don't care what they do over there, and I don't want to know. They'd better just be keeping it to themselves, that's all I have to say.

—J. R. Scarborough, *Hattiesburg American*

We really want to get along with this group. I don't know them personally. If they want to talk about it, we all would like to talk with them and carry on some positive dialogue. I'm in no position to tell the community what to do, but if on a personal level they want to talk, OK.

Just because they are homosexuals doesn't make them bad people. I don't think they are bad people. I just don't approve of their lifestyle. Their lifestyle is their business. I just hope they will keep it in their commune.

Everyone has feelings about this. We are not homophobic around here. We just want a normal lifestyle. We want our children raised in a proper environment. Everybody here minds their own business; we would like to continue that. We aren't going to have an activist organization of any sort come in and try to split the community. They should not expect us to just immediately accept them and understand that lifestyle and accept it. It is against what everyone has been taught.

—James Hendry, *Hattiesburg American*

December 6, 1993:
This group is seeking out and recruiting women. They have a sign outside their camp saying NO MEN ALLOWED. We're not used to that kind of thing around here.

—James Hendry, *The* [Biloxi, Miss.] *Sun Herald*

December 7, 1993:
If they approach any of the women of the community, they ought to run.

—Ricky Cole, *Hattiesburg American*

These people can pick up our little girls and take them to this place and do whatever they want to do.

—Clint Knight, *Hattiesburg American*

We got a report of a dead dog on the mailbox and sanitary napkins in the mailbox and shooting at the mailbox....

—Sheriff Maurice Hooks, *Hattiesburg American*

If we go to court, why can't we force them to open it up to men, and I want to be the first to join them.
—Harvey Shows, *Hattiesburg American*

It will intervene with women and girls in this community when they're vulnerable and in need of help. I believe we're dealing with something against nature.
—Rev. John (Anderson) Allen, First Baptist Church of Richton, *Hattiesburg American*

It's taught against in the scriptures. It's in opposition for what God intended for procreation of the human race.
—Ray Thornton, Baptist Ministry Association of Mississippi, *The Sun Herald*

I have a true concern about the young females in this community. There are a lot of young and impressionable girls who I fear may be recruited into this group.
—Ricky Coles, who earlier said he was afraid that his sister's unborn baby would be asked to become a lesbian, *The Sun Herald*

December 10, 1993:
Jones County might be in danger if more lesbian-type people settle here. Young people may be harmed by the camp if women teach them homosexual doctrine or ways of life.
—Rev. Terry Lee, Good Hope Baptist Church, *The Washington Blade*

December 11, 1993:
We only heard about their taking care of children and feeding the hungry after the story got national headlines. They really ought to call it what it is, a homosexual retreat. Since they don't work, the only way for them to get money is from people sympathetic to their cause. If they go on national television and say they are being persecuted, then they will probably get a lot of donations. I haven't found anything yet that would force them to leave. I don't have any quick, easy solutions.
—Paul Walley, *Hattiesburg American*

December 12, 1993:

We don't want to see Ovett turned into Lesbianville, U.S.A. They're going to be having lesbians in from all over the country. They're going to be loud and proud in our stores, and we're just terrified.... Let's call it what it is, a lesbian camp. I don't see any common ground. What can we say but we don't want you here and we want you to leave. It's a Mexican standoff.

—Paul Walley, *The Washington Post*

This ain't something we're used to. Afraid they going to start dragging neighbors' young'uns over and training them up to do lesbian things.... Women without no use for men. Trouble far as I can see.

—Ray Tucker, *Atlanta Constitution*

December 20, 1993:

They are trying to bring their way of life on us. They want to influence and change our society. These people want to change our whole way of life and are a threat to the community.

—Paul Walley, *Hattiesburg American*

December 17–23, 1993:

The focus of their existence is something I consider an abomination to nature.

—Paul Walley, *Philadelphia Gay News*

December 18, 1993:

All along we have been telling everyone what the impact of this organization will be on the community, and the local media have been portraying it as a property issue, that these ladies just want to be left alone. On the *Oprah* show, these people fully adopted the gay, lesbian, and bisexual platform. We were so aghast.

—Paul Walley, *The Sun Herald*

December 20, 1993:

A state representative, John Ellzy, volunteered to research sodomy and cohabita-

tion laws—even building codes—to find a basis for the camp's removal.
—*Newsweek*

There are a lot of nervous women out there with trigger fingers.
—Sheriff Maurice Hooks, *Newsweek*

I am a young mother with three small children—I am worried about the influence these ladies will have on our children. We don't want our small community to be known as a lesbian community. We don't want them here.
—Angela Crocker, *The* [London] *Guardian*

If it's agin God and the Bible, then I'm agin it too. If the Bible were for it, I'd be for it. So I'm agin it.
—Clayton Peters, *The Guardian*

They don't cause me any problems. I really ain't paid too much attention to it, but everybody's in an uproar. I mind my own business. I don't want no trouble. I want everyone to live peaceful. That's the way I see it.
—Eugene Creel, *The Guardian*

As long as they ain't bothering me, I ain't gonna bother them. As long as they stay on their side, I'm sure goin' to stay on my side. Everybody else wants to run them out. I don't see why.
—Ebbie Fisher, *The Guardian*

I don't know if they are as genuinely afraid for their lives as they say they are, but the fact they are afraid doesn't mean there is a real threat. You can be afraid of the dark, but that doesn't mean there's anything in the dark.
—Rev. John Allen, *The Guardian*

This must be a slow news year; but the story isn't the women, it's the town. We've been here hundreds of years, and they moved on top of us. They are trying to colonize our area, attempting to change.

—Paul Walley, *The Guardian*

I'm not afraid for the community as much as I'm afraid for our children that's going to be growing up here and having this filth around them.

—Myron Holifield, *The Guardian*

December 22, 1993:

[U.S. representative] Parker said he "agrees totally" with the position taken by church leaders and citizens in Ovett who say they do not approve of the homosexual lifestyle or the agenda of the homosexual rights movement. "That would tickle them [Camp Sister Spirit] to death, for something to occur. I'm not saying they want someone hurt, but they would want something to force federal marshals to be brought in, and that is something that none of us from Jones County would ever want to see."

—Mike Parker, *Laurel* [Miss.] *Leader-Call*

It hurt me to watch [the televised debate on *The Oprah Winfrey Show*]. It made me sick. Prior to this show, I was not involved. Now, I will join with people of this area. The people of this community have got to take a stand for the moral issues involved. I didn't know they were that radical. I thought the residents of Ovett were getting upset for nothing. After watching the show, I see that the residents had a legitimate argument.

—Ronnie Turner, *Hattiesburg American*

This is the most degrading thing that has ever happened to our community. The show displayed what kind of people they are, and in my book that's not very much.

—Maurine Pool, *Hattiesburg American*

I think the people in Jones County need to be more concerned about our unsolved murders. The people need to be concerned about more serious matters, life and death matters. They need to leave these people alone.

—Former constable Hank Landrum, *Hattiesburg American*

December 30, 1993:
They claim they're going to feed the hungry and take care of the homeless. They're out at a very rural setting, and there are no homeless or hungry people out there.
—Paul Walley, *The Baptist Record*

John Allen explained to host Oprah Winfrey that he opposes the women's activities because homosexuality is condemned by the Bible, and he therefore fears for the souls of vulnerable Ovett residents and of the lesbians in the camp.
—*The Baptist Record*

January, 1994:
When I heard that rednecks were attacking Camp Sister Spirit, I was disappointed because I think they should be attacked by all kinds of necks: black necks, white necks.
—Rev. Ken Fairly, *The* [Jackson, Miss.] *Clarion-Ledger*

Attorney Paul Walley, who has served as the attorney for the group seeking to oust the Hensons, reported on the lack of progress in finding a state or county law that could be used to force the women from their property.
—*TWISL Magazine*

January 2, 1994:
Ninety-nine percent of the people in this community are just good, law-abiding, good Christian people. All we're doing is standing up for our moral convictions. We're standing up for what is right.
—Tabitha Hendry, *The* [New Orleans] *Times-Picayune*

The group rejects the biblical morality that is the basis for life in the area. They are planning a 180-bed dorm. They're going to bring in like-minded individuals from all over the South. It's going to be a homosexual business going on out there.... We're afraid that this area of southeast Mississippi will become the center of homosexual activity for the southeastern United States. We're Christians, and we're gentlemen and ladies, and we're concerned that our community standards will be lost.

—Paul Walley, *The Times-Picayune*

We have no earthly idea what's going on in there. As a Christian, I'm opposed to their lifestyle, but that's their choice; but I don't want that lifestyle forced on me.

—Margaret Dennis Sapic, *The Times-Picayune*

January 4, 1994:

We're being invaded by activists with a radical agenda. The invasion is not coming from us. It's coming from them. We're not dealing with people that are different and want to live their lives privately. We are dealing with people who are different and want to change our community.

—John Allen, *Associated Press*

I'm the mother of four, and you can tell that I've got one on the way. I'm concerned about the teachings they are trying to promote that I find offensive and that are against the teachings of the Bible.

—Cathy Stevens, *Associated Press*

Mississippi law allows people to protect the value of their property as well as the character of their neighborhood from adjoining property owners. We're in an uproar because if their plans are allowed to go through, Ovett will become the hub of lesbian activity for the region. It is my belief they are a well-funded, organized part of the national gay and lesbian movement. People are also worried that the Hensons would require local schools to teach homosexuality as an acceptable lifestyle.

—Paul Walley, *The Clarion-Ledger*

January 5, 1994:

It's not the fact that the Hensons are different. It's the fact that the Hensons have stated that they have an agenda, and they plan to make our lives different.

—John Allen, *Hattiesburg American*

January 7, 1994:

This week, a group put up a billboard off the main highway in Laurel, Miss., that reads, "The Spirit of america is going strong, any other Spirit just don't belong," according to Gina Headrich. Headrich said all she knows about the group is that it is called the Revolutionary Force of America and that it has members from several states, including Mississippi, Florida, Alabama, and Missouri. Headrich said that the members of the group are "sick and tired of the minority telling the majority what to do."

—*The Washington Blade*

January 9, 1994:

Those people are the ones that are causing the problems. There ain't nobody threatening those people. Those people don't need but one thing. They need the Lord, Jesus Christ, in their lives. That's the only thing that will stop it.

—Clint Knight, *Hattiesburg American*

January 11, 1994:

There's been a lot of rhetoric running around, but the controversy with the Hensons centers on their radical agenda and indications that they intend to have an impact on the community.

—John Allen, *USM Student Printz*

If legal action fails, they will burn them out. They will barbecue them over in these woods. There's never been anything resolved by fighting over it, but if you don't play their tune, they don't want you here.

—R.A. McLain, *USM Student Printz*

February 12, 1994:

They want laws saying that homosexual teachers are acceptable in schools.

They want to make sex with children legal, they want homosexual couples to have equal rights. We don't need their help here. They want to totally do away with our style of life.

—Paul Walley, *World*

Paul Jones, executive director of the Christian Action Council for the Mississippi Baptist Convention, said the local Christians' best route in the future will be a legal one: "I think that the retreat center must meet the same legal statutory requirements that anybody else does—health, fire, water codes," he told *World.* Jones also said, "I think we can say to some business owners, 'You don't have to sell anything to anybody.'"

—*World*

February 19, 1994:
How can someone mediate unless they are fair and unbiased? Our President has given his unblemished support of the gay and lesbian movement, and that tells us where the administration stands on this. Why should we think we'll get a fair shake?

—James Hendry, *Hattiesburg American*

We don't know their background, their sexual orientation, we don't know anything about them. All we know is they are sent from the federal government—a liberal administration that openly supports homosexuals.

—James Hendry, *Laurel Leader-Call*

All the murders and rapes and kidnappings all over the nation and [Attorney General Janet Reno is] sending people to investigate a letter. It shows the administration is out of focus and out of touch with reality.

—Paul Walley, *Hattiesburg American*

I told my deputies anytime they are in the area to swing by the camp and be seen.

—Maurice Hooks, *Hattiesburg American*

February 21, 1994:

They're making us look like nuts and making themselves look like saints.... If the mediators plan to stay until they strike a compromise, they'd better bring a big suitcase.

—James Holliman, *USA Today*

None of us here are bigots. We're acting on what we know is morally right. They came here trying to destroy our community and create lesbians.

—James Hendry, *USA Today*

They said from the start they're loud and they're proud and they want to bring changes. Well, we don't see the kind of changes they want as positive.

—John Allen, *The New York Times*

If they're running a business where they're promoting lesbianism and running a 180-bed dormitory, that's the kind of business we don't want, just like we wouldn't like it if it was a right-wing extremist, neo-Nazi training camp or a house of prostitution or a strip joint.

—James Hendry, *The New York Times*

February 23, 1994:

In my view, these women are a threat to the community. This is not about people being homosexual per se. This is about a group of people who have endorsed the radical agenda of [the National Gay and Lesbian Task Force]. They have told us, "We are here to educate you." They want lesbian role models in schools. Their most odious endorsement is to reduce the age of consent for young people. These people are radicals who have come to change the community.

—John Allen, *The Boston Globe*

The Hensons espouse an aberrant lifestyle that is opposed to God's plan as well as Mississippi's sodomy laws. We're not trying to drive them off the land, although I'd love for them to pack up and leave. We just want to stop the construction of a 180-bed retreat they've talked about.

—Paul Walley, *The Boston Globe*

February 24, 1994:

Knowing what I know, I really don't think we'll come to an agreement. We are diametrically opposed in our beliefs, and quite honestly, I don't think the Hensons are looking for a peaceful resolution. I think they're looking for additional media attention.

—James Hendry, *The Sun Herald*

February 25, 1994:

—We don't mind Wanda and Brenda living in Ovett. We don't want a camp full of lesbians. If it were just them, it would not hurt the community. [Lesbianism] is not what Ovett is all about. They're having a 180-bed retreat. And if I know anything about what lesbians do, it takes at least 360 to fill 180 beds.

—Tabitha Hendry, *The Washington Blade*

February 1994:

It's a known fact that all your violent crimes comes from homosexuals.

—Deputy sheriff Myron Holifield, *Mississippi Press*

March 1994:

The area is a conservative religious community that has a standard based on biblical morality. Residents at Camp Sister Spirit reject that standard and have a radical agenda that would seek to change our way of life. I don't know where there is room to compromise. Our position has no compromise.

—Paul Walley, *San Jose* [Calif.] *Mercury News*

March 6, 1994:

It chaps me down to the core, what those women are doing out there. They don't have jobs, all they do is sit out there and seek out news media like you. They are professional victims in search of support and contributions. This camp is not a traditional family unit.

—James Hendry, *Miami Herald*

It's happening all over the country, homosexuals pushing for civil rights status.... We're going to push back.

—James Hendry, *Hattiesburg American*

March 10, 1994:

Somebody at the store told me that when the Hensons got there, they bought up every bit of ammunition in the store. They come here looking for trouble, and they are going to get it. We don't want lesbians and queers coming from all over the nation to Ovett.

—Vonda Hendry, *San Francisco Bay Times*

"If bigotry and intolerance means not accepting homosexuality as a moral, family lifestyle, then I'm the biggest bigot, I'm the most intolerant person you've ever met." [James] Hendry has already stated that he wouldn't be opposed to an equally large and noisy Bible camp. No, it's not the traffic; it's the lesbians.

—*San Francisco Bay Times*

March 23, 1994:

This community cannot define itself as white or male or female. Or Baptist even. We acknowledge those necessary and right distinctions. But sexual preference is not a civil right.

—John Allen, *Baltimore Sun*

March 25, 1994:

I'm going to go out and buy a gun for me and my wife. We are going to keep loaded shotguns in our cars.

—James Hendry, *Hattiesburg American*

April 4, 1994:

This ain't Selma, Ala., and Brenda Henson ain't Martin Luther King. We're just a small town with small town values.

—James Hendry, *USA Today*

May 15, 1994:

Our goal is to try to keep the lesbians from building their retreat. They want 180 there. We want to keep it to two, her and her mate. I don't want my kids to see them kissing and hugging. It's repulsive. I guess it's a fear of where it will stop. We don't want to be a town overcome by lesbians and gays.

—Darvell Hendry, father of James Hendry, *Mobile* [Ala.] *Register*

July 2, 1994:

They're not going to come hear one side of it. I'm going to tell Jones County's side, the citizens' side, law enforcement's side.

—Sheriff Maurice Hooks, on the congressional hearings, *Hattiesburg American*

July 7, 1994:

I am going to follow the law of the land. There is no anarchy in Ovett.

—James Hendry, *Laurel Leader-Call*

[Paul] Walley questioned the motives of the camp organizers, whom he said do not have jobs but travel the country raising funds from homosexual groups.

—*Laurel Leader-Call*

We are trying to seek a peaceful, legal resolution to this problem. This is not a bigoted witch-hunt.

—James Hendry, *Associated Press*

July 31, 1994:

"Anybody could tell they were lesbians, but what the hell? It doesn't matter what creed or nationality you are. You can be a good neighbor, or you can be a fanatic about things." Ray Tucker has lived on his farm for 46 years. The land has been in the Tucker family 100 years. He won't even consider selling the property, but he doesn't want his grandchildren to raise families next to a lesbian camp either. He's ready to hang up farming.

—*The Sun Herald*

[The organization has] sought guidance from other conservative groups and adapted the name Mississippi for Family Values from Colorado for Family Values, which drafted that state's controversial constitutional amendment banning gay rights laws.

—*The Sun Herald*

They are promoting homosexuality through a business with activist tactics. It's basically going to turn into a training ground for militant homosexual activists.

—James Hendry, *The Sun Herald*

Frightened by the publicity of gunshots and other threats from the Ovett community, most performers and festiegoers stayed away from the spring 1994 Gulf Coast gathering; a loyal group of some 53 women instead held a quiet celebration of tenacity and commitment, and Sonya Rutstein of the band Disappear Fear was the sole guest artist. Brenda Henson recalls that "ten minutes before that first night stage concert, upon learning that only one performer had shown up, sisters in the audience rallied together and we had a Make Your Own Festival stage. Women came forward with music, poetry, Goddess dancing, and Picard the potbellied pig assisted his mom Allison [an attorney!] in doing tricks."

In the following year, however, Camp Sister Spirit took a turn for the better. Dozens of college-age feminists who had learned of the Hensons' struggle came to Camp Sister Spirit as volunteers, assisting in the construction of several buildings as well as a security fence. As local residents gradually grew more accustomed to the retreat center, threatening incidents lessened; instead, the women living on the land received thousands of supportive letters from all over the world (where the Associated Press had picked up the story). Donations helped ready the land for the 1995 festival. I served as both emcee and performer at that festival, and the usual Seder took place without incident.

It is both startling and disappointing to note that a vocal minority of lesbian critics have denounced Camp Sister Spirit. Two women wrote in the January/February 1995 issue of *Lesbian Connection*, "We have finally had enough of the glorification of the very dangerous situation in Mississippi. The Hensons' own personal and financial choices and miscalculations in no way warrant the Lesbian community's unquestioned allegiance or the elevation of the Hensons to the status of cultural hero-

Three generations of Henson family women (clockwise from left): Wanda; Brenda; Brenda's daughter, Andrea Gibbs; Brenda's mother, "Mamma"; and Wanda's daughter, Terri Elliott.

Toni Armstrong Jr.

ines." More disturbing still are those women in the festival community who have stated that the Hensons are martyrs seeking publicity or are bad for other lesbian businesses or should simply get out. Despite Phyllis Chesler's fall 1994 article in *On the Issues*, which concluded with the important point that *no* region is safe for women, some educated feminists continue to insist that the Hensons have deliberately placed Mississippi women at risk.

Mississippi women know better. Pam Hall, a dynamic festival performer from Jackson, Miss., and one of the very few women of color to perform at the Gulf Coast festival for several years, has often pointed out that women in her home state need alternatives to the alcoholism and violence of the bar scene. Other women with barely the gas money to drive through Camp Sister Spirit's gates contributed moving statements to the camp journal after a first visit: "I thought I was the only one." "I am the only lesbian in my town." "I thought I was a sinner." "I was so scared, I turned back three times, but now I am free."

"If we're gonna take a movement from the head to the heart it's got to be through music," Wanda told me at a Halloween bonfire on the land in 1994. "We're here to teach nonoppressive life ways. There's been enough social change that Congress *could* be compelled to enact social justice legislation protecting us all…but by fleeing to gay ghettoes, removing ourselves from our own homelands, we make it easier for the government and the right wing. They say we're too hostile; I say middle-class people are too silent."

Welcoming the festival audience to the reconverted barn stage on Easter-Passover weekend of 1995, Wanda Henson stood at the microphone a changed woman, a two-way transmitter on her belt, her voice steady—the producer who was once too shy to speak sang to us.

WANDA HENSON

Saturday night speech at the Gulf Coast Womyn's Festival, 1995

Well, there's been many women before us that have decided that if they could not have their freedom, they would rather be dead. But when you get on that line, sisters, it's a real hard line to walk. And the silence of your friends is hard to take. But I'm not here to bring you down. I'm here to explain to you what has kept us going.

What has kept us going for the past year and a half has been the new sisters that have come, the feminists that I didn't even know about. I did not know about the young feminist movement that is in this nation. It's not in the lesbian press, it's not in the gay press, I'm not seeing it in the mainstream press—Mississippi's got a lot of censorship! But the sisters have come to this land, and I'll give you a sense of what we've been up to. Not only have we protected this land and made safety for each other, but this barn, in the beginning of March, still had pig sties in it. I don't know if you've ever tried to bang some of these oak boards apart, but it takes a lot of strength. And two of the three caretakers on this land live with disabilities: me and Brenda. The first person who moved in on this land was Cheri Michael. The media moved in on a sound bite that sounded funny to them, "The Hensons," but Cheri was the first dyke to be here full time. Brenda and I were here four days a week; we were going to school. I think everybody knows that we've been forced to drop out of school; we're very disappointed—we're just eight courses away from dissertation, and for women who didn't get a chance early in life to go to school, that's a real big disappointment to us. But the movement work that we're doing now is more important, and there's not enough hours in the day to do what we have to do.

Getting ready for this event was incredible. We've been trying to get ourselves out of a 16-foot travel trailer that Brenda and I and our son, Arthur, lived in for a year. We got here in March, and that's when the sisters came down from the universities. They've now left the land and gone back home to organize. We are charging them with, "You have to organize in your own community," and I'm telling every one of you that, here, now. Because if you want this event to grow or our work to continue, you have to do the organizing. We can't go into your community and have access to your friends—unless you invite us to come there and speak, and even then we're only there for hours. Movement is the one by one, the people deciding to act.

And these sisters at different universities where we spoke this last year decided to come and be on the land here for their spring break. And *my, my,* I couldn't believe it! The women from Smith College learned how to use power tools, and everybody here learned about gay and lesbian rights that we do not have. And we also talked about the human rights that have been violated against Camp Sister Spirit—17 out of the 30!

We don't have civil rights. This is one thing we have learned, and we're having a hard time trying to file a lawsuit, getting the right attorneys, and figuring out what our strategy's gonna be against this Mississippi for Family Values group. But we also want to press forward for civil rights, and the way to do it is to grow and for people to come to this land and to make a stand and for us not to be pushed off of this land. *We have to be here.* And we can only be here as long as we are financially empowered to be here.

Wanda, Brenda, Cheri, Kathy, and Pam—our fifth caretaker, now in California doing personal healing because it's been tremendously hard for us, I can't even begin to tell you—anyway, folks want to know about us. "God, they really looking good," "They got nice new clothes" is the kind of shit I've heard. Well, we got a $100 stipend the last three months of the year, and we're getting $300 a month for January, February, and March. In April there's no money. And we have worked our asses off; our personal needs have gone by the wayside for a long time now. I want y'all to go back into your communities and do what you can to organize and raise money.

Because it is important that we are here. Women come up to us on the street, look up at us, and say, "Please, you're doing it for women. You're doing it for all of us, honey, it's nothing about you being different. It's about you being a woman." Begging us; begging us. Folks that don't live here, you might not know the oppression that Southern dykes have lived under for a long time. But we have longed to be free, like the communities I see around the country. It's why we don't mind getting up at 6 o'clock in the morning, why Cheri don't mind being up here wiring this barn until midnight every night. She worked ten days leading up to festival, just getting this done. We had to have concrete, had to have a ramp; it's not completely wheelchair accessible, but I hope it has served everybody's needs for this event. Cheri can do anything!

We also put the pad into the front gate. Y'all may have noticed there's a big hunk of concrete there. Because Miss Robin Tyler of the West Coast Music and Comedy Festival made available $10,012 by passing the hat, and we have a fancy, fancy gate that's going in there, 16-foot high! And if they chase my wife again, she will have her radio with her, and she will be able to open that gate from half a mile away and come in for safety because there's always safety here. They chased her home June 1; I've never been so angry in my life. But now we have the means to get in here real quick if we need to.

We've got a mile and a half of fence up, and it's working because this hunting season, they've only been on the property three times. And we know the difference between intimidation and just regular what they do around here. So, the boys ain't messed with us this year. Our security team is doing a mighty fine job.

It's so empowering to be in this kind of space. If you don't have it, if you only get it for two or three days and then gotta go back to the patriarchy, this is so important. If it wasn't as important to us as it is, I would have been gone a long time ago. But seven years ago I walked onto a stage, and I could barely talk into a damned mike, and I begged, "I want to be a producer. This is what we're trying to do." I made circles with my arms; I couldn't explain women's spirituality. But I wanted something to happen. And I knew if we made this space available, women would make it happen. And one of these days those cars are gonna be lined up to Hattiesburg. Nobody's gonna stop the flow of justice.

〰〰〰〰〰〰〰〰〰〰〰〰〰〰〰

Wanda concluded her speech by singing "Which Side Are You On?" And since that triumphant moment, the festival has continued yearly, without incident. Artists and audience are asked to sign a liability release form (see the sample included in this chapter), but no harm has come to those of us committed to attending this festival. The buildings and performances grow every year. Performer Sandy Rapp recently recorded "The Ballad of Camp Sister Spirit," and several books on the festival are in the works. Judith Sloan, a longtime Gulf Coast festival comedian, performed off-Broadway in "A Tattle Tale," her one-woman show based on the political justice work of Brenda Henson's daughter, Andi Gibbs.

This small festival has awakened countless Americans to the need for change. Ironically, it's the Northampton Lesbian Festival which is no longer held.

THE BALLAD OF CAMP SISTER SPIRIT
© 1996 by Sandy Rapp

I went down to Ovett, Mississippi.
I flew all day then drove an ol' two-lane.
Red tin roofs and junk yards lined the dusty way,
And an ancient mill town spoke of better days.
The armadillos fled along the roadside
And a buzzard had a rattler in its claws.
Till violet tree trunks told us we were not in Kansas now,
And the barbed wire told us nor were we in Oz.
A purple gate arose to let us enter,
But only when security was cleared.

Later down the drive a dance of ribbons came alive;
Camp Sister Spirit magically appeared.
And Brenda sat amidst the flags and flyers,
And Wanda waved hello from on the run.
And I had met the Hensons who had made a dream come true;
They had built the sister camp and we had come.

CHORUS:
But did you hear Mississippi's still a burnin'
Up in flames, the sacred spaces all around.
And though you know Sister Spirit ain't a turnin',
They been shootin' at the old camp ground.

Buchanan wrote a scathing little column
Implying they were shooting at themselves
To boost attendance at the campground;
He's unaware that shellfire keeps attendance down.
Meanwhile a truck ran Brenda off the highway
And a black/white couple caught some special fire.
An automatic discharged 87 rounds one day;
And the Caretaker got shot at from a car.

REPEAT CHORUS
Well, the Hensons won a lawsuit filed against 'em,
For turning Mississippi on its ass.
And the judge is spelling womyn with a "y" now,
And the farmworkers salute them when they pass.
And a hundred people come each month to campground
For a pantry that the campfolk have on hand.
And I am told that there are those who've learned to love out loud
This living lesbiana in their land.

FINAL CHORUS:
So when you hear Mississippi's still a burnin'
Up in flames, the sacred spaces all around
Remember every Sister Spirit from the journey,
And the rainbow flyin' high and shinin' through
For that is Mississippi too.

1. Amy Horowitz, "Some Factors in the Equation," in *We Who Believe in Freedom* by Bernice Johnson Reagon and Sweet Honey in the Rock (Doubleday, 1993), p. 192.

2. Bernice Johnson Reagon, "Let Your Light Shine: Historical Notes;" ibid., p. 32.

3. Lesbian separatists in town did not take kindly to the festival's policy of admitting men and refused to support the festival. This conflict and frustration over male dominance in Northampton's annual Gay Pride event led some separatists to establish the group and newsletter *Lesbians For Lesbians*.

4. Laurie Goodstein, "Mississippi Mother to Sue Over School Prayer," *Washington Post*, December 20, 1994, p. A8.

5. Wanda Henson, "The Personal Is Political in the Deep South," interviewed by Toni Armstrong Jr. in *HOT WIRE*, January 1993, pp. 41-42.

6. Phyllis Chesler, "Sister, Fear Has No Place Here." In *On The Issues*, Fall 1994, p. 29.

CHAPTER NINE

There's a Nursing Baby in the Mosh Pit:
Generational Shift and Change

The left, or radical view, that I grew up with in the '60s is gone…gone from the everyday news, and views, but still very strong with women's groups. Since women are the new left, I can understand why everyone says the left is dead.
—Roseanne, from her autobiography *My Life As a Woman*

I'm so glad there were a few of us out on the front lines getting our faces smashed in trying to get everything to be better for you guys. I couldn't believe it when I turned on the TV last night and saw Kate Clinton.
—Ferron, at the Northampton Lesbian Festival, 1993

The oldest festivals have passed the generational watermark of 20 years, and preparations for the big 25th year celebrations are well under way. Young women who were not alive when the first National and Michigan festivals convened now serve as staff and coordinators, heirs to policy and outlook that must seem like ancient history through their eyes. Where foremothers and daughters meet in their commitment to this culture is a wry dance of conflict, mutual ageism, and recognition of the need to honor herstory while welcoming new trends. These last two chapters explore the generational shift and its meaning for the future.

In the summer of 1994, a series of dramatic events swept through the festival community. The National Women's Music Festival in Bloomington, Ind.—the oldest and longest-running U.S. festival—celebrated its 20th anniversary with a gala banquet and the live-performance recording of composer Kay Gardner's "Ouroboros" concert. Soon afterwards, hundreds of thousands of gay and lesbian activists descended upon New York City to commemorate the 25th anniversary of the 1969 Stonewall Inn uprising, and as part of this occasion, Alix Dobkin, Kay Gardner, Nurudafina Pili Abena, and Phranc performed a women-only concert at Carnegie Hall (celebrating 20 years since the release of Alix's groundbreaking *Lavender Jane Loves Women* album). The Dyke March surged down Fifth Avenue, with the Lesbian Avengers and other women linking arms to stop traffic from side streets; later, as the Avengers ate fire in Washington Square Park, Alix tenderly scrawled "Lavender Jane" on the pavement with graffiti chalk. Women's music and the lesbian movements behind it—so seldom acknowledged in public celebrations of gay American achievements—came of age in these moments.[1]

And yet elsewhere in the United States, much of festival culture appeared to be at risk. The Gulf Coast Womyn's Festival was struggling for its life in the face of community hatred. Lin Daniels was forced to shut down her East Coast Lesbian Festival due to low ticket sales and personal financial losses. Tam Martin stopped producing the Pacific Northwest Jamboree after five successful years. NEWMR, the Southern Women's Music Festival, and Sisterfire—once East Coast festival strongholds—disappeared as regularly held events (though NEWMR has since reappeared).

Furthermore, the united energy of younger and older lesbian activists that characterized much of summer 1994 underwent an unexpected test at the Michigan Womyn's Music Festival in August when the band Tribe 8 performed. The 19th Michigan festival was also Boo Price's last year as coproducer, an important farewell and leadership shift nearly forgotten during the many days of processing that followed Tribe 8's controversial performance on the night stage. The introduction of a mosh pit at the foot of the Michigan stage and the visibility of some S/M leatherwomen as Tribe 8 fans sparked a tense and yet ultimately revealing dialogue about changing music tastes and lesbian styles. The symbolic sight of Alix Dobkin stage diving into the mosh pit in solidarity with Tribe 8 was seen as a timely gesture by many festiegoers and as an end to "the olden days" of lesbian feminism by others.

In the midst of this chaotic summer of anniversaries and change, Toni Armstrong Jr. quietly released the final issue of *HOT WIRE*, concluding ten years as its editor and almost two decades of artistic and cultural journalism in service to the festival community. No other journal rose up to take *HOT WIRE's* place, and a significant vacuum developed in festival coverage and women's music journalism. The potential generation gap between festival foremothers in their 40s and 50s and the pierced and tattooed young feminists in their teens and 20s, plus the replacement of many grassroots publications with online computer discussion, altered forevermore the working definition of lesbian culture.

How would festival life be affected by all these trends?

An era had come to an end, and yet many of its own founders were still compulsively active as cultural agents. Toni Armstrong Jr. began to speak realistically about "the graying of the culture," choosing to mentor younger woman-identi-

Felice Shays, interpreter for the Deaf, at the 1997 Michigan Womyn's Music Festival.

tified performers and at-risk lesbian students. At the same time, Margie Adam was in the midst of an astounding comeback after a seven-year hiatus from performing, often sharing the stage with the younger woman-identified artist Susan Herrick and speaking urgently to the point that "there is no expiration date on feminism." Both Toni and Margie were honored guests at the 20th anniversary banquet of the National Women's Music Festival in 1994. Their speeches on that occasion are well worth reexamining here.

The 20th Anniversary of the National Women's Music Festival ⩘⩘

Toni Jr. was recognized and honored at the National festival banquet for her years of unpaid cultural labor through the women's music and culture periodicals *Paid My Dues*, *Women's Music Plus*, and *HOT WIRE*. After a music-accompanied slide show featuring selected photographs of women's music artists and activists, Toni made the following speech:

> I spent the last 20 years of my life devoted to this culture. I lived it, breathed it, spent more on women's culture some months than I paid in rent. Gone from being a young, enthusiastic, brown-haired gal to a middle-aged, gray-haired enthusiastic gal, and it really means a lot to be here.
>
> One of the things I am most struck by at this particular time in our history is that an era as we know it is coming to an end. Not in a bad way, but eras come, and they hit their peak, and then they change and another era comes. And within our 20-year era, we've had many waves of women's music: Meg, Lucie Blue. The important thing is, mostly in someone's lifetime they never ever get the opportunity to actually be part of an era, to be there at the right time and the right place with the right people. And make a difference. And you know, no matter what else happens, all of us can feel so proud that we are the generation that took a stand for feminism. We are the generation that brought lesbianism to the mainstream. No matter what happens, no one can ever take that away from any of us. That just makes me so proud and so happy.
>
> I think it's important to have herstorical perspective. If you're familiar with my work with *HOT WIRE*, and the *Women's Music Plus Directory*, that's always been my focus. We need to take the big picture. How many people remember the song "Sister Suffragettes" from *Mary Poppins*? One of the lines goes, "Our daughters' daugh-

ters will adore us, and they'll sing in grateful chorus, 'Well done, sister suffragettes!'" And we are the daughters' daughters. And 100 years from now, our daughters' daughters and their daughters will be grown and look back at lesbian feminists of the '70s, the '80s, and the '90s. And they're going to say, "Good job." How great it is to be a part of a truly *happening thing*.

Margie Adam, the keynote speaker for the banquet, then came to the stage. Her speech that night was considered so important that it was later reprinted and distributed in the Association for Women in Music and Culture newsletter, AWMAC being the closest existing organization to a festival-industry business guild.

MARGIE ADAM

It's really weird for me to be standing up and speaking to you instead of sitting down at a piano. This is my first stand-up speech—ever. And of course it's fitting that I would be giving the speech in front of you, my beloved community.

For the last 20 years, I've been asked, "What is women's music? Who makes it? And who is it for?" I thought I'd give you my opinion because there are as many opinions as there are women who make women's music. What I think women's music is is music that affirms and empowers women. Period. End. Who do I think makes women's music? Women. Seems like it should be simple.

And who is it for? Anyone. But especially women. And *any* pro-feminist man. So when I speak, you should know that this is my context. I don't care if your answers are different. This is 1994, and there's a lot of room today for all of us and our definitions.

I was reeled in by this amazing movement and network, by the passion and audacity and activism of a group of women, a gang of women who were riveted on the idea of changing the world through music. I'm here tonight because I still believe, 20 years later, in the power of women writing, singing, playing, producing, distributing, and broadcasting strong woman-centered and inclusive, life-affirming music and culture to save this world. And having had the pleasure of spending the last two days in meetings of the annual conference of AWMAC—the Association for Women in Music and Culture—having had the opportunity to talk to women about our industry and our movement, I am completely turned-on and inspired by the passion and audacity and activism of women who are in this place now, in 1994, with women's music. Completely turned-on!

But I also want to mention the names of some of the women who laid the very early groundwork for this movement. Many of these women don't get mentioned anymore when we talk about the history of women's music. But because I have this microphone, I want to be sure these names are said in a public venue. These are the

Margie Adam performing at the 1995 National Women's Music Festival in Bloomington, Ill.

Toni Armstrong Jr.

women who set the standards, who built the stage on which I stand, one plank at a time, with their lives and dreams and their reputations on the line. These are the women who created the impossible out of a complete void, in the earliest days, performers from those early years. These women—in the earliest days, I leaned on them.

First on my list is the woman who was responsible for the very first National Women's Music Festival, Kristin Lems. Kay Gardner, Ginni Clemmens, Willie Tyson, Bebe K'Roche, Casse Culver, the New Harmony Sisterhood, Vicki Randle, Maxine Feldman, Cris Williamson, Alix Dobkin, Meg Christian, Woody Simmons, Robin Flower, Linda Shear and the Family of Women, Jennifer and Susan Abod, the New Haven and Chicago Women's Liberation rock bands. I also want to name producers, managers, agents, and festival organizers who pulled us together in the earliest days: Mary Spottswood, "Spotts," who was the very first serious manager of women's music—she managed Casse Culver and scared the *shit* out of everyone else. Boo Price, who was the very first serious producer; Ginny Berson, who was a major organizing force behind Olivia Records; Amy Horowitz, the first major booking agent, who created Roadwork; Joan Nixon—she got me up at 7 in the morning on her way out of town with Linda Shear of the Family of Women Band, and she said, "Would it be too much if you just recorded all the songs you've ever written? Before we leave at 9?" She then drove all over the United States playing that tape for anyone who would listen. We were audacious, we were passionate, and we were activists. And my response to that simple call was yes. *Yes.*

I also want to mention technicians, who from the beginning made this music accessible and available. Two women in particular, one from Oregon and one from New York City, who we scoured the country to find in the 1970s: Joan Lowe and Marilyn Ries. Joan recorded Meg Christian's *I Know You Know* and Cris Williamson's *The Changer and the Changed.* Marilyn recorded Kay Gardner's *Mooncircles* and Alix Dobkin's *Lavender Jane Loves Women.* These women made all the difference; we could make up a lot, figure out a lot, but we couldn't do the recording! On sound, Margot McFedries, Boden Sandstrom and Myrna Johnston, and all the women who have mentored other women. It's part of the power of women's music and culture that we continue to mentor and pass on what we know to new generations of women coming up.

So, these are the earliest girls. It's a painful truth to me that women's accomplishments continue to be minimized and, worse, left out of the historical documenting of this country. But I think we have to be really clear about what's going on. The patriarchy has absolutely no interest in encouraging women to be engaged in this culture or the politics in this country. They *do* understand that women *will* change things once we get inside. They do understand that we will turn things upside down. It is in their best interest, as the gatekeepers, to ignore women's accomplishments, to marginalize our culture, to ridicule our efforts, to distort, co-opt, and defuse the best of our culture for the continued dominant world view white straight men control. Let us be really clear about the context in which we create this beautiful culture of ours!

Just observe the distinction between Sting, Peter Gabriel, and Bruce Springsteen—all of whom are creating music that is engaged in this world, that is socially conscious, sensitive—and then look at women's music and the complete intolerance for women singing about the world as *we* see it. When women express our involvement in the world from an empowered point of view, it is called protest music. It is discounted, marginalized, or dismissed. A complete double standard.

Is there a women's music movement today? I'm not sure. I have some thoughts. There certainly is a network of independent women in the music business. Again, I think a movement requires passion, audacity, and activism. And a women's music movement requires women inspired into action by other women in music and a commitment to act out of service to a community, a vision, and a belief system. Since the women's music movement grew out of the women's liberation movement, as a translation and a manifestation of feminist values in music and performance, maybe the first question really is, Do we still need a movement for the liberation of women in this world? Do we need feminist activism today?

Toni Armstrong Jr.

Two Nice Girls members Kathy Korniloff and Gretchen Phillips at the 1991 Michigan Womyn's Music Festival.

Violence against women in this country is increasing. There are more rapes, murders, assaults, more domestic violence, more incest than ever. Eighty percent of the refugees in the world are women and girls. There are 3,800 animal shelters in the United States and only 1,800 battered women's shelters. The Equal Rights Amendment has still not been ratified by a minimum of 38 states. A woman's right to control her reproductive functions is still subject to the control of both the federal and state governments. Of all the money given by all the foundations in the United States, only 5% goes to women's and girls' programs and organizations. We are still paid significantly less for the same jobs men do. Women are routinely sexually harassed on the streets and at work. And finally, the media continues to inundate us with images of women and girls that are demeaning and woman hating. Clearly, the work of the women's liberation movement is not done.

So we still need a culture that reflects and supports the work and the women who make this movement move. Just as every significant movement for social change has had its music—the civil rights movement, the union movement, the antiwar movement—so we must have our music.

Why did we create a women's music network in the first place? Because we had to. We started women's record labels, production and distribution companies, we encouraged women technicians and women in the media because we wanted to seize control of how women were defined. But there was another part: community. Terry Grant said that women's music and concerts and festivals are a lifeline to women who want to change, who want to come out, who want to take power in their own lives, who want to experience a woman-centered community.

I believe that women are a people. I believe we have a culture. We have a language. And yet women have no land of our own, no safe place in this woman-hating country and this woman-hating world. Concerts and festivals of women's music and culture are as close as we come to having our own country. *Here* we can say, "We are together, we are safe."

And yet, as I travel around the country—I've been back on the road for the last two and a half years—I do come across the attitude that women's music isn't much more than a historical artifact. There's a kind of attitude that, well, that was then, this is now. Maybe we don't need women's music; we have k.d. lang out there, Melissa Etheridge, Tracy Chapman, Michelle Shocked, even some of what Wynonna Judd was doing. Maybe our work's done because k.d. and Melissa are out there, because women's music blew a hole they could step through.

If we declare victory now and quit, we lose the ability to define ourselves in music and in culture. We have only to look at MTV to see that negative and demeaning images of women are alive and still viable in the marketplace. I want to suggest that we may be backlashing ourselves with this idea that "that was then, this is now." I submit to you tonight that there is no expiration date on the women's liberation movement or on women's music or on women's community.

Of course the style needs to change, but not the substance. Male-owned production and distribution companies are scraping the cream off women's music artists and recordings and discarding the deep catalog of women's music. There's less airplay. Women's music has become women *in* music programming, which means less or no feminist content. Corporate music industry has absorbed lots of noncommercial radio, where women's music used to be played. The integration of women's music into folk, New Age, and pop categories has submerged women all over again. Fewer women's newspapers are available to us today, and so there is less coverage of our concerts. That's the bad news.

The good news is that there are too many women's recording engineers for me to list. There are too many drummers, too many bass players, technicians, too many musicians recording in the industry for me to mention. Women's music is more diverse in terms of musical styles and different communities of women than ever before. Lesbians continue to be the major contributors and supporters of this network and movement, and it's a good thing. We can take the credit for introducing the idea of accessibility to all of America.

We're certainly not doing this for the money. It's too hard!

The audience must be agents of change, not just passive consumers. We're part of an underground feminist economy. Self-sustaining businesses by women, for women. I want to say that we can trust our feminism in 1994. We can reach into our radical feminist impulses and find them real and powerful. This National Women's Music Festival is real, 20 years later—as real as it gets. Thank you.

Margie later commented that the 20-year women's music era represented "not a style of music but a cultural phenomenon." Most women present would probably have agreed that political issues and personal commitment to the fight for women's liberation still defined festival culture, whereas musical styles linked to specific artists came and went. However, the changing *sound* of politically informed women's music in the mid 1990s, combined with younger festiegoers' generational alienation from older women's music pioneers, raised fresh questions in summer 1994.

The Tribe 8 Controversy ⇟

It took a hard-core band called Tribe 8 to remind audiences at the 19th Michigan festival that unacceptable statistics on rape, incest, and battered women sometimes call for an "angry" musical style. Aware that "riot grrl" bands (like Bikini Kill, Seven Year Bitch, and the Lunachicks) and alternative punk-dyke groups were attracting a large following among those 16- to 24-year-old feminists who had never heard of Meg Christian, coproducer Lisa Vogel invited San Francisco's popular Tribe 8 to play at the 1994 Michigan Womyn's Music Festival. One lone "alternative" band showcased among dozens of more sedate acts seemed a minor investment in the new music, exciting younger, urban festiegoers, many of whom were the hardest-working group of kitchen crew volunteers and festival staff. And Michigan had certainly hosted punkers and loud alternative rock bands before, including Punk Mary (Mary Gemini), the Contractions, Squeeze Louise, and others.

Nedra Johnson performing at the 1992 Michigan Womyn's Music Festival.

However, Tribe 8's advance publicity—which declared the band to be "blade-brandishing, gang-castrating, dildo-swinging," and so on—began a buzz of speculation that swelled into outright protest on the land. When the five women of Tribe 8 arrived for their performance on the Night Stage, they were greeted with festiegoers holding handmade banners: TRIBE 8 PROMOTES VIOLENCE AGAINST WOMEN. IF YOU ARE A SURVIVOR OF INCEST, YOU SHOULD NOT SEE THIS PERFORMANCE. No other band in Michigan herstory had ever been "welcomed" to their stage debut with such controversial indictment.

Self-titled "Tribe 8" as a sly pun on the word *tribadism*, an early sexologists' term for lesbian lovemaking, the band presented a heavy-metal sound and song lyrics invoking both delight in lesbian sex and anguish at male sexual abuse (most band members are rape and incest survivors). These two themes—positive sexuality and the injustice of female victimization—were what Michigan festiegoers had rallied around for years. So why the controversy? Some women claimed the band's lyrics objectified women sexually or drew too heavily on S/M imagery. Others believed that the starkly cathartic performance of rage against sexual perpetrators (including a simulated castration sequence onstage, with the severed dildo tossed into the crowd) was "unsafe" for women in the audience who had themselves been traumatized by sexual attack. Still, other women were simply put off by the noisiness of the band or expressed concern that after years of training festiegoers to respect the space at the foot of the stage for women with disabilities, the mosh pit would cause accidents.

To forestall further animosity, bandleader Lynn Breedlove began her show by bringing Alix Dobkin onstage with her and issuing a disclaimer:

> We are here to empower women. We love women. I don't think we'd be invited to the women's festival if we wanted to promote violence against women. We're not here to promote violence, pal. We're here to make all women realize their common enemy and to forget about their differences but *enjoy* their diversity. We're here to promote self-expression, and we definitely do not want to hurt, exclude, or alienate any of the women here at all. And that's why, if there are women here who feel they'll be triggered by some of the sexually explicit theatrics that will be happening or any of the lyrics which are sexually explicit and might not be very psychologically safe, there is an area there, at the yellow-and-white tent, called Festiewear, where all kinds of victims—survivors of trauma, including ritual abuse survivors and incest survivors and rape survivors—can all hang out together and get support.
>
> People who still want to watch this show but feel more safe if they have some togetherness can hang out right over there, and we really welcome them. We're in solidarity with them because we

have survived the same kind of trauma. And we're really glad we're here, so now we're gonna mosh our asses off. We're gonna fuck shit up and have some fun, and Alix is gonna sing with us.

Alix Dobkin later said that inviting her onstage was the smartest move Lynn Breedlove could have made. The symbolic imagery of Alix's presence eased the entire situation for some and also made it clear the band was not intended for the under 30s only (Lynn Breedlove herself is over 35). Being repeatedly selected as the symbolic bridge between the festival worker community and the Michigan audience has often put Alix at risk or in a compromising situation, as in 1989 when she was asked to read a workers' statement onstage criticizing Dianne Davidson.

Several women were appalled by the sight of Alix lending support to a band with purportedly pro-S/M lyrics and later wrote a scathing attack on Alix, Tribe 8, and the entire festival in the January 1995 issue of *Off Our Backs*.[2] However, more festie-goers were interested in dialogue than in protest, and both Alix and Raye Amour (the latter, then-coordinator of the over-40s tent, who died in a tragic scuba accident not long afterward) determined to hold open meetings about the Tribe 8 show.[3]

The result was a phenomenal series of candid workshops, some with the band present and some without. Women of all ages and backgrounds spoke with painful honesty, a few confessing that they simply resented a noisy, rude band getting night stage exposure when classical musicians didn't and others reacting angrily to the notion that rape and incest survivors were too weak to withstand lyrics addressing their struggle. A few women suggested that the contemporary urban streets were less safe for young people than ever before, that young women's experiences with violence and fear were moods appropriately expressed in performance, despite others' preferences for light folk tunes. One woman wept that she had spent 25 years as a feminist activist and yet the collective efforts of all her colleagues in radical feminism had not prevented a skyrocketing rate of rape and incest among the present generation of women and, Was that why everyone disliked the band's message? Because reality hurt?

Many months before, bass player Nedra Johnson wrote in *HOT WIRE*, "I used to love slamming—it was a great release. What attracted me was the emotion, which at 17 was rage. I liked the humor and the irony that I heard in punk bands. Take a band like Tribe 8, for example. I think they're great because they challenge the status quo of the women's music scene. I don't think of myself as a 'gentle angry person.' I'd much rather be thought of as dangerous and not to be fucked with."[4] This excellent point about the advantages of being perceived as tough also came up in the festival workshops: Was it healthier for survivors of sexual assault to bellow about it onstage rather than holding it in? Was a fantasy castrate-your-rapist scene a good theatrical release or against the festival's principles of nonviolence? What about all those leatherwomen in the mosh pit—was this S/M music? Ironically, many Michigan festiegoers seemed more concerned with the symbolic power relations of the S/M subculture than with the street realities for young women in the cities.

Ultimately the debate boiled down to issues of freedom of expression at the festival. By the third day of workshops, the band members, if weary from defending their show, had gained a larger number of supporters than ever expected. I attended one open discussion with tape recorder in hand and thus managed to capture a spectacular example of processing, Michigan-style.

So You Got a Problem With Tribe 8? An Open Workshop
Friday, 12 August, 1994

Members of Tribe 8—Lynn Breedlove, Lynne Howard, Slade Bellum, Lynn Payne—introduced themselves in turn and then opened up the dialogue. (Band member Leslie Mah arrived later to join the discussion.)

LYNN BREEDLOVE: Individual freedom of expression is individual government, self-government. And I think that's one thing that Michigan represents. Everybody really seems to be working hard to find out how to live their own lives without stepping on each other's toes. Everyone has to create their own physical space to do that, and they do—with workshops like this. Here, we can discuss what hurts each other's feelings, what our boundaries should be, what our differences are, and what our common enemy is.

That's what Tribe 8 is about to me. It's about joining forces with all kinds of women, whether straight, gay, or bisexual. I don't care what you do in bed; the fact is that if you're a woman—of any size, shape, or color—you have endured a lot of oppression. What I would like to do and what I find is happening is for all of us to realize that the reason we're here at Michigan is to escape oppression. There's something common to us all, and it's not just physical, it's psychic. And however we choose to express that, I think we still love each other on some level. The fact that you're here at this workshop—I fucking love you, man! I don't think there's anybody here that I could define as my enemy. And when people identify me as *their* enemy, it really fucking hurts my heart.

I've worked ever since I was 17—and that's 18 years—to understand feminist theory, to understand women on an individual and group level, to allow the freedom of every woman I know and don't know to be herself, in living through whatever shit she's been subjected to in her life. So that's basically what my thing is.

LYNNE HOWARD: I just want to say something before we open it up for discussion: Try to have an open mind and break down the stereotypes we have of each other. Let's see each other as individuals instead of as categories in boxes. People are surprised we're nice because we play punk music. We're not nice *all* the time, but we're really into meeting people *here,* talking to people *here.*

SLADE BELLUM: I'm Slade. I'm the drummer. I'm really glad to be here and to see that people are here and interested. It's very important to me to get a moment to stand up in front of everybody. It's the first time that I've been to Michigan, and it's my birthday today—I'm 34.

I have been an out dyke punk rocker since I was 18. It's taken this many years to get to where people would notice me because I've had a lot of shit given to me; today is also my nine years without a drink.

I, myself, and the people in our band work on recovery, if you know what that is. And that includes recovery from the rapes I've had—and incest and emotional and mental abuse from my family, who are also alcoholics. We've all been there, and I just want people to know that. I also come from an all-white upper-class small town in Wisconsin; I'm a completely white person, and I have to say that I don't want to own a lot of that white stuff. But I love myself. What I represent, I feel. And I follow a spiritual path.

See, there was a sign yesterday about our "promoting violence." Personally, that's not where I come from. I come from a place of trying to love myself and everybody else. And I love rock and roll. I love to play drums, and this was the biggest opportunity of my life! I've been very happy to have this opportunity to be at Michigan. I hope you can hear our point of view and just accept us.

LYNN PAYNE: I'm Lynn Payne. I've only been playing with the band since January, so I too am still in the process of figuring out what Tribe 8 is really about. All I know is that Tribe 8 has given me the opportunity—for the first time in my life—to find my own voice, to figure out who I am. Their philosophy is giving women the freedom to find out who they are. I want you, out there, to understand that. But I feel a connection to a lot of people here who are not really sure what Tribe 8 is doing. *I'm* still confused, even though I'm in the band.

LYNN BREEDLOVE: I also do worship the Goddess, and I too have a spiritual path. I'm not some fucking Satan worshiper or infant killer—I'm your pal.

OK, are there any questions? Raise your hand if you want to make a statement or have anything to say. [*A young African-American festiegoer volunteers to facilitate, calling on the various women present.*]

A WOMAN SPEAKS: I don't know why so many people are mad at you. I saw your show. I loved it, I'm into it. What's the problem?

LYNN BREEDLOVE: Well, let's find out. Who's mad at us?

A WOMAN SPEAKS: To me your show's eroticizing violence. And this means that violence gets turned on the rest of us in the community. For thousands of years the patriarchy has eroticized violence. That's the way I see it.

A WOMAN SPEAKS: The patriarchy is selling violence to us; there's no turning it back. There's no dissolving the violence that's out there; and if we transform it into something else—I'm saying that the patriarchy will always be interested in taking any of our creative impulses and finding ways to market them.

A WOMAN SPEAKS: I think girl children have to learn to channel aggressive energies rather than *hate*.

A WOMAN SPEAKS: I'm not angry, but I have some questions. If I don't get it, I'm not ashamed to say, "I need a translation on this." And I *do* need translation. My question, first of all, is in terms of your lyrics. I'm in the performing arts, and I could understand only about 40% of your lyrics. I want to know where you're coming from. OK? I have some questions about the, ah, demonstration with the knives and the violence. And I just want to know, basically, about the anger that is being expressed. I'm not questioning your justification, but I need to know whether you're going through the anger into the daylight or if this is just art for art's sake.

LYNN BREEDLOVE: I have a whole spectrum of feelings. Anger is one of them. The song "All I Can Do"—all I can do is cover you—is about the helplessness and frustration of loving my girlfriend who's been incested as a little girl. Her father thinks he loves his little girl, but obviously he's raping her. That's not love, that's wrong. And I'm mad about that. To me, anger is a totally necessary, cathartic step in the revolution. It's one of the first steps that can heal, a first step in transformation. And for me, this kind of music—some of our lyrics are funny, some are mad, some are sad, but they're all totally self-indulgent. Because I had to work through every feeling. Hopefully, when there are women in the crowd who can relate, they'll say "Yeah! I've been through that. I've felt that." That empowers them. I want to make a connection between us and the audience. There's an endless energy; we reach out to each other. And I want other people to feel that anger because a lot of them might have been raped—or their girlfriends or their moms have been raped. My mom was raped. And we're taught *not* to be angry; *not* to be aggressive. I hope I don't have to feel angry all the time. But I sure feel a lot better if I jump around and yell!

A WOMAN SPEAKS: So you would be willing to say you're against incest?

EVERYONE ASSEMBLED: Duh!

LYNN BREEDLOVE: No, I encourage incest and think that all women should be just blown off the face of the earth. *Yes,* I'm against incest. Yes! Yes! It's fucked up! Yes!

SAME WOMAN SPEAKS: Well, see, this is my first time here, and it would be a lot easier if I know where you stand at the outset.

LYNNE HOWARD: As an incest survivor in the band, I would have to say most definitely that playing in the band is a part of healing for me. Being able to express anger and then being able to express humor on another topic—being able to go through all these emotions has been really, really healing.

A WOMAN SPEAKS: As an incest survivor myself, I always loved punk music. I latched onto it in the 1980s as a way to express my anger. And at that point there weren't a lot of women actively in bands. Women didn't do a lot of punk or slam dancing or moshing, and I find it very helpful to me to *move* through my anger and get it out. I see your band as very affirming.

A WOMAN SPEAKS: I'm also a survivor, and I don't know the band; I didn't attend the show. I guess I was a little scared off? But I also really respect the power of anger. It's been an important part of *my* healing. I think a lot of times we see what looks like violence, when it's righteous anger. There's a distinction. Sometimes violence and anger go together, and sometimes they don't. Now, I also had a question. I read the description of the band in the festival program and your use of the word *ho* to describe women. You said, "Fight for your right to stage dive, mosh, riot, sabotage, and generally fuck shit up to the head-banging beat of Tribe 8—and don't forget your steel toes, all you naked punk-rock hos." I didn't understand what that meant. That description was one of the things that caused me not to attend your show. Could you explain? Are you reclaiming the word, like reclaiming *dyke*?

LYNN BREEDLOVE: It's like this: In the punk dyke community, we call each other all kinds of things that the straight world wants to use as epithets to put us down, derogatory words. So, yeah, it's a reclaiming. But I also don't think that whores are bad people.

MANY WOMEN AT ONCE: Thank you!

LYNN BREEDLOVE: I don't have a problem with sex-industry workers; some are my best friends. If they decide that because they're lesbians, they're emotionally detached enough from men to use men for money, I'm totally behind them on that—if it's their decision.

A WOMAN SPEAKS: I like your music very much, and I like the volume because it gets inside of me and I can feel the beat, but I don't like to hurt my ears.

ENTIRE BAND AT ONCE: Earplugs!

LESLIE MAH: [*Arriving late*] We use earplugs, we rehearse in earplugs. At a lot of shows these days, they're promoting earplugs, and we're all trying to learn to take care of ourselves. A lot of us have lost some hearing after all those years without thinking. You can use earplugs and still feel the vibration and really get into it. Take extras if you start going to rock shows. Think about it ahead of time. They've got foam ones. Or use toilet paper.

A WOMAN SPEAKS: The thing that I don't get is how the whole boycott or flip out over your show happened. Because, as a survivor, I don't understand what the big protection is, like how if there's one sexual reference, somehow that's an intrusion? To me that's creating a fragile flower image—you're broken, damaged, can't be sexual, can't be angry, only fearful. I guess I'm interested in hearing from women who really were upset, what they thought.

LYNN BREEDLOVE: Is there anybody here who was really disturbed or really has something they want to say? And could you speak really loud?

A WOMAN SPEAKS: OK, um, I didn't go to the show last night because I saw the banner. I read in the Michigan program what your show was about. I'm an incest survivor and have endured a lot of violence in family relationships, and I really like to be informed. If I'm not informed, I've gone through experiences where I have been mentally triggered. I realize that's my responsibility, but I have to be in that space. I have to know beforehand. Now, last night I was back at my tent, and I could hear everything word for word. And it sounded great! But I did see that one banner that said you might not want to go if you're a survivor, and I had to think. So I just want to say that I'm really glad that some people had the nerve to put those banners out to help get people informed. Even if it caused controversy. This kind of controversy is really good because people talk about it. And I also think it's great that you have a band where you deal with these issues.

SLADE BELLUM: I want to respond to that real quick. There were two banners. One of them said, "Tribe 8 promotes violence against women, children, and animals." That's what was upsetting to me. The other one said that you might not want to go if you're a survivor of incest. Now, before the show started, we did a disclaimer and talked about where people could go to watch and feel *safe*. So there was a lot of awareness besides that banner. I'm interested if the people who were holding the banner that said, "Tribe 8 promotes violence against women and children" are here and want to speak up. Because that was hard on me. By the time I got onstage, I was shaking, I was so upset. A lot of us were crying. I requested that those women come to this workshop. And I'm curious to know if they're here.

LYNN BREEDLOVE: I think the only possible triggering graphic image in the show—which we use to empower women and to strengthen ourselves—is the gang castration scene, where I slice off a rubber effigy phallus, which makes me feel really good. Now, I'm not promoting violence against women. What I'm promoting, personally, is violence against violent men. I think that is the only thing they understand. And I think that the only way for me to run my revolution is violent overthrow. I think [at a recent political demonstration] in Atlanta, you all did a really good job of holding hands. I think that's lovely, but a lot of people got stomped. And I'm sick of being stomped. I'm over that.

A WOMAN SPEAKS: So is there anybody here who was holding the protest banner last night?

A WOMAN SPEAKS: I'd have put up the banner if I'd known about it. You advocate violence against men who are violent. You eroticize violence. How many times will the violence that you advocate through sadomasochism contribute to violence against women? That's my question.

A WOMAN SPEAKS: Are you talking about consensual or nonconsensual? Do you take issue with consensual interaction?

PREVIOUS WOMAN: I take issue with consensual sadomasochism.

A WOMAN SPEAKS: I don't want to get into a discussion of S/M; I really don't care. I went to your show last night. I really didn't know who you guys were, and I didn't know what to expect. And I had fun. It was just fun. I saw those protest signs, and I really didn't understand, so I went to the show to know. My first reaction was that even if I didn't like their music, the signs were kind of like—censorship. I'm an artist. Even if I hated Tribe 8, I could go, or I could do something else. There's so much here: The producers of this festival bend their backs over to provide something for everyone. We've got some things people think are cool, and we've got other things for other people. Why should we take issue?

A WOMAN SPEAKS: Yeah, let's not get into S/M issues—they're a *band*.

LYNN BREEDLOVE: We're not promoting any kind of sex between anyone. I don't want to be recruiting anyone to do anything.

LYNNE HOWARD: I sure would not like to speak for women in terms of what they want to do in their personal lives. Their sex is really up to them. I don't think we are here to speak for the S/M community.

LYNN BREEDLOVE: Not at all.

A WOMAN SPEAKS: I think, for me—for anybody who's an incest and rape survivor— one of the best gifts they can give themselves is a happy, healthy, like, wild, creative, fun, fulfilling sex life, OK? I don't want to limit any women because there are a lot of sex abuse survivors who deal with it in all different ways.

A WOMAN SPEAKS: But when sex includes violence—

A WOMAN SPEAKS: But that's violence to *you*—

LYNN BREEDLOVE: We're not doing sex to you. You don't want us to do violence to you? We're not. You don't want us to—we're going to respect that. Now, my girl-friend and I—if she wants me to tap her on the butt and that's what she wants, that's consent. I think we're grownups and can decide for ourselves.

LYNN PAYNE: I really think that banner is saying, "Here I am, I have a problem with this, and because I have a problem, I want to tell all these other people that they shouldn't go either." And I really take offense to that. If you didn't want to go to the show because you think we're advocating S/M, that you think that's all Tribe 8 is about, well, then you really shouldn't have gone. But I really take offense to you say-ing, "I can't see it, so, hey, everybody else come and join *me*."

A WOMAN SPEAKS: I don't think she was saying that. I think she was expressing a fear that this is not only going to promote violence against violent men but that this could also promote violence against women. I don't think there's an answer to that—if we can know whether their movement does effect violence against women.

LYNNE HOWARD: I gotta say that we do play in front of men. OK? And when we play, they're scared shitless. The girls stand up front, the boys stay in the back. A lot of the boys leave, and some of them talk to us after the show. And if we feel patient enough, we'll talk to them. If these men are gonna rape, they're gonna rape anyway; it's not our responsibility.

LYNN BREEDLOVE: You can be nice and bow down and lick their boots every day, and they're gonna kill you anyway. I say, get in their face.

A WOMAN SPEAKS: But I was offended by the castration part of the show. I'm not about censorship—and I would never ask you not to do this ever again—I just need to understand why you did it. This [punk dyke music] is a subculture I know nothing about. And, actually, I'm a survivor, and I'd like to know how other people are feeling. I'm still in my opening stages.

Leslie Mah of Tribe 8 performing at the 1996 Michigan Womyn's Music Festival.

Toni Armstrong Jr.

SLADE BELLUM: Can you tell us what was offensive about it?

SAME WOMAN: Yeah, um, to me, it was, *Oh, my God—violence.* The people who did violence to me, I should go back and do violence to them? You know? I like to know how people deal with their anger, and anger and pain are definitely part of our selves, although there are other parts too. But what I heard you saying is, gang rape equals gang castration.

LESLIE MAH: It's symbolic. If you've ever gotten angry and punched the pillow, that's getting it out.

PREVIOUS WOMAN: But that's not the same as gang castration.

LESLIE MAH: Gang rape—the song "Gang Castrate" is "Fuck you!" to the gang rapers. It's a lot of symbolism but not literal.

LYNN BREEDLOVE: The effigy is a ritual. I don't actually go out and cut off penises. I put on a dildo, I cut it off—it makes me feel better when I'm disillusioned. When I'm jumping around, singing, dancing, I don't *have* to go so far as to actually cut off a human penis. I haven't yet!

LYNNE HOWARD: A lot of it is symbolism. Part of my recovery was to imagine my perpetrators and imagine just stomping them out of my head, out of my existence. And then, after that, there's grief. Even forgiveness, in some part of me, and understanding. But I can't get to that other side until there's an expression, or acting out, of that anger—the appropriate anger towards something I didn't ask for.

SLADE BELLUM: I really want everyone to think about the power men have to intimidate. We're talking about taking their power away from them and empowering ourselves. That is the symbolism. Take their penises away, and what do they have? And if you could see the expression on men's faces when we do that act in front of them! They grab their crotches in fear, OK?

LESLIE MAH: Strong men too! It's not an exaggeration. It's happened time after time. And their girlfriends come up to us later and say, "My boyfriend went like *this*."

SLADE BELLUM: And this is the pitch: We want women to realize how much men's penises mean to them. OK? We want you to realize it, acknowledge it, and take your own power back. We have our own power from our own energy. Don't give them that kind of satisfaction. That was the symbolism, for me, of cutting a "penis" off—our own little dildo.

A WOMAN SPEAKS: I just think that, well, it seems to me that a lot of you are survivors. And you're acting out what you know. If my perpetrator came to me and said, "Well, that's all I know because my dad did it to me," I'd say "Then why did you want to do it in turn?"

LYNNE HOWARD: It's a show! Sort of like play therapy.

A WOMAN SPEAKS: There's obviously a huge difference between cutting off an effigy and cutting up a real person. I'm a ritualist who encourages women to do enactments, to facilitate righteous anger against perpetrators. And I did not attend the show because I was with two young women and, mainly, it's not a style of music I listen to. It wouldn't have mattered if I knew what was planned; it's just not my cup of tea. But I heard that you're great musicians, and so at this point I wish I could have gone. Now, what you said at the very beginning of the workshop—that you're not the enemy? I want to say that again, for women who came later. What you have dared to do in the show, with this ritual enactment, is what a lot of women are really afraid to let themselves feel.

MANY WOMEN AT ONCE: Yeah!

PREVIOUS WOMAN: And the feeling, the purging of emotion, is part of recovery, part of a *healthy* response. Sometimes, rather than dealing with what one is feeling, you [the band] become the focus, the enemy, by reenacting this bad thing. I'm sad to have seen that happen, and I think that's what you've triggered in a lot of people. Because I came to the festival with women survivors of ritual abuse and also some very young girls, I was happy to see signs saying the show might not be suitable. Because then we had a choice to turn the channel. That's really basic. Like I don't watch horror films—

A WOMAN SPEAKS: Yeah, but with television, first you see what is on, and then you change the channel. You don't have someone else interpret it for you.

PREVIOUS WOMAN: That's true. But having that rating—that this is not suitable for a young audience—I know I can make a choice and not see it if I don't want to. I appreciated that. *And* I appreciate you for what you are doing. I've learned a lot today.

LYNNE HOWARD: I'll just say one more thing. We did an introduction that said there would be explicit scenes. We did not just get onstage and start immediately. In fact, a woman who was involved with the survivors group here gave us a statement to read—and we were going to do that anyway. That's why I wished that the people who had a problem, who made the banners, would have talked to us first.

Of course, music was not the only issue simmering in 1994. As discussed in Chapter Six, Leslie Feinberg's explosive bestseller *Stone Butch Blues* and the ensuing discussion on female-to-male transsexual and transgendered women led to greater pressure on the Michigan festival to recant its "womyn-born womyn only" policy. Some supporters of Feinberg's pro-transgender politics set up an educational area, Camp Trans, across from the festival gate, urging the festival to accept all those who identified as women (including transsexual males).

And among the festival staff, a workers' concern was the impending departure of co-producer Boo Price, whose graceful farewell address from the night stage ("There is old, old, ancient matriarchal energy here") belied not a hint of her troubled business separation from Lisa Vogel. Could Michigan survive all these assaults? As cold weather and rainstorms forced arguing festiegoers together around smoky campfires, it was a time to reflect on festival challenges. The Gulf Coast festival, finally on its own land in Mississippi, was primarily threatened from without. But the Michigan festival, long on private land, was being rocked from within by its own differing forces.

Yet to their credit, Boo Price and Lisa Vogel, who had served as festival coproducers for years (and who seldom—if ever—spoke onstage), ensured that only those closest to them knew that their professional separation was fraught with unpleasant feelings and accusations. In a private letter sent to a select group of longtime festival workers the preceding winter and in a shorter letter printed in the 1994 festival program, Boo Price declared only that it was time for her to move on, toward whatever exciting ventures might lie ahead. Onstage at the 1994 festival, a lineup of

Kate Clinton and Therese Edell at the 1986 Michigan Womyn's Music Festival.

Toni Armstrong Jr.

Michigan artists sang a medley of songs praising Boo, including "This Little Light of Mine" and "A Natural Woman (You Make Me Feel Like)." Beloved artist-emcee Therese Edell, who had faithfully served as the backstage "voice of Michigan" since the mid 1980s (when multiple sclerosis began to limit her performances as a musician), reemerged to honor Boo with these words:

> I know that I told you I would not be talking to you again for the next 100 years or so. But one more time! My name, for the two or three of you who don't know, is Therese, and I've been here for a long time. I would not be coming out and talking to you again except for a very special occasion. We have something that we want to tell you and have you understand. Are you listening this time?

Ah, you always make it seem as though you're hanging on my every word. I always did love that.

In the last 19 years the Michigan Womyn's Music Festival has become the most powerful, the greatest gathering of women on this planet. And this is because of tradition, inspiration, and the extremely hard work of Lisa Vogel and Boo Price. As many of you know—have you read your program?—this is to be Boo Price's last year at the festival. And there's no way that we can begin to thank you, Boo, for this huge and wonderful gift that you've given us—to us, and I can say, especially to me, for letting me be here, and letting my voice be this fucking big. That's the reason I keep coming back. If you can just take this spirit that you all give to each other home with you, this is going to be a better planet rather than a messed-up planet, and one of the people who really did this is Ms. Price. There is no way we can thank you but with much love from all of us.

Boo Price then came out onstage to give her farewell speech. For most women in the audience, it was the first time they had ever seen this festival producer or heard her speak. Yet the collective awareness of an era's end, coupled with the mass release of emotional tensions surrounding Tribe 8, created an almost audible group sob as Boo spoke and the heavens opened simultaneously:

This is sacred ground. That's what I kind of want to say. What we call Michigan and the Michigan spirit is brought here by every woman who comes and is held here by every woman who's gonna come. It's a call. No woman comes here by accident; every woman who comes is called.

There is old, old, ancient matriarchal energy here, that comes here when we're here, that calls us, and that we call up. It's so important, what we do here, and that means coming together as women and sharing that. It's a spirit and an energy that we're very blessed to have in such concentrated form when we see each other in August. But it is, as Therese said, something we all carry with ourselves and within each other when we go.

I feel that in this next period—whatever that is—that part of the "call" for all of us is taking the Michigan spirit and the Michigan energy into more of our world. I know everybody carries it home each year, but it is a part of our work now to take it out there. I feel so blessed, so honored to have grown up here at the Michigan festival, as I have. This little spot here has been the center of my home. It seems fitting that it would rain tonight—but, you know, these are Mother's tears, and they're cleansing and joyful. We come here to be safe so we *can* cry with each other and hold each other and have joy, peace, and safety.

The first time that I stood on the Michigan night stage was 1977, just several miles from here, in Hesperia. Rain, rain, rain—all throughout that festival—and we learned our chops right there. All these women when it rains do their jobs so well now; they really know what they're doing. So I figure I'll come in on the rain, go out on the rain.... And we got a show to run now. Love you!

During her special concert for the workers at Michigan that summer, Alix Dobkin (who has not returned to Michigan since) also gave an eloquent speech, heard by far fewer women but valued for its message to the staff:

I feel so privileged to have been a worker here for 13 years. I watch you walk around doing your work and being so good at what you do, and the way you relate to each other and get along—it makes me so proud that I don't think my skin can contain it. There are so many incidents, so many stories. So many of us have grown up here. I see women that I've worked with for years. They came here as 20-year-olds, and now they're in their 30s; they're not kids any more. And I'm talking about the worker community. The festival itself is an amazing miracle, known throughout the world as "Michigan" by women who don't even know that Michigan is a state. And it is because of our work here and the kind of power we create.

1996 HEART OF THE SOUTH PRODUCTION SCHEDULE

THURSDAY JUNE 13

3pm	Load in Main stage ballroom 16th floor Lights & sound
5pm	Load in Cabaret lights and sound 2nd floor

FRIDAY JUNE 14

10am	Piano tuning John Smith Ballroom

SOUND CHECKS

Cabaret Stage

12:30pm	Crew Call
1:00-1:30	Robin E
1:30-1:45	set change
1:45-2:15	Pam & Maggie

Ballroom Stage

3:00pm	Crew Call
3:15-3:45	Suede
3:45-3:50	Amy Boyd no wireless (arriving 2:19)
3:50 –4:45	Light Focus/K.C.
6:00-6:30	Heather Bishop (due to travel problems)

A sample production checklist.

For me, this gentle speech by Alix was a generational work tribute that felt quite personal. I had first come to Michigan at 20 and was in my 30s at the time of Alix's speech. Along the way I had founded the Jewish women's tent at Michigan, adding an institution to the land. That summer of 1994, I'd coordinated the first-ever bat mitzvah at the festival, and all of us had celebrated the fine passage from girlhood to womanhood of a worker's daughter.

There was one more symbolic shift during festival season 1994. Maile Klein and Marina Hodgini, popular country-and-western dance instructors who had facilitated workshops at several festivals for years, began producing a festival of their own in a hotel casino on the Strip in Las Vegas. Offering luxury and comfort to the slightly older and more affluent festiegoers who had "graduated" from camping and wanted a ballroom floor, the Heart of the West became the new festival on the block, and a Heart of the South festival in New Orleans was added in 1996. Although lesbian pride and spirit still dominated the event, with Alix Dobkin at the microphone, offering familiar festival songs, many women attending acknowledged their choice to leave Porta-Janes and camping behind forevermore. Sue Fink, as emcee on opening night, summed up this change: "When you compare it, we've come a long way from tents and tofu to glamour, glitz, and greed. How many of you have been to some of these festivals out in the woods, out in the middle of nowhere? And sometimes the people don't wear too much clothes! But *this* is *my* idea of camping."

Onward Into 1995 ⋩⋩

The potential generational split into young Lollapalooza-style, moshing, MTV-raised festiegoers versus graying Amazons whose bladders were unhappy camping too far from a toilet hole actually proved to be an unfair polarization. With Lisa Vogel carrying on the work she and Boo Price had once shared, the Michigan festival continued uninterrupted into its 20th year.

There were no controversies at the 20th anniversary of Michigan, beyond the usual dilemma of slack work-shift volunteers (and worker Pyramid's unique proposal to open a real bordello in a parked bus on the land). Instead, the large

Pat "Raffle Rose" Dodson showing support for Tribe 8 at the 1995 Michigan Womyn's Music Festival.

turnout of younger women—some, the daughters of past festiegoers—at Michigan 20 created great optimism for the future. One startling visual was the nursing infant in the day-stage mosh pit (during a Girls in the Nose concert), a single representative of the many babes in arms and toddlers present. The plethora of new lesbian moms prompted changes in festival facilities. Michigan now offers not only a special campground for mothers of toddlers but also two child-care day programs, Buttercup (toddlers, including boys under 3) and Gaia Girls Camp. Many adolescents at Michigan—and young women on work exchange—do their shifts on these demanding child-care crews. Michigan 1995 celebrated the festival's 20th anniversary with lavish fireworks, a sky diver, and the return of many old favorites to the concert stages: Ferron, Rhiannon, Kate Clinton, Holly Near, Margie Adam, Linda Tillery, Nancy Vogl, Vicki Randle, Toshi Reagon. In the midst of the celebration, however, Toshi reminded the contented audience of the danger in complacency: 1994–1995 had seen the introduction of Newt Gingrich's Contract With America and attacks on welfare mothers, affirmative action, gay rights, and public arts funding. That festivals like Michigan should be a springboard for social change, not just fantasy retreats, was a concern that one festiegoer had written in my journal long ago. Toshi's speech echoed that concern:

> At the minimum—at the minimum—make a phone call or drop a postcard in support of your favorite issue. At the minimum, we all owe it to whatever our important issue is. I bet everyone in this audience has something that's being attacked right now. It could be the arts, it could be welfare, it could be abortion rights, it could be gay and lesbian issues, it could be

support for education, it could be the environment—all these things, as we sit out here in this beautiful atmosphere, are being attacked viciously. Viciously. And we really can't be fooled by the comfort level of seeing lesbians on TV and making records and on magazine covers and think for one goddamned second that shit is OK. It is not OK. We are not doing well in this country. We are not thriving as lesbian and gay people and people of color. We are under attack. Don't let the commercialization and marketing fool you. Just because somebody put out a catalog with somebody who looks like you on it don't mean you got no rights. The same people still running the country; you can't even get rid of these fools.

Festival culture, in short, remains vibrant, proactive, attracting likewise vibrant and proactive women of all backgrounds. After 20 years—a full generation—the oldest festivals, Michigan and National, show every likelihood of continuing as cultural institutions, as valued pilgrimage sites for creative regeneration. But as Toshi Reagon points out, festivals' roles as annual (and hence temporary) lesbian-affirming zones still stand in sharp contrast to woman-hating and homophobia in our daily lives.

Toshi's call to activism and Boo Price's call to carry the festival spirit home make plain the challenge and the difficulty of living *daily* as we live during festival season. Even the most popular festival artists can't always make an economic living from their music or writing. And powerful right-wing political forces will be very much with us in the new century to come, whether threatening visionaries like Wanda and Brenda Henson, interrogating "alien" festival performers and lesbian visitors trying to enter the United States, or denying child custody to lesbian moms. Festival gatherings will thus continue to make plain our collective rage as well as our talent, hope, and love.

1. The mainstream press made much of nongay celebrities who spoke or performed at Stonewall 25 ceremonies. Openly lesbian comic Karen Williams, as emcee at the Lavender Jane reunion concert pro-

duced by Lin Daniels at Carnegie Hall, commented on the irony of straight performers winning publicity for their appearances while few lesbian performers from the festival community had been hired
for the Stonewall 25 stage.

2. Caitlin and Gunilla, "Seps' Letter on Michigan," in *Off Our Backs*, January 1995, pp. 18-19. 3 See also
Trish Thomas, "Five Years of Tribe 8: From Three-Chord Songs to the Night Stage, MTV, and Beyond," in *Girlfriends*, July/August 1995.

4. Nedra Johnson, "Renegade Rhythm and Blues," in *HOT WIRE,* January 1994, p. 16.

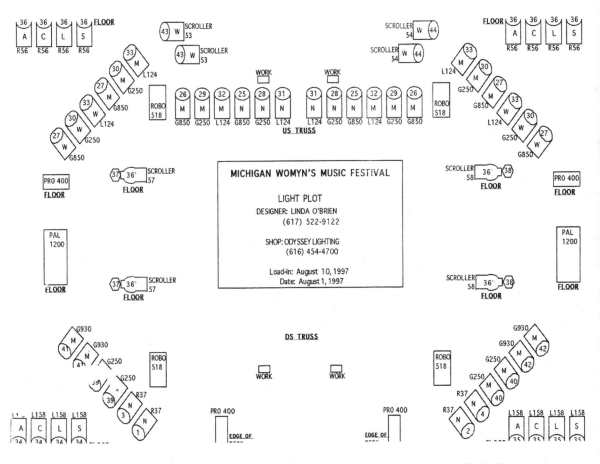

Light plot by Linda O'Brien for the 1997 Michigan Womyn's Music Festival.

Jamie Fóta
Singer, Songwriter

Music for the Soul

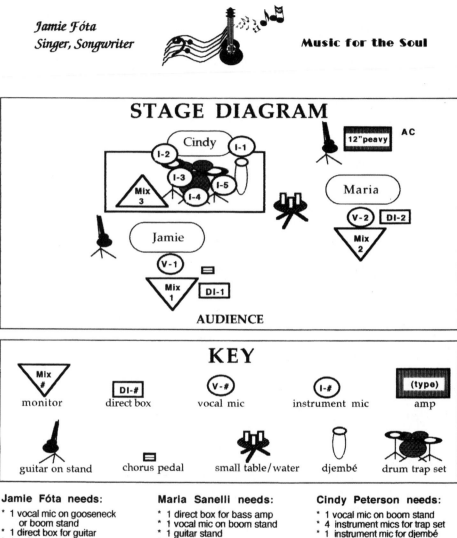

STAGE DIAGRAM

KEY

Mix # monitor	DI-# direct box	V-# vocal mic	I-# instrument mic	(type) amp
guitar on stand	chorus pedal	small table/water	djembé	drum trap set

Jamie Fóta needs:

* 1 vocal mic on gooseneck
  or boom stand
* 1 direct box for guitar
* 1 guitar stand
* 1 monitor
* 1 bottle of water on table

Maria Sanelli needs:

* 1 direct box for bass amp
* 1 vocal mic on boom stand
* 1 guitar stand
* 1 monitor
* AC grounded outlet
* 1 bottle of water on table

Cindy Peterson needs:

* 1 vocal mic on boom stand
* 4 instrument mics for trap set
* 1 instrument mic for djembé
* 1 monitor
* 1 bottle of water on table

Staging for Jamie Fota, 1997 festival season.

CHAPTER TEN

How I Spent My Summer Vacation

We came up in the 1950s at zero. And look what we have now: the freedom to be in your face! Just keep hope. Just keep going; don't let it get to you. When we first wrote Lesbian/Woman, an editor rejected it by telling us, "You act as though your lifestyle is good, and that's impossible."
—Del Martin

Our survival depends on our not being predictable; we have to take ourselves off the marketing curve.
—Alix Dobkin

Every wise woman buildeth her house; But the foolish plucketh it down with her hands.
—Proverbs 14:1

In the 21st century, women's music festivals will compete with multiple other entertainments to attract lesbian consumer dollars. This predicament reflects progress: There are more lesbian entertainment choices than ever before, including independent film festivals, cruises and travel expeditions, bed-and-breakfast getaways, clubs, and not-officially-lesbian-but-obviously-so galas such as the Dinah Shore Golf Classic. However, what this aforementioned menu reflects is an increase of choices for affluent women. Gone are the days of the $2 dance and the $3 women's music concert, mainstays of 1970s lesbian separatism. Since class remains an oddly taboo subject in a community ostensibly attentive to race and gender difference, festivals' real contributions go unremarked: They are still the most afford-able entertainment value per hour of women-only space. The sliding scale, the work-exchange option bringing a young techie in training right onto her favorite singer's stage, free child care—these are outstanding features, offering working women a full day of concerts for less cost than a single k.d. lang show. Don't like the food included in your ticket price? Bring along your own cuisine, your birthday cake, your jar of olives or buy from the festival snack bar; compromise is possible. Car trouble at the gate? A hundred women will pitch in to mend your air filter. Payment flexibility and community assistance make festivals uniquely user-friendly. These factors will continue to be festivals' competitive edge in the future.

The 1990s draw to a close with better lesbian visibility in the media, with les-bians as White House guests and presidential appointees, with new support groups for gay and lesbian high school students. It's no longer necessary to at-tend a festival to find radical women, and the Internet helps connect even the most isolated. Publisher Barbara Grier, performer Lynn Thomas, and several other women all shared the same observation with me: During the 1970s and 1980s, lesbians needed festival gatherings as antidotes to feelings of isolation and shame, but today's young women are boldly coming out in high school, as-suming and acting on their civil rights. Lesbian separatism is not their solution, and 1970s folk music is not their sound. Today's young women enjoy main-stream entertainment images we never had—for instance, an out lesbian who is cute as hell (Ellen DeGeneres) on TV, in the family living room, every Wednes-day night at 9:30. Yet ABC's decision to cancel *Ellen* after the historic 1997–1998 season demonstrates the fickle nature of Hollywood. Like so many artists, Ellen found herself first embraced and then rejected by the "liberal" media, with its mixed messages regarding diversity and tolerance. Network ex-ecutives, insisting America "just isn't ready" for lesbian visibility, sent a homo-phobic message to the same young people affected so positively by Ellen's deci-sion to come out on national television. Of course, dejected fans console ourselves by reasoning that Ellen is now free to accept festival gigs.

In this changing artistic market, must festivals reconstruct what they offer in order to stay solvent, to attract new numbers? Or, as Jean Fineberg has argued, are festivals determinedly cultural rather than musical events, defined by a fixed aesthetic? Most importantly, as we pass the 25-year mark, will we be honored and remembered for what we contributed or vilified as outmoded by feminism's next wave?

The problem is that no outside observer can really judge festival culture's "success." One festival with great friendly appeal and a fantastic ratio of attending writers, theorists, artists—Lin Daniels's East Coast Lesbian Festival (1989–1993)—developed unexpected financial problems and vanished, leaving the producer broke. But loyal ECLF festiegoers were left with five years' worth of glowing memories. Did that festival fail? Ironically, when festival producers begin to make money, they

At the National Women's Music Festival, Del Martin and Phyllis Lyon, accompanied by ASL interpreter Ariel Hall, receive the Jeanine Rae Award for the Advancement of Women's Culture.

Toni Armstrong Jr.

sometimes lose the trust of their own community—a community so accustomed to the volunteer ethic and female poverty that lesbians with money to invest (and lose) become class enemies. Robin Tyler has experienced such suspicion. Some women are baffled by the festival community's ambivalence toward profit. Throughout 25 years of women's music and culture, few topics have invoked a more confused political response than the concept of lesbian artists actually making money. For so long in radical communities, wealth has been equated with selling out.

The music and entertainment industries have always been about making money. But throughout much of the 1960s and 1970s, even well into the antiapartheid 1980s, all the "folk" musicians (and their followers) I knew were also active in the fight for civil rights, the Movement. I grew up in that cultural parenthesis, knowing from my parents' approving nuances who was a Movement person, and knowing the full range of art and politics that moniker implied. The Movement people swirling around my childhood and adolescence changed from civil rights activists to peace marchers to feminists, the pronounced shift in the gender of progressive people (once the draft no longer threatened young males) occurring around the time I entered a Quaker alternative school at age 11. Coming of age in 1970s feminist and lesbian culture, I found the perfect segue into another community concerned with freedom and justice. And like the civil rights and peace movements, lesbian feminism had its music and its musicians.

Yet by the 1990s, although there were more women's music festivals than ever before, peace and love were definitely out of fashion in the media's version of counterculture, where caffeine-fueled cynicism greeted any reminder of move-

At the National Women's Music Festival, Kay Gardner receives the 1989 Jane Schliesman Award for outstanding contributions to women's music.

Toni Armstrong Jr.

ments past. A 1997 television commercial for IBM's Lotus software showed decrepit members of 1960s folk-rock groups, with this unforgettable ad line: "Everyone in those bands is either dead or not talking to each other. Work the Web. Make money, not war." Love, communication, and the collective approach seem impossibly retro concepts in a society with too few jobs and outright political hostility toward affirmative action and feminism.

The '90s ridicule of '70s feminism (although '70s clothes have been inexplicably reintroduced as fashion) demonstrates how each generation enjoys rejecting its predecessor. But when today's independent women artists mock or ignore the legacy of festival culture—the longest-running venue for independent women artists—we find sisters dissing sisters. That's more than a generational rejection—it's dishonesty. And it's a challenge to the collective memory of lesbian achievement in the late 20th century.

The Age Question: Does Death Begin at 40? ⪢⪢

"I think the feminist movement is dead," proclaimed singer Tori Amos during a 1996 radio interview. "Is Womyn's Music Dead?" asked a 1996 cover of *Girlfriends;* inside, editor in chief Heather Findlay put the question even more specifically: "Is the lesbian festival circuit dead?" One women's bookstore lured customers by advertising, "We seek used CDs.... Want to trade in Meg and Cris for Melissa and Ani?" As though June Millington, Tret Fure, Toshi Reagon, Sherry Shute, Gretchen Phillips, and hundreds of other women hadn't been wowing crowds at festivals for years (or decades), the mainstream media touted Ani DiFranco and Alanis Morissette as the first independent and/or successful kick-ass women recording artists. Even in the notoriously queer-friendly Bay Area, home to a large percentage of the original women's music pioneers, it was the 1997 Lilith Fair that prompted the *San Francisco Chronicle* to report: "Female rock 'n' rollers are finally being heard!... First, there was Alanis Morissette."[1] When *Time* magazine put new singer Jewel on a July 1997 cover with the subheading "the all-female Lilith festival is taking rock's hot new sound on the road," thousands of women already were on the road—en route to the 22nd annual Michigan Womyn's Music Festival. Fed up with lesbian invisibility, political activist Urvashi Vaid talked back with eloquence in an issue of *The Advocate:*

> Grunge? That was lesbian-feminist clothing and fashion in the 1970s. The Lilith Fair tour? Olivia Records and Roadwork began that in 1978 with the Varied Voices of Black Women tour. The

Michigan Womyn's Music Festival has averaged 9,000 lesbians a year for 22 years.... Ani DiFranco and artist self-distribution? Alix Dobkin did that in 1975 with *Lavender Jane Loves Women,* and Ladyslipper distribution still does it today....

Lesbians confront the paradox of enormous visibility accompanied by total silence about lesbian ideas, history, politics, and culture.[2]

Meanwhile, *Rolling Stone* dedicated its 30th anniversary issue (November 13, 1997) to "Women of Rock," profiling 28 different artists. Of these, two had performed at women's music festivals: Ani DiFranco and Melissa Etheridge (although Gerri Hirshey's overview of women in rock history also quoted or mentioned former Michigan performers Tracy Chapman, the Murmurs, the Lunachicks, Bikini Kill, and Tribe 8). There was absolutely no mention of women's music festivals as an independent industry phenomenon, although *Rolling Stone* mentioned "the so-called 'womyn's' music collective of lesbian singer-songwriters like Holly Near." Of course, in this same *Rolling Stone* issue, typical sleaze ads in the back pages offered "horny oriental bimbos," "horny high school seniors," and "submissive young girls," in lurid contrast to the presumed focus on empowered women in the music industry. Perhaps most distressing was that a majority of the 28 "women of rock" distanced themselves from the feminist label. Joni Mitchell and Joan Baez both declared bluntly in their interviews, "I'm not a feminist." Only Courtney Love called herself a militant feminist, with Bonnie Raitt, Ruth Brown, Fiona Apple, and Sinead O'Connor also proud to claim the name. Ultimately, k.d. lang came closest to addressing festival politics: "The reaction from the media to the whole concept of Lilith Fair is a perfect example [of double standards for men and women rock musicians]. The idea that a whole tour of women performers would be so strange, when you think of how many thousands of entire bills of men we've had to endure...."[3]

Today's older lesbian artists continue to live between a rock and a hard place, their rightful legacy overlooked by mainstream periodicals, which endlessly recycle k.d. lang, Melissa Etheridge, and the Indigo Girls as proof of lesbian power in the entertainment industry. Using mail order and Web pages, women's music distribution companies Ladyslipper and Goldenrod work ceaselessly to overcome the limited visibility of less famous artists. Yet with mainstream fame now established as a lesbian possibility, the lesser-knowns attract even less interest for having situated their achievements in the "underground" lesbian music network. Lacking a traditional royalty of our own, presumably democratic Americans are instead socialized to worship celebrities—even homophobes will show a modicum of respect for gay and lesbian celebrities who succeed in mainstream venues. It's the homegrown Movement types who raise hackles for being modest folk singers, a point raised in a homophobe's hostile letter sent to Ladyslipper Records in 1997: "I see that you are celebrating a 20th anniversary.... What a sad commentary it is that gay people are so musically disadvantaged that they have spent 20 years making you rich."[4]

Of course, nobody at Ladyslipper ever got rich marketing women's music. But notice the writer's assumption that lesbian audiences are empowered to make successes of their own institutions. That's an accurate perception. While lesbians have sustained festival culture in the past, will they in the future? Do we respect our own "underground"? Or as Margie Adam has said, Is there a general trend toward "overground" marketing and stature in gay and lesbian arts today?[5] Radical lesbian playwright Carolyn Gage, whose works have been staged at the East Coast Lesbian Festival and at Campfest, told me, "I can't believe I'm being treated like I'm passé now because that implies I was *in* and got some real attention at one point. Did I?"

Here's the punch line: Festivals, lesbian feminism, and women's music are all far from dead in America. But they are supported and sustained in no small measure by women age 35 and older, which, in a youth-focused market, is the same thing as being dead. The women who birthed these movements as 20-somethings in the 1970s remain actively involved today, but they have had "the bad taste and poor judgment to grow older," to use advertising critic Jean Kilbourne's apt phrase. To the next generation, festival culture looks like a movement in gray these days. And due to those gray hairs, the sheer radicalism of all that festival workers have accomplished gets marked down; the motherly or grandmotherly age of the 1970s pioneers brings out stunning condescension from younger women inheriting our dyke-rock legacy. "Why should I be held to festival policies written before I was born?" demanded an arrogant new crew member during a 1996 worker meeting at Michigan.

Recent columns on festival culture in magazines aimed at younger women include unkind inaccuracies rather than incentives to attend. Early in 1997, Elizabeth Davis, a member of the "riot grrl" band Seven Year Bitch, described Michigan for readers of *Women in General* magazine:

> There were more than 6,000 women. But the very first image we saw of the festival, after barreling through the trees and dust, was not exactly encouraging. The van practically smacked into a bored-looking girl in tie-dye banging forlornly on a drum in no particular rhythm....
>
> Now, Caroline was someone I knew immediately we could relate to...one of those crazy young dykes who appear to me, as an outsider, to be part of a new wave replacing the older "PC" cuddles 'n' code-pendency lesbians with a freshly brazenly sexual breed, if you will.[6]

Describing her own first festival (1996), *Girlfriends* editor Heather Findlay marveled that "even fat babes and women with canes" leaped into the Michigan mosh pit. (In *WIG*, Elizabeth Davis had gaped at "middle-aged women stage diving.") Findlay added: "If it hadn't been for the fact that would-be divers politely queued up and even self-policed the line (God, I thought, lesbians can be such *nerds*), I would have been forever and completely disabused of my image of Michigan as ultrarigid, puritanical, and politically correct."[7]

Longtime stage security workers ground their teeth over the ridiculing of safety precautions as "nerdy" in an outdoor concert venue of 5,000 women and kids. And longtime festiegoers roared at seeing the definitions "ultrarigid" and "puritanical" applied to their 22 years of experiences as naked Amazon party girls making love in the Michigan woods. Longtime artists blinked when Findlay went on to name Ferron "the grandmother of women's music." Ferron was not quite 45 years old and had made her mark at U.S. festivals a good seven years after Holly Near, Cris Williamson, Alix Dobkin, Meg Christian, Margie Adam, and many others had founded the U.S. women's music recording and performance networks. While the May/June 1997 issue of *Girlfriends* gave an approving nod to Cris Williamson and Tret Fure's new album, the compliment contained an anticompliment: The new album, apparently, was "devoid (this time) of mood-killing politics."

Outright hostility to longtime festival performers also surfaced in *Spin* magazine's review of the Michigan festival. Detracting from what might have been an exciting moment for festival fans (finally, Michigan makes the pages of *Spin* !), reporter Alyssa Katz praised Tribe 8 while sneering at Holly Near and Cris Williamson, calling them "High-gloss folksingers...who can sound an awful lot like Christian pop if you're not listening too carefully."[8] Katz entitled her piece "Gynosaur Rock," an inside joke for those who actually attended the 1997 Michigan festival. Cris Williamson had declared onstage that with so many "older" artists performing that year, Michigan resembled Jurassic Park. Howev-

ASL interpreter Ariel Hall at the 1990 National Women's Music Festival.

Toni Armstrong Jr.

er, Cris had warned her audience, "We're the velociraptors: We still have all our teeth, and we can run real fast."

Compare this defensiveness with the sold-out Rolling Stones tour, also in summer 1997, featuring 50-something rock icon Mick Jagger. Those "grandfathers" of rock made $89 million on their "Bridges to Babylon" tour (the Lilith Fair earned $16.4 million). To see groundbreaking and productive lesbian artists in their 40s pigeonholed as dinosaurs and grandmothers by younger women demonstrates the ageism even feminists subscribe to. If one is a dinosaur at 45, what lies in store for the artist hitting her stride at age 50 or 60 in a society with increasing longevity for women? Interestingly, in the lesbian community the age question has much to do with respect for one's work and political experience rather than sexual appeal. Conventional wisdom holds that ageism as sexual rejection is more of a problem for the gay male community (see Johnny Symons's 1997 video *Beauty Before Age*).

However, ageism is a two-way street. It's also true that younger and newer festival workers often feel "bad daughter" vibes aimed at them by older staff. Younger women entering festival culture find that their behavior and appearance receive more scrutiny than the insights and experiences they might bring to the body politic. Theirs is a harsh social reality, a world with schoolyard gun violence: Gretchen Phillips once invoked the spirit of young women's frustration with dead-end jobs by appearing on the Michigan day stage in combat boots, a Catholic schoolgirl uniform, and a paper McDonald's hat. More recently, Gretchen and Alexis Vaughn had younger festiegoers cheering when they introduced a song entitled "The Michigan Anthem":

> I fear there'll be a community meeting
> About my behavior on this land
> I can't walk to my tent without being SHUSHED!
> I didn't quit my job and drive cross-country
> Just to have a woman go SHUSH-SHUSH-SHUSH
> I work a ten-hour day and I'll speak what I may
> Don't give me SHUSH!
> Don't give me SHUSH!
> Don't give me SHUSH!
> I'm sorry if I woke you up, with my brilliant insight
> Outside your tent!

Finding the sisterhood of festival culture at last, only to be shushed, brings up all the old memories of being ordered (by one's parents) to turn that noisy music down. It invokes the despair of being categorized as noisy whilst never being heard at all.

Hence, the ongoing scenario of 20-year-olds confronting 40-year-olds cannot help but reproduce the motherphobic issues addressed in Chapter Three. On the one hand, middle-aged women remain the least glamorized and celebrated of all, while hip teens and white-haired crones win the lion's share of cooldom. On the other hand, some resentment between the young and those over 35 is simply profession-al: the ongoing competition for very few stage slots. Plenty of artists over 35 still hope for a shot at night stage; "new" and "young" artists are not always the same. Some performers found their voices as artists (or came out as lesbians) after 30. They must now vie for stage time with those who are out and proud at 17.

Nedra Johnson and Lynn Breedlove, both of whom perform music that younger audiences can slam to, are themselves over 30. And both used their time on the 1996 Michigan night stage to remind younger festiegoers that older staff and festival founders deserve respect. Lynn, as emcee, invited the entire audience to a cross gen-erational salon where older women could relate how they had radically "fucked shit up" as activists in the 1960s and '70s. "Come and listen, so you punkers don't think you invited the wheel," Lynn advised the crowd. The next day, the Over-40s tent (soon to be the Over-50s/Over-60s tent!) bulged with festiegoers of every age, will-ing to learn from one another's tales.[9]

Yes, festivals require new blood. In fact, they are dependent upon attracting bold young women as future staff and visionaries. The appearance of new, young producers, like New York City's dynamic Mehuman Jonson, is a blessing. But let us also consider the viewpoint that it's OK for women in their 30s, 40s, and 50s to have a stunning institution where they are the majority, that it should be unnecessary to apologize for events that attract middle-aged dykes, that not everything must be defined by the young.

At the Virginia Women's Music Festival one year, I watched the generation gap drama unfold during a minor incident that nonetheless left a lingering impression. A circle of older lesbians who had worked all day on carpentry tasks for the festival sat down, built a campfire, and began telling the kind of authentic dyke survival stories I wish every one of my college students could hear. I settled in for the greatest night of tribal storytelling in my life. Suddenly, over the hill came a group of college-age festie-goers armed with bongos and guitars. Without preamble they took over the campfire space and began drumming and singing Indigo Girls songs. Of course it was impossible for the older women to continue their conversation, and although they had just relaxed for the first time all day, they fell silent and soon afterward left the fire pit. I ached to think that none of the younger women realized what a gold mine of lesbian heritage they had stumbled into—that no one had even acknowledged the older staff, let alone asked, "Will we interrupt your conversation if we drum now?"

But these younger women were also deeply invested in issues of art and culture. Another snapshot from the Virginia Women's Music Festival that same year: a workshop, led by artist and Ladyslipper worker Tracy Drach, on the future of

New Zealand's Topp Twins, Lynda and Jools Topp, performing at the 1993 National Women's Music Festival.

Toni Armstrong Jr.

women's music and its definition. Younger and older festiegoers—about half of whom were musicians—spoke out passionately while I grabbed for my fountain pen:

"We're negotiating who we are as a culture."

"Yeah, there's room for mediocrity in the mainstream but not in women's music, meaning we have to be the best just to earn a living."

"It doesn't matter what you call women's music or festival culture because it will always defy definition."

"Sure, I perform for men back home—I can no longer rely on the women's music community to fill an audience."

"Can we agree that art changes? That's what I see happening now."

Today much of the best cross generational dialogue takes place in cyberspace. Younger and older artists increasingly use the Internet to discuss festival politics. Denise Bump, the new co-owner of Lammas women's bookstore in Washington, D.C., told me about the detailed "Michigan gossip" she found in her E-mail box each August after women returned home from the festival. The Michigan festival itself had a temporary Web site for the first time during the 1997 festival. Also in 1997, University of California, Irvine, graduate student Chelsea Starr set up an Internet discussion group for women conducting research on festival culture and women's music, thus linking young academics with seasoned artists like Laurie "Slim" Ryan of the Fallopian Tubes. Slim, who runs a community radio show in Minneapolis, wrote in to the group:

> How do we define and describe "lesbian music"? Mostly I have to settle for music by lesbians; sometimes I do emphasize music with specifically lesbian themes—a much narrower area.... When *HOT WIRE* was still in business, it was easier to figure out who the lesbian musicians are. Now, I have to read between the lines of liner notes or the Ladyslipper catalog or wait for gossip or an interview in one of the lesbian mags. Sometimes I just guess. Ironically, *Curve* and *Girlfriends* don't only highlight lesbian musicians—just bands that they think an audience of lesbians might like.... I'm really interested in regional folks who never make it big time—those local lesbian gals-about-town who have a tape or two.

That smart young women are now writing dissertations and theses on festival culture and approaching over-30s artists as important resources gives me great hope that our herstory will receive respectful treatment after all. Legitimizing the study of lesbian culture is surely a sign of the times. JEB (Joan E. Biren), a festival photographer for many years, jokes that "it used to be that if you were interested in taking notes or pictures—preserving the culture—you'd be accused of being an FBI agent."

When the dust of debate settles, I find I have taken the same notes at every festival since I began attending them in 1981. My notes tell me that women committed to what Wanda Henson calls "making festival" have maintained the Amazon Nation model using three basic principles.

The first festival principle is temporary apartness from male society—separatism. And women-only space continues to raise hackles as "reverse discrimination" or simply as unwelcoming to men (there's an androcentric interpretation), though such space is temporary, fleeting. In contrast, the most traditional and heterosexual cultures of the world (Islam, Hasidic Judaism, the Vatican) require men and women to occupy separate spheres culturally and socially throughout their lives. Festivals, however, give women total control over what a (temporary) women's sphere looks like. This apartness connotes power. It is inherently defiant because there are never any men higher up in the chain of command.

A second festival principle is education in the ways of the world's women. Without question, women have been written out of most history books, kept from political power, and have thus found alternative means of protest and memoir. Whether information on women's lives comes to the participant audience through song ballads, drama, political speech, or workshops on the roots of racism, festivals offer the gynocentric school day we never had. Each festiegoer is an anthropologist and herstorian for her own people; each artist brings some sort of new piece to the puzzle. What have we *not* learned about our foremothers? Who were the heroines, the martyrs, the silenced ones? How can we remember and transmit their names, their knowledge? This is perhaps the most threatened aspect of festival culture. Sadly, the equation of loud female rock bands with progress/hipness has gradually pushed out groups like Libana and Kitka, who perform Balkan vocals and other songs with traditional Eastern European arrangements. While most younger women are open to what has been called "world music," there is less interest today in the a cappella sound of threatened peoples—the women's music from Bosnia, South Africa, Tibet, Burma. Have we become attention deficient to any sound that lacks a homogenized, Westernized amplifier beat? If so, we stand to lose the former festival celebration of passing along the ethnic traditions of our mothers. Perhaps ethnic folk music has lost its

"Yike! She's a dyke!"
Lynn Thomas
performs at the 1992
National Women's
Music Festival.

Toni Armstrong Jr.

radicalism because we are farther than ever from the European immigration waves of the early 20th century and from the Red-baiting protest music of the 1950s, when to sing a Russian song was to invite political investigation. Fortunately, there are also young women working in bands like Charming Hostess and the Billy Tipton Memorial Sax Quartet, who are creating "Hasidic hip-hop" for festival audiences.

Finally, festivals operate on a unique work principle, training and cultivating and rewarding ability—not appearance. While the stage artists are admired, women's competence in any job around the land wins support and encouragement, particularly where workers succeed at unpleasant or difficult tasks. Exposure to this alternative workplace inspires many women to leave unsatisfying careers or to challenge climates of harassment back home. The woman-friendly environment offered at festivals alters the very meaning of work, bringing to mind festiegoers who annually sign up for every work shift available, like Campfest lovebirds Carol and Leslie, whose interview appeared earlier.

Many of us will keep at it—renegade Amazons giving the best years of our lives to a festival culture rarely recognized, even in women's studies texts or queer girl glossies. Yes, the emergence of festivals as institutions has been a significant, late 20th century movement. But that's not why we go.

We go for the walk in the woods, the experience of light and leaf and shadow on bare ribs, not felt since first grade. We go for the collective hush when a performer sings a love song, for the drumbeat up the spine that kundalini enthusiasts never imagined, for the perfect spray of water drops across a prebreakfast cobweb on a beach chair. We go because the weight of the hammer, the call of the whippoorwill, the log falling apart and scattering fresh spark light across faces all remind us of a preindustrial era when time went by the season and not according to the Timex Indiglo. We go to hear the word *lesbian* spoken as often as possible into a microphone in a university building, to hear writers and role models we had only read about— even to ignore them in order to kiss our dates passionately throughout a scheduled presentation. We carefully pack clothes we'll remove immediately for the thrill of remaking ourselves as travelers to inner space—the inner space of "Wombstock," as Elizabeth Ziff (of BETTY) called Michigan in 1989.

For half my life I have spent my summer vacation accumulating such images, spread out now like snapshots in my mind:

Campfest: I walk down the hill carrying a broom, on my way to sweep the stage, but a woman yells cheerfully from her cabin, "Going for a ride?"

Campfest: A woman who has lost a breast to cancer slowly removes her shirt and climbs into the pool, drawing about her a ring of other cancer survivors in ritual dignity.

Michigan: Margie Adam sits down at the piano, and a giant meteor shoots across the sky above her stage, purple and gold dragon colors; 6,000 women scream ecstatically, and Margie walks out onto the runway and looks up.

National: The age category "90 and above" has to be added for competitors in the road race when Miss Ruth Ellis decides to jog.

National: The sky turns green, the tornado warning alarm goes off, and everyone's evacuated to shelters downstairs, where Jamie Anderson entertains sleepy-faced artists and staff until it's safe to resume a "normal" festival day.

Gulf Coast: All the teenagers and young girls on the land coat themselves in mud and become "swamp things," dancing in primeval leaf and vine outfits; later, I chase an armadillo through the bayou.

Rhythmfest: Workers spread hay over the ground in the crafts area, where rain has turned the paths into a sea of mud—but the hay turns out to be full of mice, and we're all slipping, flailing, and roaring with laughter.

Michigan: Four women stand under a tree eating fire, and interpreter Felice Shays calls out to them, "Say, anyone got a light?"

East Coast: Hundreds of shirtless women sit side by side in a boathouse, chanting the names of goddesses.

Sisterfire: I watch my father try to blend in at the only festival he's able to experience; a worker, or "sisterspark," yells at him to put his shirt back on, since women can't enjoy topless privileges in that public space.

Michigan: My mother and I are trapped in a tent for three days of a stationary thunderstorm during the Harmonic Convergence; my tape recorder captures our insane giggling and the heavens exploding above.

NEWMR: I seduce a new friend in a cabin filled with sleeping women, and we stay on the land for two days after the festival has ended, honeymooning and homesteading.

West Coast: Another meteor shower, this time high above Yosemite's peaks, and Karen Williams demands from the stage, "*What* are you all looking at?"

Michigan: Vicki Randle is strumming her guitar and singing lullabies around the worker campfire pit, and I watch the festival producers' faces soften into a euphoric trance.

Campfest: I roller-blade naked for two hours, then drum onstage in Ubaka Hill's orchestra, then swim laps and ostentatiously chin myself on the pool diving board, then fall asleep knowing every muscle has been used.

Gulf Coast: I lead a Passover Seder and ask the youngest girl child present to read the Four Questions; after she does so, perfectly, her mother informs me that the kid has struggled with a learning problem and never read aloud in public until that day.

Michigan: I conduct a bat mitzvah ceremony for the young daughter of a worker; she reads a letter of love and appreciation to her mother, while all of us sob aloud.

Sisterfire: A woman has put up a sign asking if there are any other Ukrainian dykes attending, and immediately one walks up to her.

Michigan: Two Sanitation/Recycling workers create a hot tub out of the baby pool used for washing vegetables; they float red candles on the water and have a romantic soak after a long day of picking up bottles and cans.

NEWMR: Sue Fink and I canoe across the lake to spy on the summer camp for boys on the other side.

Gulf Coast: Dorothy Hirsch casually pulls an espresso machine, turkey teriyaki, and Toblerone chocolate out of her knapsack, befriending the entire bunkhouse at once.

Virginia: It's my birthday, I'm wearing very little, and two women walk up to me—

one tells me she was in my ninth-grade English class, and the other reminds me that I brought her out in college.

Michigan: Kate Clinton leads 7,000 women in chanting, "This is the best time I've ever had in my whole life."

Campfest: artist liaison Sara Woolf brings a welcome feast of hors d'ouevres to the "techie gazebo," and I watch tired stage workers eat crab and smoke cigars at 2 A.M.

Michigan: A klezmer band performs on the night stage, and hundreds of Jewish women and girls dance in the "nosh pit" surrounding the stage.

Actual conversations, overheard:

"The problem with the mosh pit is that we're trying to regulate something that's not a regulated experience."

"I made the mistake of telling this woman I had cramps, and she made me drink the juice of some plant."

"Check out the Goddess choreography going on over there."

"I have a fetish for bras; I counted before I came here, and I have 37."

"How your tent is doing, eh? Mine is 15 buckets wet."

"After the rain crew put up that tarp so efficiently, I got a competence crush."

"Those security gals have cast a psychic web around us. Don't scam them."

"Hey, some of the craftswomen learned to flirt this year."

"We're all going to go home with squeegee elbow."
"Last week feels like two years ago, you know?"

"Our last album went wood—it petrified."

"Gray hair and gray matter are all that interest me now."

"We need to create music for lesbian families who live in hetfest their whole lives."

"I've been attracting women like me to me all my life, and I didn't know it. I didn't know it!"

"Sacred work and having a sacred life are equally important."

"Sorry to interrupt your sunbath, but we need 50 women volunteers for the kitchen—right now."

"Tell me your best rutabaga story."

"If I keep laughing, my lips are going to fall off."

"You wanna ride shotgun with me on garbage?"

"That boom box belongs to One World."

"I can't eat fire; I have a gag reflex."

"This music is for Generation Lambda."

"Can you help me translate this goddess language?"

"I don't have a highlighter, but Over-40s does."

"You get big points for not using my witticisms to charm her."

"The first three days at Michigan I'm Jello, the rest of the weekend I'm dancing."

"I have all the multi-X-sized women to thank for my expanded sales line of tie-dye."

"Well, Helen, you're going to get mighty sunburned like that. And I'm not going to lotion and love you because it'll be your own damn fault!"

The additional remarks of hundreds of festiegoers can be found in Appendix A. Perhaps Mimi Baczewska put it best: "It's a very long song that we can sing, to celebrate the women of the world." But I'll let June Millington have the last word, an E-mail message she shot across the country to me just as I was finishing this book:

> The Michigan 1997 experience with Cris and Tret, both on night and day stages, was kind of a watershed event with respect to the feelings "then" (mid '70s) and "now" ('90s). Something came together: Some need reemerged and coalesced with the entertain-me-like-I'm-watching-*Bound* factor that has so permeated a certain aspect of women's/gays' culture in the last ten years. Know what I mean? Women's souls were sort of looking at each other and rebonding and going, "Yeah, that's why we're all here. These are the voices we need to hear. This feels great— it's us!" I know I had a shit-eating grin when I looked at Cris and then at the audience as they were on their feet, cheering; and I yelled, "Dinosaurs rule!"

1. James Sullivan, "How Women Have Muscled in on the Male-Dominated Music Industry," in the *San Francisco Chronicle* "Datebook" section, July 6-12, 1997, p.32.

2. Urvashi Vaid, "Last Word: Calling All Lesbians," in *The Advocate,* September 16, 1997; p. 88.

3. k.d. lang, in *Rolling Stone,* 13 November 1997, p. 129.

4. Ladyslipper Catalog, Fall 1997, p. 5.

5. Gay men also face mockery as a consumer audience for music recordings. *Newsweek* magazine reported in 1995 that "this week Teldec becomes probably the first major recording company to aim an American release specifically at gay men.... Teldec executives expected record dealers to be reluctant to carry a 'gay CD.'" Lucy Howard and Carla Koehl, in *Newsweek,* February 13, 1995

6. Elizabeth Davis, "A World Without Men?" in *WIG,* Winter 1997, p. 13.

7. Heather Findlay, "Inside Girlfriends," in *Girlfriends,* November/December 1996, p. 8.

8. Alyssa Katz, "Gynosaur Rock," in *Spin,* November 1997, p. 112.

9. Unfortunately, misunderstandings arose even at the cross-generational mixer. One older woman tried describing her experiences as the daughter of an original "suffragette" only to be interrupted immediately by a younger woman who barked, "You mean *suffragist.*" "No," apologized the older festiegoer, "*At that time* we called 'em *suffragettes.*" Having been invited to tell her tale, then publicly corrected, she struggled to pick up the thread of her story.

APPENDIX A

The Voices of Festiegoers

There is no "average" festiegoer; women's music festivals have as their goal the celebration of diversity. The greater the range of difference—in age, race, ethnicity, ability, skills, and interests—the more a festival congratulates its success as an institution of the American feminist melting pot. A good festival includes in its parking lot license plates from many states and Canadian provinces, girls hand in hand with grandmothers, access for women of varying abilities and needs. No one is average here because each woman is welcomed as unique, important. However, based on my interviews with festiegoers during the past ten to 15 years, it is clear that four particular aspects of the festival experience (in addition to the great music) do attract the "typical" festiegoer to return time and again. These four aspects are:

1) The personal safety of women-only space. The temporary reprieve from fear of rape and assault is exhilarating, particularly for urban women. By extension, this dropped guard includes the freedom to change clothes in public or to go naked, the freedom to walk through pleasant woods after dark without concern, relative assurance that one can leave valuables unattended, and the knowledge that if one is injured or separated from one's child or Mom there are hundreds of women around to help. Nearly every woman who has ever been to a festival comments on this sense of safety.

2) Freedom to love other women openly. No need to hide, lie, or be in the closet here, and for lesbians that is a rare and unforgettable taste of being in the majority, accepted as normative. The public affirmation of women's relationships includes

hearing one's lifestyle celebrated in song after song and sitting in an open field kissing without public censure—the ultimate liberation for many.

3) A focus on female spirituality and healing. Festivals offer a powerful sense of being held in the palm of a loving Goddess, as opposed to a patriarchal and punitive God. There is ample opportunity to explore alternative woman- or earth-based forms of worship and an artistic focus on matriarchal images common to all pre-Christian civilizations. For ecofeminists, finding the Goddess in nature *and* culture dovetails with the political responsibility to care for our Earth's resources. For others the power in feeling part of a spiritual chain linking past and present women is best summed up in a popular bumper sticker: THE GODDESS IS ALIVE AND MAGIC IS AFOOT.

4) Seeing what cooperative and creative energy can accomplish. Festivals offer the chance to participate in an alternative to society's more competitive and destructive institutions. Here women relish being heard as contributors with skills and ideas; young women gain much from observing other women in charge. At all levels there is role modeling and mentoring during the process of building a holistic city. For new festiegoers there is a profound sense of awe in seeing myths about female weakness or incompetence blithely disproven in every arena.

The music performed at festivals celebrates each of the aforementioned aspects—in songs including Alix Dobkin's "If It Wasn't For the Women," Ova's "Some Little Girls Say No," Mimi Baczewska's "Women of the World," Ubaka Hill's "Motherbeat," Ruth Pelham's "You Can Be a Lesbian," Maxine Feldman's "Amazon," Linda Tillery's "Chosen Ones"—lyrics reinforced summer after summer on stages under the stars.

The Festiegoer Journals ⪼

How did I collect written responses from over 1,000 festiegoers? In the summer of 1986, when I turned 25, I began carrying a blank journal to festivals I attended, asking random festiegoers to write briefly about what festival culture meant to them. I gave no formal instructions, other than suggesting to those with writer's block that they might describe their favorite "festival moment" (a sneaky way, I will admit, of getting others to provide the minutiae of festival herstory for me). I chose many different times and environments for passing around my blank book: twilight at Michigan, as women waited in the audience for night stage concerts to begin; poolside at Campfest; the dinner line at the West Coast festival; front row of the Indiana University theater during the National Women's Music Festival. If I saw a solitary or unoccupied woman, I engaged her with this writing request. I often passed the journal around on shuttle buses headed back to airports after festivals ended, when grimy but glowing campers, apprehensive about "reentry," were eager to add comments on the contrast between festival culture and the outside world. Best of all were certain orgiastic research moments I recall, when I had my tape recorder running, my own journal in my lap, *and* the festiegoer book passing around the audience at a night stage concert—every part of the festival experience being documented and experienced simultaneously.

Some women proudly signed their full names and addresses; others asked for complete anonymity. Some wrote with poetic care and gusto about how festival culture had changed their lives; a few simply scrawled an enthusiastic "Yee-hah!" and then asked for *my* phone number. Others read through the entire journal first and then disappeared into deep thought for hours, trying to find just the right words for their own contribution. Many first-time festiegoers thanked me for the opportunity to clarify their reactions to this new culture. And more than a few women were up-front about refusing to write, explaining that their poor educations had left them with fear of writing; because I was a college teacher with a Ph.D., they did not want me to see their possibly "wrong" spelling and grammar. For these women I turned on my tape recorder and switched to oral herstory. Still, the book grew and grew, until its last page was crammed full at the 1991 Michigan festival.

When I flew home from Michigan that August, cradling the collected writings in my backpack, I had a sense of foreboding and worried that my apartment might have been damaged by fire. This proved inaccurate. Instead, someone followed me from the subway and seized my backpack when I arrived at my building—taking, among other things, my Minolta camera (full of festival photographs), my wallet, my address book, my own journal, a complete set of the 1970s women's music journal *Paid My Dues*, the manuscript I was writing that summer, and the precious leather-bound book of festiegoer comments I had collected for six years.

During the next three days, I lay motionless on my bed, unwilling to believe what had happened. While I might replace my credit cards and camera in time, there was no way to reproduce the hundreds of festiegoer reflections written by women from all over the world. I had not even had the opportunity to read through the last pages filled at Michigan. Six summers of networking lost in one instant to a thief who could not possibly understand or care. Why? Why? What is the value of one woman's story? Of ten? Of 200? How many women's thoughts were now condemned to a trash Dumpster or, worse, being read aloud by laughing hate-crimes types who might threaten us all? No other incident could have better illustrated the contrast between the safety one enjoys at festivals versus the threats to our work and our persons in the "real" world. No other incident could better illustrate the devaluing of women's cultural contributions in a violent and predatory world.

And now the miracle ending: The phone rang. A woman in my neighborhood had found my backpack. The thief had removed my wallet and camera, then thrown everything else under somebody's back porch. All my other belongings were intact and unharmed. Within minutes of that astounding phone call, I was reunited with my book of festiegoer writings, and believe me, I kept that journal under my pillow the rest of that fall. Eventually I wrote an article about this harrowing experience for *HOT WIRE*, mentioning that a Therese Edell album I'd bought at Michigan was the only item damaged in my backpack. Therese Edell, reading my article months later, insisted upon mailing me a new album.[1]

I believe there is a reason the festiegoer journal was not lost or destroyed but, instead, returned to me: It is an artifact owned by us all. The moral of the story is that women must continue to be our own best biographers. Only *we* acknowledge, value, and record the lives we lead. And sadly, the physical threats to our lives that accompany woman-hating can imperil the archival herstory we collect and save. Recording even our conflicts as well as favorite memories ensures an honest record of what festival culture means to us in these times.

Since then I have continued to ask for festiegoer writings, filling a second (and much larger) book between 1991 and 1995, and now a third has just been filled— with the last inscription by Alice Walker, who attended Michigan in 1998. I began to type the festiegoer writings onto computer disks in fall 1995, finding that at that point I had contributions from almost 1,000 women—including performers and festiegoers from as far away as Japan, Ireland, Germany, Australia. I had extraordinary written comments from children, workers, couples in love, Deaf women, lesbians in the military, teachers, students, activists, even French and Spanish speakers whose entries I had to translate. All expressed articulate responses to the question, "What does festival culture mean to you?"

From these once blank books, I have chosen approximately 300 excerpts to include here. These display the best range of festiegoers' backgrounds and interests and convey the most thoughtful and powerful sentiments about the appeal of women's music festivals.

There is no way to go back and contact each individual woman to thank her for the gift of her prose. And mindful of the need for anonymity and privacy in a homophobic world, I have not identified the writers' full names here—except for those few women I know personally, who granted their consent. But I have kept the writers' home states, towns, and countries wherever these were noted in the journals as pleasant proof that we truly are everywhere and from everywhere. Let these unself-conscious writings from 40 different festivals held throughout the 1980s and 1990s serve to express the audience's collective tribute to festival culture:

Free to love women—thousands of them, and one special one.
—C., from Ontario, Canada, at the Michigan Womyn's Music Festival, 1986

This land we love. The womyn who come from this land—we work together, live together, love together. We come from far away places, but we all have the goddess of the sun, earth, wind, and moon. May we never forget the great Goddess in our lives.
—D., from Wisconsin, at Michigan, 1986

Water/rain/moon/and sky
May womyn love each other until we die.
—D., from Minnesota, at Michigan, 1986

Great goddess energy
renewing, strengthening
filling us up with white light
we womyn who love one another
receive and claim the
power to create, mold
and shape our own realities.
—S., from Wisconsin, at Michigan, 1986

Wildflowers, trees, deep woods, quiet ferns, lightning, conversation, electric feet—first comes free-
dom, and with it, unlimited growth.
—B., from Buffalo, N.Y., at Michigan, 1986

My first festival here—my heart is dancing with music and good talk. How we have learned to
take care of one another! Through the hard lessons, we dream our dreams and make them real. A
teacher from San Francisco, I need to remember that we can grow and change and love one an-
other through our struggle to create this sylvan of joy.
—K., from San Francisco, at Michigan, 1986

Being naked, my soul is naked. I feel breath, wind, trees, birds, flowers, green grasses, sky—
I am now a part of nature.
—Machiko, from Japan, at Michigan, 1986

Thank you, Great Mother; it feels great to be back on the land. Last summer I arrived on the land
differently abled. I went to the Womb and was worked on by an osteopath who healed me. Today
I come with both hands working and no disability. It's through the love and healing energy that
we all share this life-enhancing experience! I thank with love all the wonderful women who work
so hard to create this environment. I am one of your lesbian sisters.
—L., from San Francisco, at Michigan, 1986

The Goddess has given us this land so that we may continue her work.
—D., at Michigan, 1986

Damn good cold showers. Baby, see you there.
—T., from Dallas, at Michigan, 1986

Ah, Amazon Nation, blessed be. I could stay here forever.
—L., from Dallas, at Michigan, 1986

Amazon womyn rise: Next year we will beat drums in the jungle of womyn.
This rhythm is the blood of life.
—Anonymous, at Michigan, 1986

This is the best: the East Coast says so! Come back and bring more womyn for my airport shuttle.
—T., from Boston, at Michigan, 1986

We can create our own reality: love and power.
—S., from Austin, at Michigan, 1986

You are perfect today/This very moment, you are perfect.
—B., from Minnesota, at Michigan, 1986

It was a village—it was our village—we created it.
How empowering—how fulfilling—
And the drums were everywhere
And the drums were everywhere
And the drums were everywhere.
—J., from Provincetown, Mass., at Michigan, 1986

So, this land is a gathering place for Lesbian Nation. It has gone through changes and growth. It is far from "ideal," but it is a wonderful place. The land was once under the water; it is special just by itself. And then the wimmin's energy transforms it. Michigan is an important part of my life, and I've come eight out of the 11 years. Sometimes I miss the intimacy of the earlier festivals and how we used to play music in twos and threes in the woods, on the paths and around the campfires. Now it's almost all on the stage. But at the same

time, I have seen the growth in resources for sober support, emotional support, differently abled. I love the festival, and it is in my blood.
—S., from New York City, at Michigan, 1986

Another gathering, amidst changes, personal and in our community, on this wondrous land that is nurtured by us and nurtures us in turn. Standing/dancing/yelling/singing/crying/laughing, earthbound but extending outward to one another and to the sky, stretching so far along the horizon. I carry the energy and safety of this home and through the year.
— C., at Michigan, 1986

Living in the moment…Breathing…Celebration of the Source.
—C., from Toronto, at Michigan, 1987

Glistening skin, in the sun, in the rain,
Bright energy smiles,
And warm love, aglow.
—D., at Michigan, 1987

Because I am good and belong, like every other woman, at the center of things, I will no longer deny my living, my loving, my relationships, or my abilities. I am completely good, I am fully feminine—I AM A WOMAN/I AM A LESBIAN.
—K., from Madison, Wis., at Michigan, 1987

My first festival, and I never knew women came in so many sizes and shapes and colors. Delightful!
—C., from Boston, at Michigan, 1987

We called the earth, the fire, the air, the water—and they blessed us with their presence.
—K., at Michigan, 1987

Energy follows intent. "We are the subversives!"
—H., at Michigan, 1987

We're lesbian life lovers.
—K., from Sacramento, at Michigan, 1987

The hawk just flew over, and we are blessed, and I will come to this place again and again. Spirits are soaring as women come together to transform the world.
—Anonymous, at Michigan, 1987

The Harmonic Convergence: Some laughed and called themselves Harmonica Virgins. Others, with reverence, love, and hope, sang, danced, and meditated to Mother Earth. (I hugged a tree.) Did our planet respond? Are lightning, thunder, and drenching rain galactic conversation? Was there hail, sleet, hurricanes, or tornadoes at the seven sacred sites? And did the promised downpour of enlightenment come through? Those of us who believe will hope.
Those of us who hope, we believe.
—Anonymous, at Michigan, 1987

This peaceful, restful land gave me a dose of serenity. These lively, loving, and strong wimmin gave me a dose of hope. I am thankful for my first festival experience; now I know what so many have known.
—A., at Michigan, 1987

Two years ago I came to Michigan for the first time and really started to believe that women can be different. After my third and hardest Michigan, I still think so. I want to figure out why some women don't think they need this as much as I do. And I want to make it happen every day.
—J., from New York, at Michigan, 1987

After a first festival, my heart is smiling, my shirt feels weird, and my mind is blown.... Amen.
—E., from Tucson, at Michigan 1987

Every year, whether rain or shine, women's energy keeps bringing me here and keeps the dream alive.
—A., at the North East Women's Music Retreat, 1988

There once was a festival, and it rained, and the power went out. But I will always remember: The spirit is a woman, it goes on and on.
—D., at NEWMR, 1988

Here in the rain with these women it feels like I'm 13 in the rain at camp. We carry all things with us, always; this is a good place to bring them home.
—C., from Vermont, at NEWMR, 1988

Freedom is one of those things like trust—to have it you must give it away.
—Anonymous, at NEWMR, 1988

There are only two things, two types of things, in all the world—those things born of love and those things born of fear. You know the difference. Which will you choose?
—Anonymous, at NEWMR, 1988

My first festival: Women empowerment, that's what I'll take with me. May it continue to heal me, and may I send it out as a legacy to other women.
—D., at NEWMR, 1988

Life begins at your first Michigan Womyn's Music Festival. And I have been reborn! Born again lesbian in 1989.
—K., from Rhode Island, at Michigan, 1989

Women and magic. Carry the love, dream the peace, love the similarities, but look at the differences. Plan on it.
—Anonymous, at Michigan, 1989

Dreams turn into reality—under the August moon.
—M., from Tucson, at Michigan, 1989

Hot. Incredible energy, incredibly beautiful womyn, fabulous fabulous strong soft funky wonderful time for experiencing the dream come true of womyn loving womyn loving living love. I'll bring

you home, Michigan, inside and outside me.
—Anonymous, at Michigan, 1989

If we dare to live our dream of womyn's strength and power and beauty every day,
we will transform this little planet.
—C., from Colorado, at Michigan, 1989

This commemorates the first (but hopefully not last) Norwegian lesbians' caucus
at the Michigan festival. And for posterity, here's how to say
"I want your hot body, you beautiful woman"—
"Jeg vi ha din hette knopp, din nejdelige kvinne!"
—E., from Norway, at Michigan, 1989

This is the real world. I don't want to go back to that other one. Michigan—
I'm an awestruck festie virgin.
—P., at Michigan, 1989

This festival should be a springboard for social change and activism, not some fantasy island.
Let's take it away!
—Anonymous, at Michigan, 1989

May the vision of the Festival inspire you all year long to become the most radical
lesbian, the most politicized dyke, speaking out your lesbian truth in every situation.
Be on fire with the desire for freedom for all womyn. Love yourself deeply.
—B., from Canada, at Michigan, 1989

This festival seems to bring out the best of woman-loving energy. My stay here as a performer has
been like being in a long embrace. What energy to play to and to have coming toward me!
—Charlotte, of the singing group Libana, from Boston, at Michigan, 1989

This is my first over-40s pickup experience. It's a trip to watch.
—B., from Minneapolis, at Michigan, 1989

My first time here and I am more empowered now than a year of therapy would do. Amazon Nation is alive and well—and beautiful!
—B., from Minnesota, at Michigan, 1989

I want to have Vicki Randle's children. A girl can dream, right?
—Jamie Anderson, from Tucson, at Michigan, 1989

Once my hair was dark as night
(Change is coming around)
Now it's silver as moonlight
(Change is coming around)
Winter's earth is dark and lorn
(Change is coming around)
Summer's earth is green and warm
(Change is coming around.)
—Marsha Farmer, at Michigan, 1989

Treetops, quaking aspens, love, womyn feeding one another—knowing the truth and taking it home with me every year. This is the year of my aspen dream.
—K., from Virginia, at Michigan, 1989

This was truly, oolee, oolee beautiful—driving shuttles, singing gospel, lying happy in a hammock getting over FMS (fear of missing something).
—E., from Washington state, at Michigan, 1989

To know what it feels like to be safe
To know that I can walk naked in the woods
To know that I am a part of an international community
To know that all this and more is not only possible—but a reality.
—H., from Philadelphia, at Michigan, 1989

Bless these women—Boo and Lisa—for sacred womyn's land to share. I grow with each festival,

becoming more womynly; may it continue ad infinitum.
—M., from Connecticut, at Michigan, 1989

Now I'm feeling too hot and too dirty and too filled up with experiences—seen, heard, thought,
felt, eaten. And it's been wonderful, and I hope to come back.
—U., from Germany, at Michigan, 1989

This was my second Michigan, and as I sit here on the airport shuttle, I can already
feel the "magic dust" begin to rub off. So thank the Goddess we have a space where we
get "dusted" anyway!
—K., from Los Angeles, at Michigan, 1989

No better way could I transition my life from prostitution to freedom of choice
than to be in the company of women who, because of discrimination, may
appreciate freedom of choice.
—Anonymous, at Michigan, 1989

From Girl Scout to Gynivore! You can take a woman out of Michigan, but you'll never take
Michigan out of a woman.
—D., from Vancouver, Canada, at Michigan, 1989

We are the flow, we are the ebb; we are the weavers, we are the web.
—Anonymous, at Michigan, 1989

California's hot, hot, dry sun. A women's concert, patches, layers of clothing in my bag. Notes,
laughs, aluminum chairs in soft dirt. Hot and cold flashes!
—S., from Seattle, at the West Coast Lesbian Festival, 1989

It's a high that I'll take home with me! The first het I see after this weekend,
I'm going to let them know I am a lesbian!
—A., from San Jose, Calif., at West Coast, 1989

I knew I needed to surround myself with woman energy, but I could not have envisioned the reality of it. I am revitalized, renewed on an energetic, intellectual, spiritual level.
A lot to take home, and I get to go home with Sue.
—K., from Santa Rosa, Calif., at West Coast, 1989

Sitting in this high meadow with pen in hand—women are gathering for this evening under twilight skies as the sunlight graces the green mountain—in shadows and patterns, and one's partner-lover–soul mate is near—sitting beside each other, women's lives together.
A world tapestry, a love in this life.
—A., at West Coast, 1989

I will certainly take the energy and these varied experiences back with me to Placerville, California—a place known as "Old Hangtown" and not exactly known for its progressive community. There is much work to be done. This festival helps recharge me and makes it possible for me to continue the domestic violence and sexual assault work that I do. I will miss this freedom but look forward to returning home to see our children.
—K., at West Coast, 1989

All day, all ways, this makes us able to go back to that other world, with a strong sense of where reality is.
—A. at West Coast, 1989

Yay for recovery from drugs, alcohol, and codependency.
—K., from Santa Cruz, Calif., at West Coast, 1989

This event is such a clever idea. I love it; I feel so great when I leave. I wish there was an island where we could all live in peace, in happiness of each other.
—C., from San Bernadino, Calif., at West Coast, 1989

Spirit lives us, knows us, keeps us—loves us. I hope your walking is filled with the beautiful experience of this.
—Mindy Ray, performer, at West Coast, 1989

Robin Tyler's workshop today was wonderful. She sees women healing and taking responsibility for themselves as a general trend, as opposed to coming to this land to escape the angry world and then direct it at each other!
—L., at West Coast, 1989

Wimmin can change the world only if we change the game of men. But we need to cleanse ourselves first. The pitfall would be to continue their poisons.
—I., from Ithaca, N.Y., at East Coast Lesbian Festival, 1990

Pizza...lettuce...dishes...carrots...celery...more dishes...Thank God kitchen duty's over.
—S., from Chicago, at ECLF, 1990

Lesbian womyn—queens on the scene—with our power and our womyn gynergy can shatter their world.
—Marilyn T., performer, at ECLF, 1990

Come the winter of 1990, Echo Lark Camp grounds will echo with the voices of many proud lesbians. These lesbians are proud to be among the voices.
—C. and K., at ECLF, 1990

It is the 15th Michigan Womyn's Music Festival, and I'm sitting at a table wondering who else I'll run into during the next few days. The variety of women is, as always, comforting—the different styles, energy, shapes, sizes, all here gathered together. Hair is still important—very popular is a shaven look on the sides and more hair on the top—mohawk-like—and it seems that longer hair is more popular than a couple years ago. Colors—pinks, blues, reds—seem less popular in hair, although there was one woman I noticed at the orientation tent who looked very punked out with long hair and reddish streaks throughout. The workshops are as varied as usual, topics as varied as the women. Two-stepping going on in the background, grapevine, 1-2-3, touch, sashay. The lights in this cafe are truly sweet—pink and green Chinese lanterns—I am blissed out. Oh, yes, the trees know, and the stones for sure know what we will never know, may realize someday but will probably pass by in thinking that knowledge is power.
—L., from Cambridge, Mass., at Michigan, 1990

Gidday mate! This land is wonderful—the heat feels like home.
And s-o-o-o many womyn; WHOA!
—A., from Australia, at Michigan, 1990

As I sit waiting for food in the dinner line, I am contented.
—Anonymous, at Michigan, 1990

I only wish I came out earlier. But, oh, well, this is heaven anyways.
—Anonymous, at Michigan, 1990

I'm a first-timer who came with returnees who couldn't prepare me well enough for this safe and
loving experience. We are the earth, the goddess, the breath. Let's breathe deeply—Motherpeace.
—R., at Michigan, 1990

As I walked through the woods last night alone and saw the fireworks through
the trees and heard the cheers of thousands of womyn, I realized,
"This place is magical."
Carry that magic out to that "other world" out there.
—C., from Cincinnati, at Michigan, 1990

This festival, my dream of many years to attend, has been the best feeling in my heart and mind
ever. The planet should be like this.
—T., from Detroit, at Michigan, 1990

Il faut y etre pour le croire…et j'y suis la fierte et le bonheur de croitre avec mes
souers lesbiennes me marque a jamais.
—H., from Ottawa, at Michigan, 1990

Michigan is the most special of places, spiritual, harmonious, sensual;
and I want to come back forever.
—M., from Connecticut, at Michigan, 1990

Esta fue mi primera festival; me gusto mucho.
—R., at Michigan, 1990

*My favorite memory is the standard of excellence that women have achieved in
their art, music, and patience.*
—Anonymous, at Michigan, 1990

My memory was day care and skipping rope and sitting by campfire.
—E., age 6, at Michigan, 1990

*My favorite time was sitting outside my tent and hearing some woman playing
a sax somewhere in the woods.*
—G., from Seattle, at Michigan, 1990

*Running around and dancing shirtless! With 8,000 womyn! Most of them dykes!
So great to be in the majority for once!*
—T., from San Francisco, at Michigan, 1990

*Rhiannon and Judy Grahn's powerful work on incest brought up lots of emotion for me.... Won-
derful music, especially jazz.... And the Dyke Scientists workshop, where I got to meet some other
womyn who love science!*
—B., at Michigan, 1990

*Ah, Rhiannon's set on the acoustic stage—there are simply no words—the acoustic
stage setting itself—the intimacy.*
—S., at Michigan, 1990

WED I spent pissed at my ex-lover and looking for my navy blue tent at night.
THU I spent playing the congas all over in the grass, like fruits all over in the grass.
FRI I spent getting laid.
SAT I spent learning that Friday night had a lover and saying it was OK.
SUN I spent keeping a girlfriend warm. I talked to my ex. I kissed Friday night. My best memory

was Friday night, although I also liked telling my friend Kathy, a full-bodied woman, that I felt like a rail for the first time. There's that song by Sweet Honey in the Rock that says, "I'll be loving you like a patchwork quilt." I didn't mind so much being a rail in Michigan, where all the sizes are like patches. My other best memories were difference and respect.
And one can't forget the children!
—L., at Michigan, 1990

Transformative and informative, transcendental and yet existential, women-loving-women–only space—I felt safe and nurtured for once in my life. I will carry the wisdom and strength of the lesbians who touched me—a favorite memory is Casselberry and Dupree, whose music has helped me through harsh emotional weather and storms. I will return to this space from now on; forever starts now with my first Michigan experience.
—R., from Ohio, at Michigan, 1990

This is my first festival, and I think it is a joy to be among other sisters. I have enjoyed every minute of my coming into being.
—P., at the Gulf Coast Womyn's Festival, 1991

As time goes, my destiny is still at reach, but remember true life's pleasure is being in love with a woman. For I am a woman. May you spread love to a sister, no matter what race, and remember that love is the key to all woes, no matter where you are.
—A., at Gulf Coast, 1991

As humans, we are constantly searching outside ourselves for happiness. The treasure lies within.
—R., at Gulf Coast, 1991

Fantastic, marvelous, sad, joyous, filling, enlightening! Wonderful, wonderful, wonderful—life is wonderful.
—Anonymous, at Gulf Coast, 1991

We're queer, we're here, get over it. Clits rule!
—Diane Germain, at Gulf Coast, 1991

I too am here because I love women. I am here because I need grounding. I am here because I need energy to fight my "Southern burnout."
—G., at Gulf Coast, 1991

Continue to teach the reality of all our herstory.
—B., at Gulf Coast, 1991

This was a very liberating experience for me due to the fact that I skinny-dipped in a "public" pool for the first time!
—J., at Campfest, 1991

This new experience was one of the best in 46 years of life and living.
—Anonymous, at Campfest, 1991

The women from N.Y. were here
To enjoy Campfest, good friends, and good cheer.
The women were hot,
We partied a lot,
And we'll all be back next year.
—Cabin V (eight women), at Campfest, 1991

It brings me such joy and strength to continue with my own struggles with identities and definitions. Stay delighted. Keep baring those breasts.
—O., at ECLF, 1991

Take it out there, sister.
—L., at ECLF, 1991

I've been going to camp since I was a little kid in Athens, Greece. Always the last day was very difficult for me. This space of women loving women is very powerful; that finally brings tears to my eyes, and this last day of camp for me is warm.
—N., from Athens, Greece, at ECLF, 1991

First year here—as a city woman, I was ready to hide my money, watch my stuff, and I was (am) astounded by the trust of this community. Next year I will bring more young lesbians from Boston with me.
—N., from Boston, at Michigan, 1991

First time here, enjoying the whole thing; it's definitely something I shall pass on to my other Kansas sisters. Reactions from Auntie Em? Dorothy surely would have liked it!
—M., from Wichita, Kan., at Michigan, 1991

I learned a lot. I found out about two lesbians who legally married because one of them "passed" as a man! Anything is possible.
—R., at Michigan, 1991

1991 was my eighth festival as [the We Want the Music Collective's] *documentary photographer, and as my eyes see and record our woman power and energy, it grows in my heart. We need to keep that energy flowing and growing as we go to our homes! Be loud, be proud—be wild!*
—Phoenix, at Michigan, 1991

I love coming to this largest festival every year. This time I met women from Germany, Holland, Japan, Canada, South America, France, etc.! I love sharing in their wisdom and insight. I've made myself a promise I will come every year (this is my eighth or ninth time) to recharge and heal and return refreshed. I feel ready again to contribute to the world through my work and with wings, eyes, ears, and heart. Thank you, all of you who come to live and love and play here every year. I love you, in all of your diversity.
—J., from Tampa, Fla., at Michigan, 1991

I feel inspired by all the variety of creativity that women bring here—it is empowering to my own unique expression. I also feel I was blessed by the Goddess's magic wand and met a very beautiful woman—heart, body, mind, spirit—and we shared gently as we explored ourselves— alas, she lives in Toronto, and I live in California! I shared my heart with this woman for a brief time, and my spirit feels kindred with her for infinity. Maybe I will see her again, I don't know. What I feel is the fountain of profound love that grows within and without—all women are

beautiful—let's bring caring and honesty into all our interactions, with ourselves, with our Earth.
Passion of life is growing!
—L., from California, at Michigan, 1991

Yes, Sisters, for always, I take it back now to my Amsterdam.
—M., from the Netherlands, at Michigan, 1991

I listened more and gained more at this festival than I thought I would. I learned a lot about op-
pression and my part in it. Now I have to figure out what to do with this knowledge! Keep
learning and growing, I guess. Being a woman at Michigan is such a freeing experience—what
an incentive: a year-round Michigan somewhere, eventually?
—C., from Texas, at Michigan, 1991

Another path I have walked down for the first time. It will change my life! I take strength, power,
and woman energy—I will regenerate that energy in a world that needs us.
I am a woman warrior, a survivor.
—J., from Los Angeles, at Michigan, 1991

My favorite memory: lying on the earth listening to the womyn drummers, especially Edwina.
I drifted into a beautiful place.
—C., from Los Angeles, at Michigan, 1991

I feel most myself at this festival, free, unjudged. And I love having my favorite person with me.
—D., from New Jersey, at Michigan, 1991

My favorite moment: 2 A.M. Friday night, outside and safe and laughing to lift the sky with a
very special loving woman friend.
—B., from Oakland, Calif., at Michigan, 1991

I love it—a women's city, great music, wet feet, wet kisses.
—M., from Australia, at Michigan, 1991

This was my first festival. It's part of a dream I've had since childhood—living together in peace and harmony, celebrating and releasing the reality that has been created on this earth. Thanks for a new reality, and Goddess bless us all.
—K., from New Jersey, at Michigan, 1991

This is the living, loving vine that brings us all together.
—T., from California, at Michigan. 1991

The calm of the women in the kitchen really inspired me as a way to combine my interest in cooking with antiracist work. The spirit of NEWMR always allows my soul to rest in a way it is unable to in any other time or space.
—B., at NEWMR, 1991

This place centers me, focuses me so that I can go back into the real world and breathe.
—H., at NEWMR, 1991

I've finally found my life partner at age 43; I've been coming to festivals for many years, and she's never been to one. I brought her to Campfest, introduced her to all of my friends, got to go swimming with her for the first time, and thoroughly enjoyed watching her face as she watched all the women.
—Anonymous, at Campfest, 1992

This is the third time I've been to Campfest. Every time, I am amazed by the beauty of all the different sizes and shapes women appear in. Here, together, in the wilderness, we create a safe space where we can all be ourselves freely—even if it's fuckin' butt cold, man!
—M., from New York City, at Campfest, 1992

All the funny moments, the lovely ladies close dancing together.
—K., from Cambridge, Mass., at ECLF, 1992

At my first festival it's been wet for three days—and not in an unpleasant way. Sort of the dyke version of Woodstock. I liked it—and my lover and I finally found our wedding rings.
—T., from Philadelphia, at ECLF, 1992

My favorite moments of the festival are seeing my all-time favorite performers, lesbian legends, simply walking through the land. One minute I'm saying, "Ooh, there's Jamie Anderson! There's Sue Fink! Wait a minute, there's Margie Adam!"—and then I'm sitting down, and Pam Hall asks if I mind if she sits next to me. Life is good!
—J., from Staten Island, N.Y., at ECLF, 1992

I enjoy the community of women that this festival offers along with the very many diversities, being a person who not too long ago found her place in the sun in all aspects of herself as well as her rich Native heritage. There is much to celebrate and be proud of; most important to be very grateful for—I met my friend, my lover, my partner here, at the first East Coast Lesbian Festival close to our home.
—S., at ECLF, 1992

Throughout the rain and all the craziness, I remember the reason I do this: the feeling of pure joy that came over me when Margie Adam began to play.
That's why I'm here—that and all the wonderful, loving womyn.
—Satya, at ECLF, 1992

It's about time that the Lesbian wimyn of the world (or at least U.S.A.) get it together and set an example of peace and harmony and celebrate diversity among all colors, religions, personalities, etc....so "society" as it is can see how wrong exclusion is! And how wonderful lesbians are!
—J., from Maine, at the Northampton Lesbian Festival, 1992

Two days of freedom out of the closet, beauty and diversity, seeing all these women celebrating each other.... It's always great to be out with so many dykes!
—B., from Boston, at Northampton, 1992

The complete memory is my favorite part...to be surrounded by such comfortable dykes.
—A., from Connecticut, at Northampton, 1992

Festivals make me think continually of sex. Perhaps that is because I picked up a hot woman at my first music festival of this season.
—Anonymous, from Maryland, at Michigan, 1992

It's wonderful to meet so many women from all parts of the world. I noticed that if you get a woman talking about home, her accent intensifies. Cool, huh? Do festivals keep getting better at this rate?
—Allison, at Michigan, 1992

One performer asked me how to use a sleeping bag.
—M., at Michigan, 1992

I turned around because a voice told me to and saw my girlfriend, whom I'd not seen in 12 years, among the trees and sun.
—D., from California, at Michigan, 1992

Looking up at the stars, listening to Vicki Randle, with a cup of coffee in hand—it doesn't get much better than that.
—Julie Homi, at Michigan, 1992

The clouds threaten fierce rain, but it only falls at night after the concerts; I am all tucked into my lover's arms, and I listen to the night rain.
—Z. Budapest, at Michigan, 1992

Fireflies and shooting stars brighten the night sky; I work all day, listening to great music all night, finally fall asleep tangled in my lover's arms.
—H., at Michigan, 1992

Freedom, retreat, acceptance; all the womyn witches dykes.
—L., from Vancouver, Canada, at Michigan, 1992

I worked at the box office and was able to watch an 18-year-old from Iowa be given a ticket that another woman donated to the festival.
—A., from Lancaster, Pa., at Michigan, 1992

Playing cowbell with my pals in the performer tent on Sunday afternoon…percussion heaven.
—Linda Tillery, at Michigan, 1992

My memories of the women's festival include beautiful sounds, beautiful things, beautiful people. I cannot remember a time in my life that I was as totally relaxed. Even though I got lost every day—it was still a grand, fantastic experience.
—Bettye Casselberry Vance, at Michigan, 1992

I hate camping, it's raining, they ran out of syrup, and my utopia includes a microwave and television. I'm missing the Bills game this very minute!
—Leah Zicari, Buffalo, N.Y., at Rhythmfest, 1992

I wake up in the clouds, the tree frogs, the moans of pleasure.... Hers...Mine....
—V., at Rhythmfest, 1992

My favorite everlasting images of Rhythmfest: naked women playing volleyball in the rain, in the mud; rain rain rain, mud mud mud; a naked woman riding a mountain bike.
—E., at Rhythmfest, 1992

The number of lesbians there are, as different-looking as each and every one of us are; the laughter and uplifting attitudes carrying us through such wet conditions; being in the woods camping with no anxiety of a man walking through, nor my beeper going off with an emergency phone call; drumming, smiles.
—K., at Rhythmfest, 1992

Like all women's gatherings, Rhythmfest is like an electrical charge for me, rejuvenates me so that I may again go out into the hetero world and remain sane.
—B., at Rhythmfest, 1992

She was at the night-stage concert Saturday night. She was slightly over to the left. She was using a yoga pose—actually standing on her head. The green backdrop, her tapestry clothing, and her long dark body made a visual image for me that I hope I never forget.
—Anonymous, at Rhythmfest, 1992

*Great space—soothing space—warming space—healing space—loving space—womyn space—
wet space—muddy space—wet, muddy womyn space—supportive space—more spaces!*
—Anonymous, at Rhythmfest, 1992

Here I am able to hold hands with my sweetie.
—S., from Houston, at Gulf Coast, 1993

*Who can determine the length of a moment? Mine was the feeling of riding a giant wave of
laughter, love, and communion with wonderful womyn that stirred my waters inside. Thank you,
all womyn, for this journey.*
—L., from Houston, Gulf Coast, 1993

*Remember these times, swamp thing, mud queen, prancing about
butt mud naked; influence, honor, divine.*
—J., at Gulf Coast, 1993

*The opportunity to openly express my lesbian sexuality with other lesbians is so rare that I
cherish every minute I spend in such an environment. The sense of belonging, the sense of
being a part of a much greater whole both touches and nourishes my spirit. I will never take
such moments for granted.*
—S., from New Orleans, at Gulf Coast, 1993

*I have been coming out in the past year, and my interactions with other lesbians have been so val-
idating and feel like such a "homecoming." I finally have found women like me and have found
the courage in myself to let the real me be expressed in all the spaces I enter, including my workplace (a law firm). Sometimes it is scary, but it is so freeing. No longer can I play other roles because of what I think others expect of me. I am so awestruck that in every interaction that I have
with another lesbian, no matter how diverse we happen to be, I find something "that is me" in
her—a common identity. Thank God that I have been given this awareness and opportunity to
discover this about myself. I have found home and my family.*
—L., from New Orleans, at Gulf Coast, 1993

Many years have passed in my life that I have lost, forgotten, or missed the unified feeling of women. Together this weekend has rejuvenated this feeling in me.
—G., at Gulf Coast, 1993

Sun women music food, oh, this is livin'!
—M., at Campfest, 1993

A little bit of Mecca.
—C., from Jersey City, N.J., at Campfest, 1993

I'm having a relaxing, comfortable weekend with my aunt and sister, who are straight but not narrow, and my wonderful lover of four years.
—N., at Campfest, 1993

For the love of bugs and dirt, I camp.
—Julie Wheeler, at Campfest, 1993

Here I sit by the pool watching a woman with a large megaphone instruct women in the art of watermelon wrestling as she proudly displays today's colored ribbon, delicately bowed, in her curly ginger pubies. Yet another heart-warming, zany event in the festival world. Other such memories: nipple printing, vagina making workshops, chatting with ex-nuns, sweet jamming until sunrise, and the freshest, most open little kids this side of the universe.
—Zöe Lewis, at Campfest, 1993

I live for festivals, always have. We as lesbians, as a group, are slowly learning that what you spend your energy on is what comes about.
—Leda Shakti, at Campfest, 1993

This festival represents part of my dream come true: to be in an all-women environment. The realization of the full dream is the world led by women's values. To the women-future!
—M., at Campfest, 1993

My most moving moment was in Ruth Barrett's workshop about women's sacred mysteries. We made a circle, did some chanting, some rituals, and I really felt a part of something bigger than myself: something old, something essentially woman-oriented and part of a loving family of lesbians and women. It made me high the rest of the day. Magical, powerful, wonderful.
—A., from Cincinnati, at the National Women's Music Festival, 1993

I think memories of the festival-at-large don't tend to settle in until days and weeks later—as the spectacles on the stages and the larger images fold in and find their proper spaces to nestle in one's mind and heart and soul. Until then it's the one-on-one interactions, the smaller, momentary human connections that, like an impressionist painting, create an almost surreal picture held together in a magical gestalt.
—Marcy Hochberg, Chicago, at National, 1993

My favorite memory is driving all the women around, driving the van with a beautiful vest on and no shirt underneath, and loving every minute.
—S., from Northampton, Mass., at National, 1993

I bought the Martina Navratilova Fund-raiser dinner tickets in the auction; it felt really good to take a risk and be extravagant. Then, to top it off, I made a date with the auctioneer!
—S., at Northampton, 1993

From an English lesbian—I love the pride, the noise, the extroverts; we can learn much from our sisters over here.
—V., from London, England, at Northampton, 1993

Individually we are all pretty cute.... Together we are beautiful.
—J., from London, at Northampton, 1993

I think my most favorite thing about the Michigan festival is that it allows me to get away from city homophobia and be me and free one week out of the year—to run naked if I please and enjoy the beauty of women!
—K., from Chicago, at Michigan, 1993

The view! Thousands of women! The wonderful comfort of not looking over my shoulder, of going without a shirt and feeling safe.
—D., at Michigan, 1993

I love to walk alone in the woods at night without any insecurity—the freedom, the feeling of such safety, the oneness I feel with everyone, even the famous-ish gals. Walking down the path without a shirt and realizing that the people walking behind me are Holly Near and a friend. How cool—this is home.
—D., at Michigan, 1993

Hot, beautiful weather; hot, beautiful womyn—the total freedom to be in my body. Such acceptance, of being only with womyn, feels like being at home with myself. Between Margie Adam and shooting stars, I'm in heaven.
—J., from Ontario, Canada, at Michigan, 1993

We are dykes from Ireland. We are everywhere. But after this, bodies, sun, drums, we don't want to go back.
—Anonymous, from Ireland, at Michigan, 1993

What's the best part? Whew—so many—safety, love, sharing, power, energy, even tofu—and the absolute best—shopping.
—G., at Michigan, 1993

I am choosing freedom here, taking a part of this home, keeping it all in my heart. The pulsing of 8,000 is so ready for the rhythm of the drums; it builds and builds and then lets me go, free fall.
—C., from Texas, at Michigan, 1993

Hey, so many Canadians, eh? I'm one too. Michigan rules: the talent, energy, trust, spontaneity, and fun are blowing me away. Womyn rule! I have many reservations and criticisms, but it's OK because I also feel very free, safe, sexy, and happy. And I love the fact that total strangers chat each other up. Mais j'aimerais mieux si il y avait plus de Quebecoises!
—Anonymous, from Montreal, at Michigan, 1993

The unity that is being created among all women here is beautiful. Political correctness has its place, but honoring diversity and tolerance is a joy.
—S., from Illinois, at Michigan, 1993

I am attending my first Michigan festival at age 47 and have only been in the lesbian community one year. Wow, what a smashingly wonderful experience of women and nature, music and peace! Serenity…Energy.
—Anonymous, at Michigan, 1993

The joy of seeing lesbian feminist culture as the norm.
—Anonymous, at Michigan, 1993

I love the gentle, loving, woman energy all around. It's like being back in the womb. After spending a week here at the festival, I will never be the same. Most of all, I appreciate being in this private space where I can be honest and open and feel more in touch with what's most important to me in life: being me, contact with other women, especially lesbians—s-o-o-o special.
—Anonymous, at Michigan, 1993

A feeling of completion, loving, sensual touch—an orgasmic place of women.
—L., at Michigan, 1993

It's thrilling running into such wonderful players. I had no idea I'd find jazz jam sessions where I could play and drumming sessions that were ripe for listening. I'm glad I finally made it here, to this beautiful land, with a killer staff taking care of me.
—Julie Wolf, at Michigan, 1993

Listening and watching all the women—women loving women joining in evolution. The voices of the singers blend with the turning of days into nights. All of us stars in a brilliant canopy of wonder: The goddess is alive in Michigan.
—Ruth Barrett, at Michigan, 1993

Opening the festival as a four-legged stilt walker, walking down the aisles of screaming womyn,

being dubbed a "puppet dweeb," having crushes on all the foxy babes, going topless all day long.
—Wise Fool puppet makers, at Michigan, 1993

My favorite festival memories are all the sexy womyn I've had the pleasure of holding in my arms, but most of all, one particular black beautiful sister who turned all my lights on green and opened my heart to a new love.
—L., at Michigan, 1993

I had my lover say she loved me from the stage. Merry meet and merry part and merry meet again.
—M., at Michigan, 1993

I danced in the meditation circle with my sweet girl in the rain.
—Melanie DeMore, at Michigan, 1993

I met a brilliant pianist from New York—we jammed for five hours nonstop and transformed the kitchen into a hip jazz club!
—Mimi Fox, at Michigan, 1993

I was sitting watching the festival gospel choir in the rain. They did a song called "Rock Me, Hold Me," and I started crying. It was raining, and they were singing, and I was crying, rain and tears on my face; it was good.
—Anonymous, at Michigan, 1993

I can't think of anything better than womyn coming together to be with each other and nature.
—L., at Campfest, 1994

Work hard. Play harder. Find friendships new and old: You never know.
—Anonymous, at Campfest, 1994

My favorite image from this year is Lucie Blue Tremblay dancing with my granddaughter.
—P., at Campfest, 1994

Campfest is the one festival where I can relax and network by the pool. I like it because it's my "community" festival—all the Long Island girls who support me come here, so I can hang with them. I also like to walk around and talk to everyone; I like being a celebrity and dressing up!
—Retts Scauzillo, at Campfest, 1994

I went to Justina and Joyce's incredible workshop on voice. Singing like a dolphin and knowing that notes are not "high" or "low"; singing from below the womb, the whole body resonant. Great spirit, great words from great women.
—Chris Vinsonhaler, at Campfest, 1994

This women space gives me my energy for the year to come. This last year was hard, trying to pass a domestic partnership bill in Baltimore and dealing with Baptist ministers. Thinking about coming to Campfest got me through!
—B., from Baltimore, at Campfest, 1994

I came out in the '60s; there were only bars and drunks. This is refreshing—and empowering.
—G., from Baltimore, at Campfest, 1994

I will remember hearing Ubaka Hill call us all to work for a world of peace and justice and hearing Margie Adam remind us of the special vision of womyn, of the incredibly beautiful music that womyn create.
—Anonymous, at Campfest, 1994

I gave an engagement ring to my beloved woman while Margie Adam was singing a love song.
—L., at Campfest ,1994

I see the blended spirits in harmony everywhere and the wonderful ability to laugh with ourselves.
—K., at Campfest, 1994

Thank you, Goddess; I am feeling, laughing, playing, touching, dancing, and strengthened.
—L., at Campfest 1994

All those breasts.
—J., at Campfest, 1994

I've had lots of good times, but one that really sticks in my mind is the first year I got up enough courage to bring my paintings and be a craftswomon. That first time a womon bought my painting will always be dear to me.
—K., at Campfest, 1994

My spirit waits for this and then takes off for the summer.
—Barbara Slater, at Campfest, 1994

Life is from Campfest until Sisterspace. Then I hibernate.
—J., at Campfest, 1994

There is good food, sprit-filled air, sex—or no sex for some, like me—memorable meetings, a lovely lake, and geese, geese, geese.
—L., from Richmond, Va., at Campfest, 1994

Let time work the magic of rekindling and revealing many things.
—B., at National, 1994

I've been coming to Michigan for ten years now. I can't imagine not coming here— it's where I feel at home—a world built by womyn—with all the struggles, there's no place I'd rather be.
—M., from Cleveland, at Michigan, 1994

Michigan is energy—women's energy. You can feel it, enclose yourself in it, add to it.
—S., from Cleveland, at Michigan, 1994

I like the music, and I like the girls' camp, and I like everything.
—T., age 5, at Michigan, 1994

This is an annual thing that I can use to gauge where I am as far as my personal,
spiritual, action life.
—C., from Wisconsin, at Michigan, 1994

I like knowing that nothing happening here was created by anyone besides women. Women can do
all the best things with or without men!
—L., from Minneapolis, at Michigan, 1994

I feel such comfort—I'm in good company, and every bit of my body and spirit knows it. I am en-
joying me and all of you.
—R., from Ithaca, N.Y., at Michigan, 1994

I never knew there were so many different size and shape boobs.
The visuals are even better in the heat.
—Piersun, at Michigan, 1994

I see more and more children each year. Hear! Hear! for lesbian moms.
—Anonymous, at Michigan, 1994

I am a first time festie, and my favorite memory is all of the happy, joyful smiling faces watching
the line dancing each day.
—M., from Maryland, at Michigan, 1994

We sat in the field at night stage and watched the shooting stars above.
—B., from New York, at Michigan, 1994

At a time when I felt depleted, a wonderful woman gave me a warm, lingering kiss on the lips—
expressing gratitude to me for teaching her to stilt walk.
—J., from San Francisco, at Michigan, 1994

Michigan is nothing short of a miracle. The land and the women and the music and the spirit are
one and the same in my memory. I will never forget the respect and love we were given; the join-

ing of such powerful women performers and workers left me tingling.
P.S.: Sex in the woods was good too.
—A., from Texas, at Michigan, 1994

Ja mirada fija de una mujer llena de amor. Asegurandome que todo iba a salir bien. Un camino
seguro, sin temores un calor de millones de anos, esperando a liberarse. Una cancion que abre el
alma. Un corazon en las manos.
—J., from Puerto Rico, at Michigan, 1994

Dialogue between the various ideas and ways of being that women think and feel. When we stop
talking with each other, we are doomed!
—Ruth Barrett, at Michigan, 1994

A dream…of what it could be like, a diverse vocabulary of women, music, art, style,
friendship, poetry. My first year: a vision into a peaceful, exuberant reality, where many
funny and talented women come together and just be. Inspiration to create more of this re-
ality. Fun as hell dancing in the rain and feeling the history of the festival seep into my
consciousness.
—N., from San Francisco, at Michigan, 1994

Open to the opinions of truly diverse womyn and consider the feminism of the young ones.
—H., at Michigan, 1994

Playing those congas and djembes has always been a blast, playing for the people, hangin' out
shuckin' and jiving, feeling the heartbeats.
—Nuru, at Michigan, 1994

I loved just talking with other women like us—couples in love.
—M., at Heart of the West Festival, 1994

I've been listening to a great salsa band for the last hour. I feel dang good. As soon as this plate full
o' food that I just ate settles, I'm going to get up and shake my thing. All my things. The music is

great, the women are fine, and best of all, it doesn't matter if it rains during my set.
—Jamie Anderson, at Heart of the West, 1994

I love the mural that snakes along the border of the land, with lots of evidence of women's hands to care for and stand on this land. A clear statement of our ability to transform a necessary boundary into a celebration of all we are.
—Anonymous, at Gulf Coast, 1995

This is my first women's festival, and thankfully I was fortunate to organize seven other women to join me. The whole experience has been like a giant "oneness" in total—I am for the first time surrounded by others who don't view my politics/personality as bizarre.
—T., at Gulf Coast, 1995

This is also my first women's fest, and I have never felt more at peace. The Seder here is the way that all of my Easters at home should have been celebrated. Yes, it had meaning for me. The storytelling as well as the sound of the drumming mesmerized me. The atmosphere was strange at first because of my heterosexual Afrocentricity, but the women are great, the vibe is positive.
—M., at Gulf Coast, 1995

A weekend slumber party at Mississippi's camp for wayward girls. To lesbians!
—Lin Daniels, at Gulf Coast, 1995

Wimin together—wimin in spirit—wimin eating—wimin loving—wimin showering—wimin just being—peace—truth—healing—creativity—music—trust—stories—mosquitoes—little girls—the concerts—the work—the message—all continuing. "We all come from the Goddess, and to her we shall return."
—Anique, from Australia, at Gulf Coast, 1995

What is my favorite thing about this festival? What isn't would be easier to answer. This is the first festival for me. I had heard about Camp Sister Spirit from the media and all. I had no idea of the power of the women that were here. I feel I have gotten stronger about my womynhood just from these women who have touched me since I've been here. The love is so overflowing. But I

also think the strength and the courage from these women is a big impact. I am so thankful and so proud of these women who make it possible for me to experience this weekend.
—B., at Gulf Coast, 1995

Moon over firelight, drums throbbing restlessly beneath my skin, and soft kisses through mosquito repellent. Sparks dancing like fairy sprites into Mississippi sky. And magic—real magic, uncontrived and knifing home to my heart.
—Anonymous, at Gulf Coast, 1995

I come back to Camp Sister Spirit and see all the changes and progress the women have made with the land and buildings, doing sound in an old beautiful pig barn. I meet the brave women friends from last year's fest when we were few and brave...I love this space!
—A., at Gulf Coast, 1995

My very first festival and the first time I know that there is a place for a woman like me—like us. The most beautiful experience of my life—freedom, singing, dancing, finding my voice in a place of safety and warmth, spirit and love. Healing, we are free and fear does not live in this heart right now—love is the force.
—S., at Gulf Coast, 1995

I am coming out, proud to be a woman, and being with my family, I feel very much alive.
—C., from New York, at Campfest, 1995

Sunshine/Big beautiful womyn/Happy happy day.
—Anonymous, at Campfest, 1995

I am in womyn space with my lover and friends; this is the real world.
—Barbara Slater, at Campfest, 1995

Every time I come here I'm overwhelmed by how varied and talented our community is; it's another year to celebrate.
—B., from Maryland, at Campfest, 1995

Let's do it again and again and again—friendly hellos, delicious food served and prepared with love, great entertainment fun in front of the fire at the café, love and godlight.
—A., at Campfest, 1995

How are there any ways to choose one memory? But my favorite moment had to be Lucie Blue Tremblay singing "Ave Maria"—tears poured down my face.
—Anonymous, at Campfest, 1995

So much rain! But so many beautiful faces of beautiful women sharing love and laughter, making up for the dreary weather. I guess the message was to gather together and huddle and cuddle with one another in harmony. My first festival—Goddess bless.
—L., at Campfest, 1995

This is the first festival that I came to with someone—someone very special and close to me. I'm not single any more, and it feels wonderful. I was scheduled to do one workshop, which turned out to be so successful that they added another one—shows me how appreciative the women are and how interested they are in the subject of earth dancing.
—Anonymous, at Campfest, 1995

I always enjoy the women, the ones I bring with me and the ones I find here.
—J., from Dayton, Ohio, at National, 1995

My favorite moment was in 1994 when Ferron told the crowd, "Lighten up!"
—D., from Chapel Hill, N.C., at National, 1995

I was quite moved by seeing the film One Fine Day—*just thinking about the aura in the auditorium during the showing brings tears to my eyes. I am so proud to be a woman.*
—B., from Indianapolis, at National, 1995

This is my first festival, and the best part was realizing that we were here together and that we are all gay.
—L., from Illinois, at National, 1995

Inhaling the smell of leather in the crafts market, being in the presence of beautiful old dykes, then listening to Janis Ian as an out dyke and crying tears for my adolescent memories of her music and my life at that time.
—S., from Vancouver, Canada, at National, 1995

Drumming with Ubaka Hill is a jam session complete with hugs.
—W., at National, 1995

My first festival is empowering—"it's OK to be gay"—realizing being a lesbian is more than who you sleep with; it's a culture, complete with art, music, creative expression.
—K., from Illinois, at National, 1995

Chest full, of feeling full, of silver-haired loveliness, lovingness, pounding the raging beauty of our sacred spaces—finding the secret places where I am, she is, we are, singing with life.
—S., from Vancouver, Canada, at National, 1995

I feel like I'm in heaven watching lots of beautiful women on the earth.
—P. (Deaf), at Michigan, 1995

Surely, all of shapes of boobs got my blue eyes—said wow! I think this festival made me feel like a woman. Believe or not, I am coming back next year, smile and grin.
—K. (Deaf), at Michigan, 1995

Whee!!! Smile! Loads of Hot Women—heat from those bodies enough to cause the Arctic ice to melt. Definitely will be back next year, and...whee!!
—E. (Deaf), at Michigan, 1995

Wowee, like a village without (eek) men.
—L. (Deaf), at Michigan, 1995

I feel honored to be in Michigan's Deaf community. I've never felt so safe. This is the best place to be for womyn from all over, the best opportunity for us. I love it here and wish not

to leave the land. Pfft!—it's so safe away from men!
—M. and D. (Deaf), at Michigan, 1995

On Saturday morning, I saw a tiny red-spotted newt slithering through the rain-soaked leaves near my campsite. It was inspiring to see a bit of nature carrying on within all the human activity.
—J., from Austin, at Michigan, 1995

My first festival—driving down the dirt road to the gate—seeing the "no trespassing" signs and realizing that this land is reserved for us—this is just for us....
—K., from Cleveland, at Michigan, 1995

I have always known that women can do anything. This place is proof of that. I am able to show my lover and say, "See, it is possible."
—P., from Cleveland, at Michigan, 1995

My heart will forever shine brighter. Every moment here is a memory unto itself.
—B., at Michigan, 1995

It was schwell stage divin' and hangin' in general.
—Nedra Johnson, at Michigan, 1995

When the thunderstorm came this year, I stood under a tree as the black clouds rolled, lightning every few seconds. On my right, about 30 women had stripped and were screaming and leaping and dancing in the rain. On my left, 20 or 30 workers were rushing to ready the night-stage tent for the rain, shouting instructions to each other, using their bodies to steady the huge posts. I loved the contrast—summed up Michigan for me.
—A., from Aotearoa, New Zealand, Michigan 1995

It has to be the only place in the world where I could get a whole long line of naked womyn to clap for me as I burst out of line (on a double dog dare) and ran to the semiwarm showers just before the festie worker turned them all off to clean them.

I sure loved having all those gorgeous, fabulous, all shapes and sizes of naked womyn
clap for me. What an affirmation!
—K., from Minnesota, at Michigan, 1995

Summer camp revisited, girls girls girls, stage diving lightning storm.... Next year in Michigan.
—Felice, at Michigan, 1995

At the 19th Michigan festival, Boo Price walked out onto the runway and bowed as the crowd
cheered wildly. The rain stopped. The moon shone brightly, and Boo was elegant, positively regal.
We gave her our love, and she received it humbly.
—Jo W., at Michigan, 1995

Favorite festival moments:
Overheard near the main kitchen: "Did you see that woman with the dildo between her breasts?"
"Where?"
"Over there."
"Isn't that the same woman who had the dildo on top of her head the other day?"
"Yeah, I think so."
Seeing my friends, my wonderful friends, many of whom I correspond with during the year
but rarely see, and meeting them at festival and hugging and carrying on exactly where we
left off last year. The realization that I don't have to pierce anything, and I can still
be a real lesbian!
—Ruth Simkin, at Michigan, 1995

My favorite things are the dances that go on here. They're totally filled with energy and joy—and
people dance as hard as they can. I've never been on a dance floor that feels this way—a lot of
love. It is a bit overwhelming here, and also it's hard 'cause I'm young. But I think I'll come back
in a few years—with my mother, maybe.
—J., age 16, from North Carolina, at Michigan, 1995

One of many highlights: loud, pulsating drums combined with lovemaking.
—Anonymous, from Toronto, at Michigan, 1995

I know I'm an elder because the place is full of young womyn I don't recognize. But those whom I do recognize…other elders and longtimers—are s-o-o-o beautiful. What a joy to bring East and West Coast womyn together to play in an "out there" free-form improv. Goddess, I'm happy to be alive and well and still at Michigan.
—Kay Gardner, at Michigan, 1995

I loved seeing the woman with guitar serenading her beloved in the workers' shower, oblivious to the others showering and dressing around them. And it is great (and gratifying) when a woman tells me how attending a workshop saved/changed her life.
—Denslow Brown, at Michigan, 1995

Learning all about "body shots" (tequila drinking game) from Cherie, who parachuted down to the night stage wearing nothing but leather chaps and a black bra…. Dancing under the Michigan August stars on the night stage ramp while hundreds of workers writhed on the stage…. Knowing enough basic ASL to hang out with the gorgeous Deaf women…. Being the first in the mosh pit this year during Team Dresch (thanks Nedra Johnson for stage-diving tips: wear a bra, take off jewelry— unless you don't mind them finding your nipple ring in the mosh pit the next morning—turn over on your back as soon as possible for a long ride)…. The number of babies and toddlers along with the teen workers/festiegoers makes me feel like this cultural torch will in fact be passed to the next generation.
—Toni Armstrong Jr., at Michigan, 1995

1995 Impressions

Ferns
trampled, bent, temporarily crushed aside
circling rounded homes
for many womanly bodies

The faces at the airport, play
spot the dyke, searching for sisters going to "the land"

The sisters in the village

weave like naked ant colonies
laughing and playing and working
swallowing the new arrivals in their rhythm

Faces from many pictures
of festivals gone by
unfreeze from the printed page
and walk, laugh, share stories
with animated eyes

"Women go to the land, women go to the land"

The circles grow
the tables swell
the showers full
and the sisters keep arriving.

Outside the barricades hold back the yearly
crush of Amazon campers
tractors and shouts
chairs and tents
they fill the green with color shape and size.
Inside the stages build like jigsaw puzzles—towers rise up.
The gates are open
the lights are up
the fields are full
and we remember
the ancient calling
we remember
the drum
we remember the gathering of our tribes
we remember the music

The songs
The dance, the beat rhythm and ritual
"The women united will never be divided"
and still the sisters pour in…
The sound, the song
the wrenching of soul
tears and laughter
The stories are shared
cultures exchanged
we network
push the boundaries of our worlds
We skydive
We firework
We drum and we sing
We work and try to sleep surrounded by energy

The full moon
on an empty field
where so many women have been

The sunrise
the heat
the breaking of storm
"O babe you are my bellybowl, my soft-shoe shuffle"

The rains came
the sisters full
start to pick up chairs
pack up stages
collapse their rounded homes
exchange the pen and paperwork
and hold each other close.

The stages
Amazon village dissembles its arms
the paths are trampled
the mud has dried
the ferns moist
and deep green
lift up from where they lay
trampled by the dancing moving and slow walking
of many sisters' feet.

—Mignon, from South Africa

1. "The Importance of Documenting Women's Music Festivals," in *HOT WIRE*, January 1992.

APPENDIX B

A Lexicon of Festivalese

"We need two 'terps and an artist liaison at sound check."

Accessible: All festivals strive to be held on sites equipped for women in wheelchairs, women on crutches, and women with visual or hearing impairments. Disability activists and Deaf women have made considerable progress in educating festival organizers about their needs, but some festivals continue to take place at inaccessible land sites or buildings. One concern is that while most festivals employ sign-language interpreters, few stages are ramped, leaving the impression that disabled women are not performing artists (though many are, as in the Axis Dance Group, among others). See **interpreting services.**

Artists: The musicians or stage performers at a festival. Not to be confused with craftswomen, who create and sell artworks at festivals.

Artist liaison: Staff workers or volunteers who care for festival performers in a variety of ways, such as driving them to and from airports or arranging for meals and living quarters.

Butt-cans: At festivals with a high risk of fire, such as the West Coast Women's Music and Comedy Festival, smokers were asked to carry empty tins, referred to as "butt-cans," for their cigarette butts and ash.

Campers: A term distinguishing those women attending a festival from staff or performers. This term may seem inaccurate at festivals where the majority of "campers" are housed in real cabins with flush toilets. However, festivals with indoor cabin beds are usually summer camps rented for the festival, so the term "camper" still applies. See **festiegoer.**

Carps: Not to be confused with the creatures my Jewish grandma kept in her bathtub in order to make really fresh gefilte fish on Fridays, *carps* is short for *carpenters.* She who can build stages and repair festival structures has the revered stature of engineer, construction worker, and tradeswoman. In festival culture there is much respect for women in traditionally male-dominated, physically demanding jobs. Never ask to borrow a carp's hammer to pound your tent stakes.

Chem-free: An area or person unsullied by alcohol, drugs, or tobacco products; increasingly, this includes perfume and other manufactured scents or chemicals. Persons choosing to sit with friends in the chem-free section of a festival audience are also asked not to get drunk or stoned beforehand. Chem-free space is important to women who are either physically intolerant of smoke or are avoiding exposure to drugs and alcohol. Chem-free space also prohibits burning incense or sage smudge sticks without permission. While more and more women are developing allergies or environmental sensitivities to products such as hair spray, cologne, or scented laundry soaps and skin lotions, it is impossible to enforce such bans in larger areas, but many festivals do encourage women to leave heavily scented products at home. Chem-free space does allow caffeine and prescription drugs. A person, as well as a place, may be described as chem-free.

Chem: Any area in which one may smoke or drink alcohol.

Coordinator: The women in charge of a specific festival area or service and its work crew. There are separate coordinators for child care, shuttle buses, security, kitchen, sound, and so on. These are sometimes paid positions.

Craftie: Short for *craftswoman;* she who sells her wares or services in the market area of a festival.

DART: Differently Abled Resources Tent; this term originated at the Michigan Womyn's Music Festival and refers to seating areas, services, and transport for disabled women, not just the networking tent. Hence, the DART shuttle, etc.

Festiegoer: Like *camper,* this term distinguishes those women paying to attend a festival from workers, performers, and craftswomen. While some festiegoers may find the term pejorative, it was never intended to be so; it is merely the result of festival hierarchy in catering to different groups' needs. Workers and performers have responsibilities and sometimes privileges that differ from those of the festiegoing audience and often camp or eat in separate areas that accommodate workers' exhausting schedules or artists' privacy. Festiegoers may be prohibited from visiting such "backstage" areas without permission. A worker picking up 30 women at a regional airport may need to know who is a festiegoer versus who is a late-arriving musician or sound crew technician due at the stage.

Festie virgin: A woman attending her first festival.

Festiewear: T-shirts, sweatshirts, tank tops, shorts, and hats with a festival's design or logo. The Michigan piano under the stars is probably the best known symbol on festiewear. Occasionally, baseball jackets, handbags, fanny packs, or other items will be manufactured for a festival. Leftover styles from yesteryear are often sold alongside new designs to raise money and spread the herstory around. And there are items that cannot be bought by just anyone but must be earned, such as worker jackets at Michigan, Five Year Jackets at Campfest. Incidentally, no festival sells products connected to another festival; however, different festivals do advertise in each other's programs.

HOT WIRE: Subtitled *The Journal of Women's Music and Culture,* this periodical served as *the* source for good festival journalism from 1984–1994. Edited by Toni Armstrong Jr., each issue contained a vinyl recording of women's music.

Interpreting services: Interpreters, or 'terps, work to make festival music and culture accessible to the Deaf community and vice versa. Interpreters are trained and certified but are frequently assumed to be altruistic volunteers or handy extensions of Deaf festiegoers instead of professionals who deserve decent wages for hard work. Several interpreters have raised concert interpreting to an art form and are raptly watched by hearing audiences as well; this artistic trend began with Susan Freundlich in the very early 1980s. There is a political debate within the Deaf and interpreting community, however, about music interpretation because music is not a part of Deaf-born culture but an obvious manifestation of the hearing world.

Land, the: Always referred to with reverence. The land is wherever the festival is held—privately owned acreage, a rented camp, Yosemite. Used interchangeably with "the festival," as in "We have women on the land who need…" or "As you move about the land, remember to…" or "Now I know there's been some talk on the land about…" or "Are there any women on the land with white gas so the Lesbian Avengers can eat fire?"

Lineup: The order of performers/performances on the stage; the artists advertised as playing at a specific festival. We all have our favorite performers and our secret fantasies of the ultimate lineup. Most festivals work hard to make both day- and night-stage lineups ethnically and musically diverse.

LST: Lesbian Standard Time. Means "late."

"Men on the land": This warning is announced by auto horns or sheer lung power; means "Get your shirt on—now."

Monitors: Not the mean girls who took down your name in school, sound monitors are part of a performer's amplification equipment, reflecting vocals or instrumentals back to the musician so she can hear herself play while onstage. A performer's frequently heard, plaintive request at festivals is, "Could I have a little more guitar in the monitor, please?"

Night stage: Sometimes a physically separate structure from day stage, this is where all evening festival performances take place, usually from 7:30 P.M. or 8 P.M. to midnight. Almost all artists want to be hired for night stage, but unknowns tend to start out on the day stage, where the audience is smaller because the show competes with attractive workshops, lunch, canoeing, and so on. Night stage performers tend to be the "big names" in women's music, and at some festivals, only night-stage artists are paid—day-stage performers win a festival pass and lots of exposure.

Porta-Jane: What is otherwise known as a Porta-John; a temporary, movable, freestanding toilet rented for festivals that lack indoor plumbing. At Michigan, men show up to clean out the accumulated waste midway through the festival, prompting the town crier's warning bellow, "Men on the land! Get yer shirts on!"

Raffle: A fund-raiser for the festival. Throughout the day and evening, festival workers stroll through concert audiences selling tickets—three for $5, typically. Craftswomen at the festival donate jewelry, clothing, art, or services, and lucky ticket holders may win these fabulous prizes. Tickets are drawn onstage once or twice a day, usually by giggling performers or beloved longtime workers.

Registration: Not as simple as it sounds; depending on the festival, when one arrives one must present one's ticket, choose a work shift, sign a release form, watch an orientation video, and only then receive the official festival program and a map to camping areas. For years festiegoers wailed, "But how can I choose my work shift if I haven't seen a schedule of concerts and workshops? I don't want to miss my favorite performer." Most festivals resolved this dilemma by stapling a sample program schedule to the work shift table.

Rumor Control: Rumors do abound at larger festivals, where festiegoers have less access to producers and aren't certain "who's in charge." Rumor control might be a table or booth or a place within the political tent, staffed by calm, informed workers. Typical questions answered at rumor control include: Will Melissa Etheridge be here? What happened to the woman who fell off the sound tower yesterday? Is that storm going to hit us? Is it true that the festival is bankrupt?

Rush hour: The period of time when foot traffic and shuttle traffic are heaviest on the land. (1) The time between dinner and the first night-stage concert, when everyone is trying to eat, shower, change into warmer clothing, and schlep a lawn chair over to the stage for a good seat. (2) The Friday evening or first day, when most festiegoers arrive at the festival and are all registering, hauling in gear, and setting up tents at once.

Seating: Festivals are infamous for complex seating arrangements at concerts. Generally, the front rows are reserved for Deaf women, women with disabilities, and one or two official photographers. The remaining audience is split into chem-free and chem-tolerant sections, with smokers perhaps set apart from both of these. It's generally accepted that the very back rows are a "loud and rowdy" area. The rush to slap down blankets and chairs as a means of reserving one's spot begins at 5:30 P.M. or 6 P.M., depending on the festival rules. Since 1989 the Michigan Womyn's Music Festival has used a policy of allowing ten women at a time to place their chairs in an orderly fashion during the first tense minutes of open seating after 6 P.M. Many women wait in line for hours to compete for a spot, although sound is usually best in the rear. At most festivals one may not leave a blanket or chair overnight to save a space in the audience. Regrettably, even pacifist festiegoers often lose their tempers and hurl obscenities at one another over seating arrangements and misunderstandings. A particular sore point is the height of folding lawn chairs, some of which block others' views of the stage.

Security: If anything happens, call them.

Short crew: At the Michigan festival this refers to workers who sign up for a ten-day staff period and who arrive just before the festival week begins. "Long crew" workers arrive earlier in the summer and commit to several weeks or more of labor, readying the land for the deluge of campers in mid August.

Shuttle: Most festivals require all women to park at the outskirts of the land in designated lots. Then shuttle vans bring some women to the interior, others walk in. This cuts down on the amount of vehicle traffic and noise in the central area of the festival. There are also shuttles to and from the airport nearest the festival.

A signing: Held at the Ladyslipper booth or Goldenrod booth or whichever women's music distribution company is selling albums and tapes at the festival, performers usually sign their CDs and chat with fans at a scheduled time in or in front of the music booth. Many artists have a signing as soon as possible after performing, not only because that is when they have aroused the most audience response, but also because they may be departing the festival to perform elsewhere.

Sound check: What every performer should have *before* she begins her set onstage. This brief run-through of sound levels and instrumental amplification takes place in the morning or the early afternoon, when festiegoers are not nearby the night stage. Because sound checks often create anxiety or frustration for both stage crew and artist as they wrangle with uncooperative wires and microphones, privacy is desirable. A sound check isn't a performance, although the artist may need to play most of a song to check sound levels. When Teresa Trull's voice begins blasting all over the land, it is a safe bet that crowds will gather to watch and cheer on the sound check.

Trash queens: The hardworking, noble women on the garbage crew. At the Michigan festival the sanitation crew is called Sano and has its own subcategory of slang (a backed up toilet, for example, is a "code brown" in Sanoese).

Vegan: A form of vegetarian diet that excludes all animal products, including eggs, dairy, gelatin, etc. Some festival kitchens label which meals are vegan and which contain dairy products or gelatin. This is also helpful to women who keep kosher or are allergic to dairy.

WOC: Women of color. Every festival now has—or should have—a designated gathering space or tent for women of African, Asian, Latin, Arab, Native American, Aboriginal, and Pacific Island descent. Jews of color are also welcome here; Caucasian–North European Jews generally defer. The point is to offer a safe and private space for women whose identities and experiences were shaped outside of white heritage and looks. Some festival workshops are open to women of color only, and this has created many misunderstandings among white women who cry "reverse discrimination" because they aren't invited. Most festivals have a clearly white majority.

Woman: May be spelled womon, womyn, womin, womoon, etc.; this language practice reflects many lesbian feminists' (and separatists') impatience with male identification. Changing *man* to *moon* in certain instances linked female identity with the monthly, or lunar, cycle of menstruation.

Womb: A common term for a festival's health center, where both Western and traditional, or homeopathic, healing practices are available to women needing medical attention. Also the place to get emergency tampons—you *will* get your period; women living together in groups often results in synchronized menses.

Work shift: Even paying festiegoers must do a two- or four-hour work shift—in an area of their choice—to help maintain the smooth operation of many services at the festival site. Work-shift areas typically include child care, security, registration, garbage, kitchen (always understaffed), health care and massage (if one is licensed to practice), lifeguard duty, and so on.

Wristband: Several festivals assign different wristbands to the women on the land, signifying either that one has paid the appropriate ticket fee or that one is an artist, worker, or craftswoman. This enables women to leave the land and get back in as necessary and indicates who has permission to enter certain restricted areas, such as backstage or crafts.

Special Bonus Festivalese Trivia:

It is common practice at many festivals to name or rename certain locations. Can you name the correct festival for each of the following sites?

Q:
Emma G's Canteen
Radclyffe Hall
The Bloomingmoon Café
Central Heating, Solar Heating, Body Heat, Space Heater
Gyrlfest

(A: North East Women's Music Retreat, Campfest, National Women's Music Festival, Michigan Womyn's Music Festival, Gulf Coast Womyn's Music Festival)

BIBLIOGRAPHY

Festival, Cultural, and Women's Music Sources

Alther, Lisa. *Original Sins.* New American Library, 1981.

Bechdel, Alison. *The Indelible Alison Bechdel.* Firebrand Books, 1998.

Cheney, Joyce. *Lesbian Land.* WordWeavers, 1985.

Clinton, Kate. *Don't Get Me Started.* Ballantine Books, 1998.

Covina, Gina, and Laura Galana. *The New Lesbians.* Moon Books, 1977.

Davies, Miranda, and Natania Jansz. *More Women Travel.* Rough Guide, 1995.

Davis, Angela. *Blues Legacies and Black Feminism.* Pantheon, 1998.

Dobkin, Alix. *Alix Dobkin's Adventures in Women's Music.* Tomato Publications,1979.

Faderman, Lillian. *Odd Girls and Twilight Lovers.* Columbia University Press, 1991.

Fitzgerald, Judith. *Building a Mystery: The Story of Sarah McLachlan and Lilith Fair.* Canada: Quarry Music Books, 1997.

Fleming, Lee. *Hot Licks: Lesbian Musicians of Note.* Gynergy, 1996.

Flowers, Charles, ed. *Out, Loud and Laughing.* Anchor/Doubleday, 1995.

Gaar, Gillian. *She's a Rebel: The History of Women in Rock and Roll.* Seal Press, 1992.

Gage, Carolyn. *The Second Coming of Joan of Arc and Other Plays.* HerBooks, 1994.

Gilbert, Ronnie. *Ronnie Gilbert on Mother Jones.* Conari, 1993.

Greig, Charlotte. *Will You Still Love Me Tomorrow?* London: Virago, 1989.

Hoagland, Sara Lucia, and Julia Penelope, eds. *For Lesbians Only.* Onlywomen Press, 1988.

Jackson, Blanche, and Amoja Three Rivers. *Cultural Etiquette.* Market Wimmin, 1990.

369

Johnson, Sonia. *Wildfire: Igniting the She/volution.* Wildfire Books, 1989.

Karvoski, Ed, ed. *A Funny Time to Be Gay.* Fireside, 1997.

Kimball, Gayle. *Women's Culture.* Scarecrow, 1981.

Kovick, Kris. *What I Love About Lesbian Politics Is Arguing With People I Agree With.* Alyson, 1991.

Luck, Joyce. *Melissa Etheridge: Our Little Secret.* ECW Press, 1996.

Maupin, Armistead. *Significant Others.* Perennial, 1987.

Murphy, Marilyn. *Are You Girls Traveling Alone?* Clothespin Fever Press, 1991.

Near, Holly. *Fire in the Rain, Singer in the Storm.* Quill, 1990.

O'Dair, Barbara, ed. *Trouble Girls: The Rolling Stone Book of Women in Rock.* Random House, 1997.

Penelope, Julia. *Call Me Lesbian.* Crossing Press, 1992.

Penelope, Julia, and Susan J. Wolfe, eds. *Lesbian Culture: An Anthology.* Crossing Press, 1993.

Post, Laura. *Backstage Pass.* New Victoria, 1997.

Reagon, Bernice Johnson, et al. *We Who Believe in Freedom: Sweet Honey in the Rock, Still On the Journey.* Anchor, 1993.

Stein, Arlene, ed. *Sisters, Sexperts, Queers.* Penguin USA, 1993.

Steward, Sue, and Sheryl Garratt. *Signed, Sealed and Delivered.* South End Press, 1884.

Stocker, Midge. *The Woman-Centered Economy.* Third Side Press, 1995.

Turner, Kay, ed. *Between Us.* Chronicle Books, 1996.

Van Gelder, Lindsay, and Pamela Brandt. *The Girls Next Door.* Doubleday, 1996.

Warren, Roz, ed. *Revolutionary Laughter: The World of Women Comics.* Crossing Press, 1995.

Wenner, Hilda. *Here's to the Women.* Syracuse University Press, 1987.

Whiteley, Sheila, ed. *Sexing the Groove: Popular Music and Gender.* Routledge, 1997.

Young, Irene. *For the Record.* Olivia Records, 1982.